Flotsam & Jetsam

A collection of Sea Stories that have washed ashore during a forty-year career in the United States Navy

By Hank McKinney

FORTIS
PUBLISHING
Jacksonville, Florida ♦ Herndon, Virginia
www.Fortis-Publishing.com

Flotsam & Jetsam

A collection of Sea Stories that have washed ashore during a forty-year career in the United States Navy

By Hank McKinney

ISBN 978-0-9845511-4-9 (hardcover version)
ISBN 978-0-9846371-3-3 (trade paperback version)

Library of Congress Control Number: 2010935124

Published by Fortis Publishing
Jacksonville, Florida—Herndon, Virginia
www.Fortis-Publishing.com

Manufactured in the United States of America

Dedication

To my father, Peter T. McKinney, who in his teens and early twenties went to sea as an Able Bodied Seaman. As a teen, he sailed aboard Great Lakes Ore freighters, and then after graduation from the University of Michigan in 1927, he sailed around the world on merchant ships with port calls in Germany, Australia, the Panama Canal and Pitcairn Island where the descendants of the mutineers from HMS Bounty settled.

He settled down for a life ashore in New York City with his parrot and sailboat in 1929. I grew up listening to sea stories from my father and set my sights on a Navy career. I had the great pleasure of taking my father to sea while in command.

My father, at the periscope of USS Seahorse, summer 1977

At the helm of his sailboat, 1930

With his parrot, 1930

Contents

Contents (continued)

Contents (continued)

Contents (continued)

Acknowledgements

This book is the result of some very special people who provided support and a great deal of encouragement.

My wife Mary and I are celebrating our 45th wedding anniversary as this book goes to press. During our voyage provided by the Navy, we shared many of the experiences that I have written about. Mary has always been there for support when I needed it. She gave birth to our two children while I was underwater in the Atlantic and Pacific. She was always there to support the family and our children when I was gone, filling the role of mother and father, counselor and mentor. Early in our marriage, I was amazed at all the things that she accomplished and problems she solved while I was gone, But later on I took these accomplishments for granted. Mary was always the perfect hostess when we entertained, gracious with our guests and an accomplished cook. She listened to my recounting of the sea stories in this book many, many times. She said that she never tired of the stories because somehow I would change the story or the ending. She encouraged me to write the stories down before they changed too much so our children and grandchildren can have them.

I started to write some of the stories, but I wasn't getting very far until the Pine River Journal, our weekly hometown newspaper got a new editor, Kelly Virden and she agreed to publish the stories in the paper. Now I had a commitment of one article every two weeks and I had to keep up with the schedule of the paper. Without this commitment, I doubt that I would have finished the book. Thanks Kelly.

After I started publishing my *Flotsam and Jetsam* articles in the Pine River Journal, I decided to include friends and family locally and around the country on an email distribution list. Many started to encourage me to publish a book. Among those, Admiral Frank Kelso, who has been a close friend and mentor since the late 1960s, Jack Gobbell a former naval officer and marvelous author of historical fiction covering our Navy during the early years of WWII. Also Bob White who taught me the rudiments of fly fishing. In addition to being one of the legendary fishing guides of Alaska, Bob is also an accomplished author and artist. And finally Ric Edelman, Barron's #1 Financial Advisor in the nation 2009 and author of several fascinating books on money management. Each of these friends has offered to write a short review my book, and I am extremely grateful for their friendship and support.

This book would never have happened without the support of Taylor Kiland of the Navy Memorial Foundation who suggested that I talk to Dennis Lowery, President of Fortis Publishing who encouraged me to complete the book and provided invaluable editing assistance and guidance in navigating the vast oceans of the world of publishing.

Acknowledgements

This book is the result of some very special people who provided support and a great deal of encouragement.

My wife Mary and I are celebrating our 45th wedding anniversary as this book goes to press. During our voyage provided by the Navy, we shared many of the experiences that I have written about. Mary has always been there for support when I needed it. She gave birth to our two children while I was underwater in the Atlantic and Pacific. She was always there to support the family and our children when I was gone, filling the role of mother and father, counselor and mentor. Early in our marriage, I was amazed at all the things that she accomplished and problems she solved while I was gone, But later on I took these accomplishments for granted. Mary was always the perfect hostess when we entertained, gracious with our guests and an accomplished cook. She listened to my recounting of the sea stories in this book many, many times. She said that she never tired of the stories because somehow I would change the story or the ending. She encouraged me to write the stories down before they changed too much so our children and grandchildren can have them.

I started to write some of the stories, but I wasn't getting very far until the Pine River Journal, our weekly hometown newspaper got a new editor, Kelly Virden and she agreed to publish the stories in the paper. Now I had a commitment of one article every two weeks and I had to keep up with the schedule of the paper. Without this commitment, I doubt that I would have finished the book. Thanks Kelly.

After I started publishing my *Flotsam and Jetsam* articles in the Pine River Journal, I decided to include friends and family locally and around the country on an email distribution list. Many started to encourage me to publish a book. Among those, Admiral Frank Kelso, who has been a close friend and mentor since the late 1960s, Jack Gobbell a former naval officer and marvelous author of historical fiction covering our Navy during the early years of WWII. Also Bob White who taught me the rudiments of fly fishing. In addition to being one of the legendary fishing guides of Alaska, Bob is also an accomplished author and artist. And finally Ric Edelman, Barron's #1 Financial Advisor in the nation 2009 and author of several fascinating books on money management. Each of these friends has offered to write a short review my book, and I am extremely grateful for their friendship and support.

This book would never have happened without the support of Taylor Kiland of the Navy Memorial Foundation who suggested that I talk to Dennis Lowery, President of Fortis Publishing who encouraged me to complete the book and provided invaluable editing assistance and guidance in navigating the vast oceans of the world of publishing.

Foreword

I was often asked what it was like to grow up as a "Navy brat". The question has always left me a bit stumped. It's sort of like asking a giraffe what it's like to be so tall. I have no other perspective to draw upon; the United States Navy's Submarine Force is the only life I have ever known. I grew up the son of a career submariner in the 1970s and 1980s and chose to follow my father's footsteps and join the "Silent Service".

My family never really knew what my father did at sea. Dad just went to sea, and returned months later, invariably with some really neat presents. He told us wonderful stories of fictional submarines and sang sea chanteys to us at bedtime. We knew we were proud of him and his service to our country, but there was a whole other side to Dad that we did not know about. This was the height of the "Cold War", well before the publication of "The Hunt for Red October". Submarine operations were strictly "need to know", and families were clearly out of the loop.

In elementary school, I devoured books about our World War II submarines, especially those by Ned Beach, and dug through all the "tell-all" books of the modern submarine force. I peppered my father with questions about submarine operations, trying to impress him with my knowledge. He usually replied simply with, "you don't believe everything you read, do you?" I did not know how close I was to the truth until my Second Class (junior) year at the Naval Academy, when we finally had the minimum security clearance required to be indoctrinated into the world of the submariner. During the briefing, the true nature of submarine operations was revealed, and I was completely floored. I don't think my classmates had the same reaction, but then again, most of them had not spent their young lives trying to figure them out!

I am now in command of my own submarine, the USS Wyoming, one of our strategic deterrent submarines. As I reflect back on the path of my career, I can see my father's influence throughout, not directly, but subtly. From him I gained my fascination with the technologies that make submarines the formidable weapons systems they are. He is responsible for my belief that the people of the Navy are our most important asset and that their development and care are our most important priorities. Most importantly, he taught me that the job is an extremely difficult one, but it still can be fun!

My father had a very successful career judged by conventional measurement. He retired as a two-star Admiral with a chest full of awards, having commanded not only his own submarine, but also all of Navy Recruiting and the entire Pacific Submarine Force. To me however, his most impressive and lasting accomplishments are the influences he had on the sailors and officers who served with him.

I have been very fortunate to not only have a father, but also a role model and mentor—the finest kind. This book is not just a collection of sea stories—it encapsulates who my father is and what he finds important. You will find in each story a positive message and a lesson to learn, not just about the Navy or submarines … but also about life. I look forward to being able to share it with my own two boys, Liam and Adam (now very precocious toddlers), so they will truly know what a great man their grandfather is, and to see his legacy in themselves.

Bill McKinney
Commander, United States Navy
Commanding Officer
USS Wyoming (SSBN 742) (BLUE)

Prologue

I suppose that it is possible to consider this collection of memories as a memoir, but I prefer to think of it as a grouping of Sea Stories. Sea Stories is a uniquely mariner's term and they are very popular in the Navy. An old salt will have many of these stories collected over the years and with a little encouragement, he can keep his shipmates entertained for hours. Most stories could be classified as "historical fiction." The setting of the story and some of the details are factual, but over time, the story has evolved into a completely different story. My wife told me once that she enjoyed my stories because they always had a different ending. So what are you to make of the stories in this book? Fact or fiction or maybe a little of both? If pressed on this point, I would say more fact than fiction, but you can't believe everything that you read. (Is that clear enough?)

I started to write these stories while I was still the President and CEO of the Navy Memorial, in Washington DC. I probably had ten stories written and stored in my computer when I left that job and moved to Minnesota. Shortly after we moved, the local weekly paper, the Pine River Journal, hired a new editor, Kelly Virden. I called on Kelly and asked her if she would be interested in publishing my stories as periodic articles under the title **Flotsam and Jetsam:** *a collection of memories that have washed ashore after a forty-year career in the United States Navy.* I felt that there would be a lot of interest in stories about life in the Navy and particularly about submarines. I wasn't sure how many stories I had in my memory bank, but enough to keep me going for a few years anyway. Kelly agreed with me and I have been writing a story for the paper every two weeks. In addition, I have been sending email stories to friends and family and keep adding to the list as I make new friends.

As you can tell from the Table of Contents, these stories begin with my first experiences in the Navy as a Midshipman and continue with my career on ships through my command tour of USS Seahorse. Every naval officer who has the opportunity aspires to the command of a ship and I felt this would be a logical ending for this book. Command of a ship is the high point of one's Navy career, particularly in submarines. Submarines as opposed to surface ships operate autonomously. They get orders from the admiral back at headquarters, but these orders are flexible and recognize that the commanding officer will have to make independent decisions without referring to headquarters. It was this opportunity for independent action that drew me to a submarine career.

I was fortunate to have several outstanding officers under my command. My first Executive Officer was Bill Habermeyer who made my job look easy because he was always just behind the scenes making things happen that needed to be done. His advice to me was well thought out and I could always count on him for the right decision. He went from Seahorse to an exceptional command tour in USS Puffer, was selected for flag rank and served as commander Submarine Group Two in New London. George Bardsley relieved Bill Habermeyer and was an outstanding Executive Officer. His patrol report for our last patrol was the best the SUBLANT intelligence office had seen in ten years. George went on to command of USS Spadefish and a major command of USS Ohio. George Voelker was the Engineer during the shipyard period and went on to a very successful career in the Navy and retired as a Rear Admiral in command of Navy Recruiting. John Bird was communications officer during my last patrol, has since gone on to an extremely successful career, and is currently a Vice Admiral and Seventh Fleet Commander. Last but by no means least in this group of superstars was Leo Falardeau who was a nuclear-trained second class Petty Officer with about three years in the Navy when I took command. I saw great promise in Leo and even though he was a nuclear power plant watchstander, for my last patrol he was qualified as a plot coordinator for the attack center and a key member of the fire control team. He advanced to Chief Petty officer and then selected for the Nuclear Limited Duty Officer program. Leo qualified both submarine and surface warfare. He commanded a dry dock, served as Chief Engineer of the nuclear Aircraft Carrier Harry S. Truman. He commanded the King's Bay Trident Refit Center and served as Chief of Staff for a Carrier Battle Group. Captain Falardeau now serves in the Bureau of Naval Personnel as a Branch Head and is the most Senior Limited Duty Officer in The Navy. An extremely distinguished record and I am proud to have had a hand in the start of his career.

I have always felt that the success of a Commanding Officer can best be measured by the growth and future successes of the officers and senior petty officers under his command. The primary goal of a commanding officer is the training and nurturing of the personnel in his command. It may take several years for this success to become evident, but if you analyze the careers of successful naval leaders, you will find a common thread of outstanding mentors who have made a difference in the success of these individuals. I am proud of the role I played in the development of officers under my command.

Hank McKinney

Chapter I - My Midshipman Days

My First Day at Sea

During the summer of 1956, I embarked upon my first Navy ship, the destroyer USS Robert H. McCard (DD 822), for a midshipmen training cruise. I was 19 and nervous about my first time at sea. Becoming seasick was probably my single greatest concern.

One day out of Norfolk, we ran into rough seas. My watch station was in the forward engine room. I was hanging onto the handrail in the upper level of the engine room with the ship rolling 15 to 20 degrees. Feeling the oppressive heat of the steam machinery all around me, I was not sure how long it would be before I "lost my cookies." A voice behind me asked, "Is everything all right, Mid?" I turned around to see the Chief Petty Officer in charge of the watch. He took one look at me and told me go topside to get a breath of fresh air. I think that he was as much concerned about my making a mess in his engine room, as he was about my feeling miserable. In any event, I did not need more persuading to get out on the main deck for some air.

After a few minutes topside staring at the horizon, I came to the realization that the rest of the world was as stable as always and it was only the ship that was trying to tip over. With that thought, I overcame my nausea, and decided that I could return to my watch in the engine room. Climbing down the ladder, I met the chief who seemed as relieved as I was that I was no longer green. I thanked the chief for his concern and resumed my watch.

Later that same day, the ship was scheduled to go alongside the battleship USS Wisconsin (BB 64) for a hi-line transfer of personnel. Though I was still on watch in the engine room, I was very interested in what was happening on the main deck. The chief gave me a nod and told me to go up the ladder but not to leave the hatch and not to go out on the main deck, as it was too dangerous.

I reached the top of the ladder, stuck my head through the hatch and I will never forget the sight. All I could see was a gray wall about fifty feet away from our ship. It was the hull of the Wisconsin and it was enormous! As I raised my eyes, I could see the men, all in crisp white uniforms, handling lines on their main deck, which was twenty feet above ours. I saw gun mounts bristling from the superstructure, more than I could count. But the thing that really got my attention was the music I heard. It sounded like a band, but it couldn't be, not at sea! Then I spotted it, a Navy band, all in white, on the main deck just aft of Wisconsin's big 16" gun mounts, playing "Anchors Aweigh." I was dumbstruck. In the middle of the Atlantic Ocean and being serenaded by a Navy Band. What a treat!

I learned a lot on my first day at sea. First, I did not have to worry about becoming seasick. Second, Chief Petty Officers take care of their men. And finally, the Navy takes its music to sea. This was a day I will never forget.

USS Robert H. McCard (DD 822)

The Captain's Therapy

The Navy ships supporting the midshipman cruise during the summer of 1956 included the battleship USS Wisconsin, the cruiser USS Albany, a large fleet oiler, a supply ship and about twenty destroyers. This task force was deployed in a circular formation with USS Wisconsin, USS Albany and the auxiliary ships in the center and the destroyers in a circular anti-submarine screen, the diameter of which was about 4 miles. We sailed across the Atlantic from Norfolk to the Mediterranean and made port calls in France and Spain, my ship, the USS Robert H. McCard moored in Barcelona.

When we departed Barcelona, I was no longer standing watches in the engineering spaces, but was reassigned to the bridge to continue my midshipman training. No longer could I wear my dungarees and not have to worry about getting dirty working around oily bilges and machinery. I shifted into my whites, all starched and gleaming, and reported to the bridge for my first indoctrination watch.

The first thing I noticed was how quiet it was. We were about thirty feet above the main deck, and the breeze was warm and gentle. As the ship left Barcelona, the Mediterranean was very calm, hardly a ripple. Orders were given by the officer of the deck in a quiet voice and just as quietly acknowledged by the helmsman. Having just left the noisy and chaotic engineering spaces, I was overwhelmed by the quiet order of this part of the ship. I found the bridge peaceful, almost serene. It reminded me of coming into a church from the busy hustle and bustle of the city street outside.

I observed the watch routine for about thirty minutes and then the Quartermaster of the Watch told me take over as the helmsman. I hadn't a clue how to steer a warship, but after about ten minutes of instruction, I got the hang of it. It is not like driving a car, as there is no road to follow. The officer of the deck orders a course to steer, "Steer 130" which means to keep the ship steady on a heading of 130 by the gyrocompass. It all sounds easy, and after a 30-minute stint at the helm, I was relieved by a fellow midshipman. The quartermaster took me out on the wing of bridge and told me to look at the wake trailing behind the ship. It meandered back and forth across the ocean for a half a mile. It was anything but straight! I had been over-correcting in steering the ship and the crooked wake was the proof. I was embarrassed, but he told me not to be, I was a rookie and he was sure that I would learn in time how to keep an absolutely straight wake.

While out on the bridge wing, I noted a special chair, with the initials CO on it. I asked the Quartermaster if this was the Commanding Officer's chair and he replied that it was, and that only the Captain was allowed to sit in it. As the chair was occupied, I got my first glimpse of the Captain, albeit from the back. He appeared quite relaxed, enjoying the fresh breeze and the view. Every now and then, he would reach into a bag of jellybeans and help himself to one or two. He also had a little notebook by his side and a stopwatch. Periodically, he would note something in the ocean, punch his stopwatch, then stare intently for a few seconds and then punch the stopwatch again. He then would make an entry in his notebook. I couldn't for the life of me figure out what he was doing, but I assumed that it must be important for him to be so absorbed by it.

Later, I asked the Quartermaster what important business the Captain was involved in with his stopwatch. He smiled, and told me that the Captain was timing the flight of flying fish. But he wasn't sure what the Captain was going to do with the results of his study. He then asked me about my impressions of my first bridge watch and I remarked how quiet it was and well ordered. He commented that I should have been aboard three months ago before the Captain started timing flying fish, as it wasn't quite so peaceful and serene then. The Captain was a tyrant and life was very difficult for the personnel on the bridge. Then he started timing flying fish and relaxing, and life on the bridge became a lot easier. I discovered that day that even Captains need a little therapy!

Shoal Waters in Guantanamo Bay

After we left the Mediterranean, we proceeded north toward the British Isles and through the Irish Sea to Belfast, Ireland for our next port call.

My sister-in-law had an Irish cousin who was a Commander in the Royal Navy, who lived near Belfast on the coast. He made arrangements with our Navy to pick me up from the ship to spend a few days with his family. My fellow third-class midshipmen were duly impressed when a Commander in the Royal Navy met me on the Quarterdeck and escorted me ashore to an awaiting official Navy car. I had a great stay with Commander Bailey and his family. This was followed by a four-day trip to London to "see the sights" and then underway again for Guantanamo Bay, Cuba.

The Navy has had a naval base in Guantanamo Bay since 1903, first as a coaling station and then as a Fleet Training Center. This base has certainly had a lot of recent notoriety as a result of the detention center there for the terrorists captured in Afghanistan. But the primary use of the base had been for underway training of Navy ships in gunnery practice and readiness evaluations. Our midshipman task force was there for gunnery training so that midshipmen would have actual hands-on experience operating and firing naval guns from 40mm anti-aircraft guns to 16-inch shore bombardment guns.

The USS Robert H. McCard had three twin 5-inch gun mounts that were dual-purpose anti-aircraft guns and shore bombardment guns. Each gun could fire up to 15 rounds per minute with an experienced loading crew, and each projectile, weighed 54 pounds. By comparison, the 16-inch guns on the USS Wisconsin fired a 2,000-pound projectile. My assignment was as a member of the crew in mount 53 and we rotated assignments between loading crew and trainer and pointer of the gun mount. Our target was a sled towed 1,000 yards astern of a fleet tug. There was a safety observer in each gun mount, whose primary concern was that we were pointing the gun at the sled and not the tug. As the ship was rolling 5 to 10 degrees in the swell, the key to success was to time the firing of the gun just before the target rolled into the crosshairs. Mount 53 edged out the other two mounts with 55% of our shots on target, which was well below the fleet average but not too bad for midshipmen trainees.

We celebrated our success that night ashore at the fleet enlisted man's club. I expect that we were a little too boisterous and must have caught the attention of a group of Marines who were in the club. After we left the club, and were walking back to the ship the Marines caught up with us and we had a minor confrontation. These Marines were assigned to the USS Wisconsin and were not happy with the way the Midshipmen onboard her were treating them, and it was clear that they wanted to take out their frustrations on us. I stepped forward to attempt to calm the situation and the next thing I knew, I was on the ground with a bloody nose and a sore jaw. I never saw who hit me. Fortunately, the Shore Patrol was not too far away, and the situation was rapidly under control. As I was the only one hit, but could not identify my assailant, the Shore Patrol escorted both groups back to our ships and no further action was taken. The corpsman on the McCard took care of my medical needs, which were minor.

The next morning, the ship's Executive Officer asked to see me. When I reported to him, the officer in charge of midshipmen was there as well. They debriefed me on the incident and then gave me some advice that has served me well in future years in the Navy. *"Steer clear of shoal waters and you will never run aground."* It took me awhile to realize that this advice applied to more than navigation of a ship.

Marines, Aviators, Submariners and Sharks

1957 saw my second summer of midshipmen training. I was now a "seasoned" midshipman second-class and ready for anything that the Navy could throw at me. The last summer focused on going to sea and learning the fundamentals of shipboard life, which I enjoyed very much. This summer was going to be different, however. The first three weeks was devoted to an introduction to the Marine Corps at the Little Creek Amphibious Base near Norfolk, Virginia and the second three weeks was spent at the Naval Air Station, Corpus Christi, Texas for an introduction to Naval Aviation. I also elected an additional week at the Submarine Base in New London, Connecticut for an introduction to submarines.

Reveille at 0500 with calisthenics conducted by a Marine Drill Sergeant was a shocker to us all, but we quickly adapted a Marine "gung-ho" mentality and by the end of our time in Little Creek we were actually enjoying our routine. We learned a great deal about amphibious warfare, including conducting an actual landing on the beach, witnessed live fire exercises and even had some time for liberty on the weekends to enjoy the pleasures of nearby Virginia Beach and its famous boardwalk. A few of my classmates elected the Marine Corps "option" for the last two years of the NROTC program and were commissioned as 2nd Lieutenants in the Marine Corps. The training during this summer certainly had a lot to do with their decision, but I also knew that most of them were very weak in mathematics and dreaded the upcoming celestial navigation course that we would take in the fall semester. The Marine Corps option did not require this course.

The second three weeks in Corpus Christie was a blast, a jet blast! We learned that Naval Aviators enjoyed a "laid back" life style, and this was thirty years before the movie Top Gun. Because of poor eyesight, I would never qualify for Naval Aviation, but I enjoyed the training we received, including demonstration rides in jet aircraft and seaplanes, as well as a Blue Angels air show. Little did I know at the time that my next summer's cruise would be on an aircraft carrier and I would have the opportunity to see two months of at sea flight operations.

I was only one of about five midshipmen who attended the optional submarine training. I think that this was due primarily to the fact that we had to pay for our own transportation to New London. (In later years, the Navy would include a week of submarine training for all midshipmen.) Because we were a small group, we got special attention and had the opportunity to go to sea for two days on a diesel submarine, USS Entemedor (SS 340). This was quite an experience as we watched an officer from another submarine go through an "at sea" practical examination in order to qualify in submarines. He was under a lot of pressure as he conducted evolutions that had been pre-planned by the ship with built-in casualties and mistakes that had to be corrected by the officer being observed. We did not understand all that was going on, but we came away impressed with the thoroughness of submarine training and qualification.

During lunch on the second day at sea, the Entemedor surfaced in Long Island sound and the atmosphere was relaxed. We were directed to go the bridge for some commanding officer training. We climbed the ladder to the bridge and met Commander Joe Skoog, commanding officer of USS Entemedor and the principal "tormentor" of the officer who was going through qualification. He explained to us that this was standard procedure for submarines and that even though it did not seem to us that it was going very well for the qualifying officer, Commander Skoog thought that he was doing fine. He told us that the key to success was keeping your wits about you during times of stress and relying on the fundamentals of submarine training. That was what he was looking for as he conducted this qualification exam.

The captain then asked us if we would like a little target practice on the sharks in Long Island sound. He had some of the cooks, topside throwing meat in the water and the sharks were very active. We all had a chance to fire an M-1 at the sharks and as soon as one was hit, the others would start attacking the wounded shark. It was quite a demonstration of the ferocity of these creatures, and a lesson I would heed later on about the dangers of sharks in the open ocean.

USS Entemedor (SS 340)

Pollywogs and Shellbacks on a Bird Farm

During the summer of 1958, I was fortunate to be selected to participate in a cruise aboard the USS Ranger (CVA 61) as she conducted a transit from Norfolk, Virginia to Alameda, California, her new homeport in San Francisco Bay. As this class aircraft carrier is too large to transit through the Panama Canal, the voyage took us around South America. This was a period of relative peace around the world, and President Eisenhower had proclaimed a "People to People" program for the military in maximizing visits to foreign ports of call. The Navy felt that the Ranger cruise was a good opportunity to meet this objective and scheduled port calls in Trinidad; Rio de Janeiro, Brazil; Valparaiso, Chile; Lima, Peru; and Acapulco, Mexico. Five midshipmen from each of the 52 universities with NROTC programs were selected to participate.

Life aboard a modern aircraft carrier was a new experience for most of us, as our previous training cruises had been aboard destroyers and cruisers. Aircraft carriers are sometimes called flattops and in Navy slang are referred to as "Bird Farms." They carry over 100 airplanes and are virtually small cities with over 5,000 men aboard. The fight deck during flight operations is extremely busy and hazardous if you don't know what you are doing. As midshipmen, we were allowed out on deck only if we were accompanied by a member of the flight deck crew and we were not allowed to leave his side. I remember being with the catapult officer as he launched the aircraft. He had a special loop attached to his belt and I had to hold onto that loop and stay with him wherever he went. His message to me was that he wanted to feel me pulling on that loop at all times. The wind across the flight deck was generally 30 knots and the noise of the jet engines made conversation impossible. Everything was coordinated with hand signals.

The ship is controlled from the bridge about four stories above the fight deck on the "island", which is on the starboard side of the ship. Just aft of the bridge is PRIFLY, which is the primary flight control center where the Air Boss who is the officer directing aircraft launches and recoveries is stationed. Both of these are very busy places during flight operations. During this cruise, there was no admiral aboard, therefore the Flag Bridge, which is three stories above the flight deck, was not being used and was assigned to the midshipmen for our exclusive use. Sitting in the Admiral's chair looking out the window watching flight operations was an experience none of us will ever forget. The ship conducted both day and night flight operations.

The flight deck, which is over 1,000 feet long and over 200 feet wide, was also the location of our "Crossing the Line" ceremony, which is a traditional event for all sailors around the world when their ship crosses the equator. Those who have already crossed the equator are designated "Shellbacks" and those who have not crossed, are "Pollywogs." It is the responsibility of the shellbacks to ensure that the pollywogs are fully indoctrinated into the "mysteries of the deep" in an appropriate ceremony as the ship crosses the equator.

The day before the crossing, Davey Jones came aboard and all the pollywogs were gathered together, charged with infractions against the law of the sea, and directed to appear before King Neptune and his court the next day. The day of the crossing, the pollywogs were fed an unpalatable breakfast of cold green scrambled eggs, cold green spaghetti, green Kool-Aid and salted coffee. We then gathered in the hangar deck and in groups of 50 or so were allowed to proceed to the flight deck to appear before King Neptune's court. To get to the court, we had to run through a gauntlet of shellbacks wielding three-foot sections of fire hoses to "get our attention" and keep us moving.

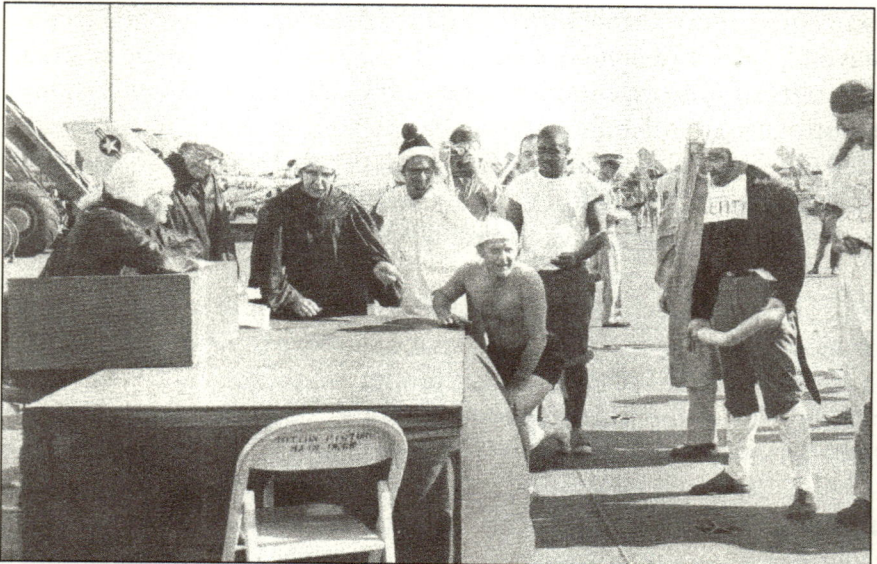

Shellbacks & Pollywogs

King Neptune's Royal Family

King Neptune and Queen Aphrodite and assorted members of the court were seated on their thrones in full regalia. Before we were allowed to plead our charges we were given a "truth serum" that seemed to be a mixture of Tabasco sauce and vinegar. We were all found guilty as charged, directed to kiss the belly of the royal baby, who was the fattest man in the crew with a greased stomach, taken to the royal barber to have our hair thoroughly oiled and greased and we then crawled through a 300-foot long garbage chute with shellbacks again encouraging us to move quickly. We finally made it to a large tank of salt water where we were immersed and declared cleansed of all our landlubberly grime and declared true Shellbacks. Over 4,000 pollywogs were initiated that day and it was a great experience for all of us, although I am sure that the 800 Shellbacks were glad to see it over.

USS Ranger (CV 61)

Black Shoes, Brown Shoes, the Southern Cross and Eight Bells

The major mission of an aircraft carrier is the forward deployment of an air striking force if required to defend our national interest throughout the world. With over one hundred aircraft on board, it is indeed a formidable force. The commanding officer of a carrier and the executive officer are both naval aviators, as well they should be as their major focus is on the launching and recovery of aircraft, but there is a large contingent of surface officers on board in charge of the traditional aspects of running a ship from navigation, deck seamanship to engineering. This alliance of two warfare specialties, aviation and surface, has always been a difficult one. Aviators have always been known as "brown shoes" because of the shoes they wear with khaki uniforms and surface officers are known as "black shoes" because of the color shoes that they wear at sea and with the traditional navy blue uniform.

The major focus of our midshipman training cruise on board the Ranger was the completion of our at-sea navigation workbook. During the previous academic year, we had taken a course in celestial navigation and we were now ready to test our skills and knowledge as navigators. The navigator of the Ranger was a "black shoe" and was ready to show us the stars. In 1958 celestial navigation was the principal means of navigation for Navy ships as there were no navigation satellites and no GPS (Global Positioning System). All we had were the stars, and I was looking forward to seeing the Southern Cross, which is only visible in the Southern Hemisphere, and using some of its stars for navigation.

Celestial navigation involves measuring the angle between a known star (Altair, Spica, Polaris, etc.) and the horizon using a sextant, which can measure this angle very accurately. This process is called "shooting the star." The exact time of the sighting is noted, then several calculations are made, and a Line of Position (LOP) results and this line is plotted on the chart. After shooting three or four stars, the resulting three or four LOP's should all theoretically cross at a common point, which is the ship's position. Theory and practice don't always match however and some of our navigation fixes put us in the middle of Brazil or near the west coast of Africa. Fortunately, the ship's navigator did not have these problems and he was able to help us find our mistakes as well.

Since one measures the angle between the horizon and the star, you must be able to see a clear horizon and a star at the same time. The period of time that this is possible is called "twilight", both evening and morning. The stars are very faint at this time with only the brightest stars visible. By the time the dimmer stars are visible, it is too dark to see the horizon. As it turns out, the four stars that make up the Southern Cross are not terribly bright stars, and I was never able to pick out one of these stars during the twilight period while we still had a clear horizon. Ten years later, I was able to shoot the stars of the Southern Cross for navigation when I was the Navigator on a submarine, the USS Shark, but that is another story.

Another important celestial observation is made during daylight, which uses the sun to determine "Local Apparent Noon." From sunrise to noon, the sun rises and reaches its highest point in the sky at noon. This is not precisely at 12:00 PM (noon), because it depends upon what the longitude of the ship is, hence this time when the sun reaches its zenith is called "Local Apparent Noon" or LAN. The method of determining this time is to continue to measure the angle between the sun and the horizon until the maximum angle or zenith is reached. This angle is noted and through some rather simple calculations, the latitude of the ship is determined.

In the eighteenth century, this determination of LAN was also used to reset the local time on the ship, as clocks were not yet used at sea. When the ship's Navigator announced LAN, the marine sentry was directed to turn over the hourglass, and eight bells were sounded. The hour glass was actually a half hour glass and it was subsequently turned over every 30 minutes at which time one bell was sounded at 1230, two bells at 1300, three bells at 1330 and so on up to eight bells at 1600. The watch rotation was every four hours, with eight bells marking the end of each watch. This would continue until the next day when LAN was reestablished. We have accurate clocks on ships today and we do not reset our clocks to LAN each day, but we still rely upon the traditional sounding of a ship's bell to mark each half hour, with the rotation of the watch at eight bells.

Chapter II - USS Wedderburn (DD 684)

Pacific Odyssey

In January 1959, I had some decisions to make about what I was going to do after graduation from college in June. Most of my classmates were trying to find a job or applying for graduate school. I knew that in June, I would be going on active duty as an ensign in the Navy, and the only decision I had to make was on what type of ship I wanted to serve. I was interested in the Navy's nuclear submarine program, but this was not possible for two reasons. The first was that there were no direct inputs to the submarine program at that time; you could only get into submarines after two years on a surface ship. The second problem was my academic record in college. I majored in engineering, but I was sure that my grades would not qualify me for entrance into the elite nuclear power training program. So I asked to be sent to a small ship, preferably a newly commissioned destroyer on the west coast.

My orders arrived in May and I was to report to the USS Wedderburn (DD 684), a World War II Fletcher Class destroyer, a veteran of World War II and 15 years old. Not exactly a newly commissioned ship, but it was home-ported in San Diego. The ship was deployed to the western Pacific, and my orders were to report to the Commander of the Twelfth Naval District in San Francisco for further routing. I arrived in San Francisco on 6 July and a few days later, left Travis Air Force Base in a Boeing Stratocruiser (a B-29 converted to a passenger plane) for a 24-hour fight across the Pacific with refueling stops in Hawaii and Wake Island, final destination Tachikawa Air Force Base, Japan. I then reported to the Naval Base in Yokosuka to await the arrival of the Wedderburn. After about ten days, I was advised that its next port of call would be Iwakuni Marine Corps Air Station and I flew down to Iwakuni on a Marine transport plane. A few days later, I reported on board USS Wedderburn on 23 July, completing my 17-day Pacific odyssey.

I reported to the captain, Commander James D. Oliver, the next morning after he had reviewed my record. I had my heart set on a division officer position in the Operations or the Gunnery Department. The Captain told me that another officer, who was a Naval Academy graduate was due to report on board, and because of his training and experience, he felt that he would be ready to take on the position as First Lieutenant in charge of the deck division. He did not assign me directly to a division officer position, but he felt that due to my engineering training in college, I would be able to fit into the Engineering Department. I was very disappointed, but was determined to carry on where I was needed.

As it turned out, this was a great assignment and I really got a great start in my Navy career with this experience in the Engineering Department. The ship was part of a division of four destroyers supporting the carrier operations of the USS Oriskany. The Oriskany needed at least 30 knots of wind across the deck to launch and recover aircraft and required her escorts to have all four boilers on the line and to be ready for flank speed of 33 knots as required. The other three destroyers (tin cans) were also WWII veterans and over 15 years old, and this demand for full power capability was very difficult to meet for these older ships. At the conclusion of each day's carrier operations, one or more of the tin cans had suffered some form of engineering casualty and had to conduct repairs at night in order to be ready the next morning. Wedderburn was no exception and I found myself assigned to the engineering casualty control team to assist in conducting necessary repairs. Leading the team was Machinist's Mate First Class Hightower and he knew his stuff, having served on tin cans for most of his twenty years in the Navy. I was very fortunate to spend my first month aboard under his tutelage.

By the end of this Western Pacific deployment in November, when we returned to San Diego, I was the Machinery Division Officer and Main Propulsion Assistant, with 30 men in the division. I also knew a great deal about the engineering plant, and was destined to learn considerably more in the next year. The Naval Academy graduate who reported that summer was Kevin Mulkern. Kevin and I became fast friends over the next three years. He knew his seamanship and was a very proficient ship-handler, and I knew my engineering and, as I found out, the captain knew what was best for his officers.

USS Wedderburn (DD 684)

Oil on Troubled Waters

After we returned to San Diego in November 1959, the ship had a stand-down period over the Christmas holiday period with a liberal leave policy in effect. When I returned from Christmas leave with my parents in Illinois, I found out that I was scheduled to attend a six-week school at Treasure Island in San Francisco. The course of instruction was titled, Atomic, Biological, Chemical Defense training, or ABCD for short. But before I departed for school, I became heavily involved in preparing the ship for an underway training period in mid-January.

One morning during January, I got a phone call from the quarterdeck watch just after returning from morning quarters with the engineering department. Petty Officer Jones told me "Senior Chief Flowers said to let you know the lubricating oil that you requisitioned last week is on the pier, but he thinks that you need to come topside to see it." I thought that this was a strange request, because there really wasn't anything to see except a tank truck with 2200 gallons of lubricating oil (2190TEP in Navy lingo), which would be pumped to our storage tanks in the engine room.

I went topside and then had to cross over the three ships in our squadron moored inboard to reach the pier. After saluting the flag and then the quarterdeck watch of each of these ships and requesting permission to cross, I finally reached the pier. I found a frustrated leading chief and his engine room gang looking at forty 55-gallon drums of 2190TEP lube oil stacked on the pier and an irate crane operator asking us to expedite moving this mess off his pier so that he could move his crane.

"Mr. McKinney," Senior Chief Flowers said, "it looks as if we made a mistake in ordering the oil and rather than a tank truck delivery, we've got forty barrels to manhandle across three ships." I appreciated the senior chief using the term "we" as it was I who had placed the order and had made the mistake. I asked him how much each drum weighed, and he replied that he thought about 400 pounds. It was clear to me that trying to get forty heavy and unwieldy drums across the quarterdecks of our three sister ships was not an option. We were scheduled to get underway tomorrow and there was no time to reorder the oil for delivery by a tank truck. Finally, I had to deal with the crane operator who was becoming increasingly agitated.

Then it occurred to me that oil floats on water, and maybe that was the answer. I explained to the crane operator that he could wait all day until we moved the oil one barrel at a time across three ships or he could help us and we could get the job done in half the time. Senior Chief Flowers wasn't sure that an oil drum full of oil would float and neither was I, but it was worth a try. He had our Chief Boatswain get our motor whaleboat underway, with the help from some of the engine room gang we got a line around a barrel and had the crane pick it up, and move it the side of the pier. By that time, we had quite a crowd of onlookers who were evenly split between "Another officer hair-brained idea that will never work" and "Give it a chance, the Senior Chief thinks that it might."

We all held our breath as the first drum was lowered into the water. It really didn't float, but it didn't sink either, it just wallowed semi-submerged. It reminded me of those waterlogged deadheads that I used to avoid with my motorboat on the lake in northern Minnesota. The Chief Boatswain got a line on it and towed it to our fantail where the deck gang had rigged a davit with a block and tackle. In five minutes, the barrel was on our deck and the whaleboat was back alongside the pier picking up the second barrel. We were finished transferring the barrels by lunch and had all the lube oil transferred to our storage tanks that afternoon.

I learned a valuable lesson that day. Let the chief order the lubricating oil in the future! The ship got underway as scheduled the next day, and I was on my way to San Francisco.

Learning my ABCs on Treasure Island

In January 1960, I had the opportunity to attend my first Navy school at Treasure Island in San Francisco. Officially titled Atomic, Biological, Chemical and Damage Control School and commonly referred to as ABCD School, the school was six weeks long with the first three weeks focused on Damage Control, firefighting and controlling flooding and repairing damage during combat. We then spent three weeks learning about defensive measures to combat a nuclear, biological or chemical attack.

Treasure Island is a man-made island in the middle of San Francisco bay, which allowed easy access to San Francisco for "liberty-runs" but only during the weekends as the Navy kept us busy during most of the week.

Damage control on a Navy ship is very important. The Navy learned many valuable lessons during World War II, and we were fortunate to learn from individuals who had survived Kamikaze attacks and submarine torpedoes. Fire and flooding are the two principal concerns and we gained a great deal of practical experience fighting simulated shipboard fires and attempting to save a simulated sinking ship by stopping the flooding. Whenever I see the movie "Titanic", I have vivid memories of my experiences at this school.

By 1960, 15 years after the atomic bomb was dropped on Hiroshima, the Navy had learned a great deal about the effects of the atomic bomb and ship survivability. Unless it is a near direct hit, ships will survive the blast effect. If the crew is kept inside the ship, then the radiation from the explosion will be minimized. A major concern is the radiation from the fallout, particularly if the bomb detonates on the surface or subsurface of the ocean. All Navy ships were being equipped with water-wash-down systems in 1960 that would create a fine mist over the entire ship, which would capture the fallout before it reached the surface of the ship, and wash it overboard.

In addition to nuclear weapons, the Soviet Union had large stockpiles of biological and chemical weapons that presented a serious threat to our ships. We learned about nerve gas, anthrax, and many other chemical and biological agents. There were very few defensive measures against attacks using these weapons in 1960, and that is still the case today. That is why these weapons in the hands of terrorists are such a serious threat.

I reported to the ship in San Diego in late February only to find that I would be attending the Commander Cruiser Destroyer Force Pacific (COMCRUDESPAC) engineering officer course in March. This is an 8-week course conducted in San Diego with four weeks in a classroom and four weeks on board a ship. As it turned out, my ship, the USS Wedderburn was the designated school ship for this particular course, which would be a great opportunity for me to build on the knowledge I had already gained from my experiences during my first cruise in the Western Pacific in 1959. These two courses, back-to-back, may appear to some to be too much training. I was very fortunate that the Commanding Officer supported this time and effort as it paid off in my ability to meet the challenges that I would face in the next few years. Today, before officers report to their first ship, they receive at least six months of advanced training much as I received in 1960.

The instructors during the classroom phase were Chief Petty Officers, each with more than twenty years, experience running destroyer engineering plants. We learned the steam cycle from boilers to turbines to main condensers. We studied turbines, main feed pumps, condensate pumps, deaerating feed tanks, lubricating oil systems, fuel oil systems and electrical distribution. We were able to study cut away models of all the machinery we would find on our ship. In short, this was an extremely well organized school, one of the best in the Navy. The quality of the instructors was excellent and their mission was to impart their accumulated knowledge and experience to a group of newly commissioned, "still wet behind the ears" Ensigns.

The second phase aboard ship was a very practical "hands-on" experience. The crew of the Wedderburn had been directed to "open and inspect" the boilers and major machinery in the engineering spaces. Our instructors then led us through the required inspections and analysis of the status of the machinery. I received "special" attention from the instructors, as I was the prospective engineering officer of the ship. We crawled through the inside of boilers, inspecting soot build up in the firebox and water corrosion problems inside the steam drum. We lifted the casings of the main turbines, did micrometer checks of bearings and thrust clearances.

During the second half of the shipboard phase, we started up the engineering plant and took the ship to sea with the officer trainees manning all the watch stations. We conducted routine at-sea operations and casualty drills. This was a particularly valuable phase for me as I was the division officer of the machinery division and the crew could see that I was learning the operation of the engine room from experts, and they knew that I would expect high standards in their performance in the future.

I reported to the ship in May, fully trained to take on any assignment in the Engineering Department. For the next month, we all were heavily involved in preparations for our next deployment to the Western Pacific in July.

Formosa Patrol

On July 7, we departed San Diego with three other destroyers from our Destroyer Squadron (DESRON 15): USS Boyd (DD 544), USS McDermut (DD 677) and USS Bradford (DD 545). The Commodore was embarked in the Flagship, the USS Boyd. All four ships had limited range and required refueling stops to make it across the Pacific. Our first stop was Pearl Harbor, Hawaii the second stop was Midway Island and then Guam. While in Guam, we had a change of Commanding Officers with Commander Lawrence A. Wilder relieving Commander James D. Oliver. This was the first Change of Command ceremony that I witnessed, and I would see many more and participate in many during my naval career. Under my first skipper, I had become well trained and qualified in the engineering department and had qualified as Officer of the Deck for independent operations (OOD-I).

When we left Guam, we were assigned to Formosa Patrol operations for the next month. There was and still is today a great deal of tension between Communist China on the mainland of Asia and Nationalist China on the Island of Formosa (now called Taiwan). The Formosa Straights separates Formosa from the mainland, and the United States was committed to a continuous patrol in the straights to ensure the security of Taiwan. Two destroyers maintained this continuous presence.

During the first two weeks, USS Wedderburn was assigned to the southern patrol. When we shifted to the northern patrol, I had the first watch as OOD. We were proceeding on a northerly course, about 20 miles from mainland China. The Combat Information Center (CIC) reported a "Skunk" (surface radar contact) bearing 355, range 15 miles. Twenty minutes later, the skunk was bearing 353, range 10 miles, and appeared to be dead in the water (DIW). I called the Captain to advise him. Ten minutes later, CIC reported a great deal of radar activity from the Chinese mainland, and that most of the radars were focused on us. I became concerned and advised the Captain, who came to the bridge to evaluate. Just as he arrived on the bridge, CIC asked if we held the skunk visually, now bearing 348 at 6 miles and still DIW. We held no visual contacts on that bearing.

The Captain and the Navigator studied the chart to see if we had missed anything. They observed that on a bearing of 345 from our current position, at a range of 6 miles was a very small, unnamed island, little more than a large rock. Another close look on this bearing with our high power binoculars revealed what appeared to be a low-lying island. Our skunk was not a ship, but an island. Then the Navigator recalled reading something in our patrol instructions about this island, and left the bridge to check. He returned shortly to confirm that this small island was claimed as a territory of Red China and we were cautioned to remain at least twelve miles from this island, which was the limit of the claimed territorial waters of Red China. This also explained the increased radar activity from the mainland. The Captain directed that I alter course to the right and proceed until we were at least twelve miles from this island. He also said that he expected that we would hear some more about our "violation" of Chinese territorial waters.

As the Captain had predicted, the next day we received a message from CINCPACFLT (Commander in Chief, Pacific Fleet) advising us that Communist China had issued its twenty-sixth serious warning regarding the violation of its territorial waters by a United States warship. The message also requested all the data we had pertaining to our track and position during the previous day. I should note here, that the United States only recognizes a three-mile limit for territorial waters, which is standard for most nations.

The Navigator and I worked up all the track and position data and prepared a message for the Captain's review and release. The Captain then met with all the officers and navigation personnel to discuss what had happened and what he expected from us in the future so that we would not make this type of mistake again. All operations and evolutions would be briefed in advance, navigation charts and operations orders would be reviewed by all watch-standers, and each officer of the deck would be responsible to review all charts and proposed tracks for navigation hazards prior to his relieving the watch. These requirements are standard operating procedures today, but had not been in place at the time of this incident.

The Captain then met with me privately, and was I worried about my future? You bet I was! But he was very encouraging. He told me that I was only recently qualified as OOD and that it was clear to him that I was not the only one to make a mistake in this instance and that he had a great deal of confidence in me as a watch officer and finally, he hoped that I had learned from this event. I came away from this meeting very relieved personally, but also with a great deal of respect and admiration for the Commanding Officer.

This approach to leadership and mentoring of his officers would continue throughout his time as our Captain and would serve as a role model for me for the rest of my Navy career.

Plane Guard Operations

"FALLBROOK, THIS IS CHILDSPLAY. STATION. OUT" Those words coming over the bridge radio receiver were designed to get our attention, and they still do 45 years later. Our radio call sign was FALLBROOK and the call sign of the aircraft carrier USS Oriskany (CV 34) was CHILDSPLAY.

After a month on Formosa Patrol, we spent a few weeks in Yokosuka, Japan conducting repairs and enjoying an opportunity to visit Tokyo and Kyoto. We then got underway as part of the carrier task group supporting the USS Oriskany. USS Wedderburn was assigned plane guard operations, which meant that we were to take station about 1200 yards nearly directly astern of the Oriskany. From this plane guard station, we could quickly come to the rescue of a downed aircraft that had a problem either during the catapult launch or during landing. In either event, the plane would crash into the water fairly close to the carrier and we would be in a position to quickly reach the plane and render rescue assistance.

At 30 knots, steaming into a 10-knot wind, there is 40 knots of wind blowing across the open bridge, with accompanying stinging spray from waves hitting the bow. Orders to the helmsman were shouted into the pilothouse, and the radar repeaters were carefully monitored to insure that we maintained station. At 30 knots, the ship covers 1.000 yards every minute and with the carrier just 1200 yards away, the risk of collision is significant. If the Captain or the Officer of the Deck on the carrier is not comfortable with the plane guarding ship's position, particularly if it is too close, then the dreaded "STATION" message would come over the radio, which generally meant that we were too close. I am sure that they had the most powerful radio transmitter in the fleet and they carefully chose the individual who would transmit the message, as his voice would be full of authority, with just a touch of disdain as if to tell us that we were probably the worst destroyer that they had seen in weeks.

There was good reason for concern. In 1952, the USS Hobson (DD 464), a World War II destroyer, very similar to Wedderburn, was plane guarding the aircraft carrier USS Wasp at night in the Atlantic near the Azores. As Wasp turned into the wind at 27 knots, Hobson turned the wrong way going to plane guard station and the 34,000-ton Wasp hit the 2200-ton

Hobson broadside and cut the ship in half. 176 men were lost in one of the worst peace time accidents in our Navy's history.

During plane guard operations, our motor whaleboat was swung out on its davits ready to be launched and a rescue crew was standing by. If a plane crashed into the water, then within a few minutes we would be alongside the spot where the plane was lost and the rescue launch would be in the water. If it was a jet plane, the pilot may have had time to eject before the plane hit the water, if it was a propeller driven plane, the pilot would attempt to exit the plane after it had settled in the water. In either case, it was essential that we get to the crash site as quickly as possible in order to save the pilot's life. A night crash was particularly difficult due to reduced visibility.

We had our share of successes rescuing pilots, but it was very difficult for us all to arrive at the crash site and find only an oil slick and some scattered wreckage and no survivors. Pilots drew hazardous duty pay as compensation for the risks that they were taking, and I don't think any of us felt that this extra pay was not justly deserved. Today, all Navy combat aircraft are jet aircraft and to "bail out," pilots use an ejection seat and parachute. Our helicopters have rescue swimmers aboard and are much more capable of at-sea rescue, and as a result, today's destroyers are no longer involved in plane guard operations. But throughout most of the Cold War, nearly every destroyer was involved in plane guarding, and there was a whole generation of junior officers who learned to hate the dreaded "STATION" radio call from the carrier.

Fill Her Up!

When a ship needs to refuel at sea, it can be difficult to find a gas station! The Navy solves this logistics problem by strategically placing tankers around the world at sea for refueling the fleet. The destroyers (called "small boys") needed to find a gas station every four or five days. Many times the destroyers were refueled from the aircraft carrier that they were escorting. The aircraft carrier has a great deal of fuel oil storage capacity, but it is not ideally suited for alongside refueling, particularly on the port side where there is an overhang from the angled flight deck. The top of our mast was about 80 feet and the overhang of the flight deck was about 90 feet above the water, so theoretically, we could fit underneath. But this did not account for the ever-present swell and waves of the open ocean.

This painting is part of the Navy's Combat Art collection and was done by Walter Brightwell in 1960. It shows the USS Boyd (DD 544), one of our squadron sister ships, refueling from USS Oriskany (CV 34).

To accomplish an underway refueling, the carrier or tanker maintains a steady course and speed, and the destroyer maneuvers from astern to come alongside either the port or starboard side of the carrier with a distance between the ships of about 50 feet. Lines are passed over from the carrier, and then two cables are rigged from the carrier to the forward and after refueling trunks of the destroyer. Finally, a 6 inch diameter hose is sent over from the carrier and fitted into the refueling trunk. When all is stable, the oil pumps are turned on.

Unfortunately, nothing remains stable for very long at sea. The destroyer is constantly making changes in course and speed to maintain a safe distance from the carrier. If the sea is rough, the waves are magnified in the space between the two ships, and everyone is quickly drenched. If conditions are particularly rough, the task of maintaining position alongside the carrier is very difficult even for the most experienced and competent shiphandlers.

It was very rough with a large swell running as we made our approach to the port side of the aircraft carrier USS Oriskany (CV 34) for refueling. The Captain was in control on the bridge and was clearly concerned about the safety of our ship and of all hands working topside. I was in charge of the after refueling station and we were hanging on to our life lines and already soaked by waves washing over the main deck..

After a significant effort by the deck gang, all the lines were secure and the carrier commenced sending us fuel. The overhang from the carrier was directly over our heads and each time we rolled to starboard, we were sure that we would have a collision. Gradually we started to close on the carrier and even though the helmsman was applying left full rudder, it was clear to the Captain that a collision was inevitable if he did not take immediate action. He backed the port engine, went full ahead on the starboard engine and ordered an emergency breakaway from the carrier. The ship twisted to port and quickly started to clear the carrier. The deck crew cut all the lines from the Oriskany and the carrier stopped the oil pumps, but not before the hoses had pulled clear of the refueling trunks and literally sprayed hundreds of gallons of black fuel oil over our starboard side. We were all drenched now in black oil as well as salt water.

As we were clearing the Oriskany, I noticed a flashing signal light from another destroyer sending us a message. The phone talker told me that the Captain from the other destroyer had just asked our Captain for the stock number of our new haze gray paint on the starboard side of our ship. Our

Captain had not lost his sense of humor, as he replied to this inquiry with his own message, which stated, "You are looking at a well-oiled machine."

USS Oriskany (CV 34)

Keeping Watch at Sea

Watches at sea are four hours long, and generally, the crew is divided into three watch sections, which means that each member of the crew mans his watch station for four hours and then has eight hours off. It has been a custom, handed down from the Royal Navy, to split the early evening watch (1600-2000) into two 2-hour watches (1600-1800 and 1800-2000), which are called "dog watches." This alters the watch rotation so that one does not stand watch during the same period each day. As an example, the 0800-1200 watch will have the second dog watch (1800-2000) and then have the 0400-0800 watch on the next day.

My favorite watch was the early morning watch, 0400-0800. Awakened at 0315 and expected to relieve the watch at 0345 the ship is dark and very quiet at this hour. On a typical watch, the stars often were brilliant, as the moon set sometime before midnight. The phosphorescence in the water spectacular, and you could see our wake for over a mile. As the ship rolls the stars are literally dancing overhead. About 0430, the sky in the east starts to lighten as prelude to an anticipated 0530 sunrise. The sea is very dark, but over the next 90 minutes, it will change to a slate grey then to a dark blue and finally to the friendly brilliant blue of the open ocean. With a fresh cup of coffee, I would settle into the bridge watch routine. If traveling with other ships, we would adjust course and speed to maintain our assigned station and routinely check for other surface contacts. Wafting into the pilothouse is the aroma of the night baker's efforts from the ship's galley. Cinnamon sticky buns are my favorites, but some mornings its hot biscuits and I would send the messenger of the watch to the galley to return with fresh hot biscuits for the watch section.

The Navigator is on the bridge with his assistant at 0500 to take his morning star sights. Although the stars are fading, the brightest are still visible and the horizon is visible which allows the Navigator to shoot these stars by measuring the angle between the star and the horizon. The sky turns a rosy color, then red and finally, right on schedule, the sun bursts above the horizon. Sunlight streams into the pilothouse and glints off the shiny brass of the binnacle and the engine-order telegraph. The quartermaster turns off the ship's running lights and the members of the bridge watch look at each other and we seem to see new faces, even though we have been standing side by side, for the last two hours…we greet the new day and each other.

Reveille is at 0600 with the boatswains-mate(bosun) blowing a long shrill bosun's pipe and then passing the word on the 1MC, which is the ship's announcing system, "Reveille...Reveille...Up all bunks...All hands heave out and trice up... Reveille...Reveille." At 0615, a few of the crew are visible on the foc'sle as they break out fire hoses to wash down the deck. At 0630, another bosun's pipe with a long trill and over the 1MC "Sweepers, sweepers man your brooms. Give the ship a clean sweep down fore and aft. Sweep down all ladders, weather decks and passageways. Assemble all trash on the fantail. Sweepers, sweepers." The ship is starting to come to life.

The Captain has a call in for 0645 even though he has been called several times during the night with contact reports and routine course changes. He comes out on the bridge, has a cup of coffee with the Officer of the Deck, and watches the crew clean the ship. He reviews the navigator's star fix and approves the updated navigation position and then goes down to the wardroom for breakfast.

The aroma of fresh biscuits from the galley is replaced with fried bacon and fresh coffee. At 0655, over the 1MC "Clear the Mess Decks." Then at 0700 another bosun's pipe and the 1MC announcement "Breakfast for the crew" and we know that our relief's are near at hand. At 0745, my relief arrives and we turn over the watch and I lay to the wardroom to report my relief to the Captain and enjoy breakfast. Another day at sea has started and I was there to see night turn into day and have the joy of seeing the ship and crew come to life. Life at sea is an experience one never forgets.

Backgammon - the Navy Way

Every Sailor learns to play various games at sea to wile away his idle time. In today's Navy, Sailors play video games and other high-tech diversions. In the Navy I joined in the late fifties, times were simpler and so were our pleasures. One of the first games that I was introduced to was Acey/Deucey. No, it isn't a card game and it isn't a gambling game. Acey/Deucey is the Navy's form of Backgammon.

Two Chiefs playing Acey-Deucey (ca. 1910)

Acey/Deucey can be played on a regulation backgammon board with regulation pieces, but Sailors at sea have created a much simpler game board; one that can be easily stored and set up anywhere on the ship on a moment's notice. A piece of canvass about 2 feet long and one foot wide is the playing board. A standard Backgammon board is painted on the canvas. When not in use, the canvas "board" can be easily rolled up and stored away in a locker.

The playing pieces are brass and steel washers as well as two standard dice along with an old wooden cigar box. The cigar box was set on its side with a hole on the top side, a series of baffles in the box and a hole at the bottom. The dice were dropped in the hole at the top of the box and then tumbled through the baffles and came out the bottom.

I learned to play Acey/Deucey from a first class Boatswain's mate named Weaver. The rules are simple. Each player has fifteen pieces (washers) and he places them on his end of the board according to the numbers rolled on the dice. The object of the game is to move your pieces around the board (in the opposite direction of your opponent), moving each piece according to the numbers rolled on the dice. If you roll doubles, then you can move one piece or as many as four pieces the number of spaces associated with the number on the dice. For example, double fours would allow you to move one piece, sixteen spaces, two pieces eight spaces or four pieces four spaces. If you land on a space occupied by a single piece of your opponent it is knocked off the board and must go back to the beginning. If you roll a one and a two (Acey/Deucey), then you move two of your pieces one space and two spaces and elect a doubles of your choice to move your other pieces as if you had rolled that set of doubles. You also get to roll the dice again after an acey/Deucey.

If you have two or more pieces on a single space, then you prevent your opponent from landing on that space and from knocking your men off the board. An important strategy during the play of the game is to set up a block of several adjacent spaces with two of your pieces on each space, thereby impeding the forward progress of your opponent. The game ends when one player has moved all his pieces around the board into his opponent's home territory and then has removed all of his pieces.

I not only learned to play from Bosun Weaver, but I also had my first lesson in humility, as I never won a game against him. As Bosun Weaver pointed out, I played pretty well for a new ensign, and after I had fifteen years in "this man's Navy" as he had, I might be able to win a few games.

Every day after lunch, the Captain and the Executive Officer played a game of Acey/Deucey in the wardroom and generally, the Exec won, much to the chagrin of the CO. The CO was a Naval Academy graduate and taught me a lot during my first tour. The Exec was a mustang who had come up through the ranks to become an officer. When I had the opportunity to ask him about his phenomenal success playing Acey/Deucey against the skipper, he just smiled and told me that he learned from a Boatswain's mate many years ago.

An Acey/Deucey tournament was a popular event on board the ship and Bosun Weaver and the Exec were generally in the finals pitting their skills and experience against each other. After twenty years in the Navy, I could routinely win most of the games in the wardroom, but rarely did I make it into the finals of a ship-wide tournament.

Who's Driving?

The helmsman is the man assigned to steer the ship. His job is to maintain the ship on a specific course on the gyrocompass as ordered by the Officer of the Deck (OOD). As opposed to driving a car, the helmsman does not really need to know what's in front of him; that is the responsibility of the OOD. On a destroyer, the helmsman stands watch inside the pilothouse on the bridge and has limited visibility of the sea around him.

The helm, or steering wheel, is not connected directly to the rudder. The movement of the helm sends an electrical signal to a remote location located in the stern of the ship very close to the rudder. This location is called "after steering." The ship maintains a continuous watch while underway in after steering. In the event of an emergency on the bridge, control of steering the ship can be shifted to after steering. The helmsman in after steering has the same responsibility to maintain ordered course as indicated by the gyrocompass. We practiced shifting steering control to after steering on a regular basis. Little did we know that this drill would one day be for real.

We had been at sea with the carrier for almost a month, and we were all looking forward to our next port, Hong Kong. We had run into the tail end of a typhoon and were in very heavy seas. A rogue wave engulfed our fantail. The helmsman reported, "I have lost steering." The watch-stander in after steering reported a significant amount of water had come through the ventilation system and had shorted out the switchboard. The after steering watch shifted to manual steering, and we regained control of the ship. We later determined that the flooding in after steering had shorted out the synchronous follow-up motor that receives the electrical signal from the bridge, and we would have to continue to steer from after steering until we could get the motor repaired at a shipyard.

It looked as if the Hong Kong trip was off and that we would have to go to Subic Bay in the Philippines to get the motor repaired. Morale really dropped at this point as Hong Kong was to be the high point of our entire six-month deployment. The Captain got on the radio with the aircraft carrier and asked about their electric motor repair capability and their reply was that it could be done on the carrier while in Hong Kong as long as we provided the manpower to do the job. The Commanding Officer of the aircraft carrier made it clear that he did not want us within a mile of his ship with our current steering casualty, but we were welcome to "tag along" to Hong Kong.

This left only one problem, and that was the need for refueling at sea from the tanker in three days, just before we arrived in Hong Kong. Our Captain decided that we could easily accomplish this task, the misgivings of the carrier Captain notwithstanding. After all, he was an aviator and not really experienced at handling a small ship. We practiced for three days with control shifted to after steering. The officer of the deck would give his helm orders to the helmsman on the bridge who would pass these orders by sound-powered phones to the helmsman in after steering. The bridge helmsman could constantly monitor the course to ensure that the orders were followed. We were ready for a refueling.

While refueling from a tanker, the ships are side-by-side separated by about 50 to 75 feet. Minute changes in course are made to ensure a safe separation between the ships. The risk of collision is high and everyone is particularly alert. Our approach to the tanker went smoothly and we came alongside, passed over the lines, and commenced refueling. I was in charge of the after refueling station. The phone talker told me that our Captain wanted to speak with the Captain of the tanker on the phones. I watched the bridge of the tanker as their Captain put on the headset. The conversation was very short—15 seconds—and terminated by the Captain of the tanker removing his head set and departing to the other side of his bridge, not to be seen again.

We completed the refueling about 20 minutes later and returned without incident to our station with the carrier. The next day we entered Hong Kong harbor and the crew enjoyed 5 days of hard-earned liberty. First Class Electrician's Mate Gresham and his division officer (yours truly) spent most of our time on the carrier rewinding the motor, but we both got ashore to do some shopping.

I asked the Captain about his short conversation with the Captain of the tanker. He told me that he had determined that he was an aviator as well, getting his first ship command experience before he took over an aircraft carrier. Our skipper decided not to tell him in advance about our steering problems as he could have denied our request for refueling, but rather to tell him personally as soon as we were alongside. When he explained that we were not steering the ship from the bridge, the tanker skipper couldn't believe it, but he couldn't tell us to stop, so he went to the other side of his bridge and ignored us. He sent a strong message of protest to our commodore. The Captain received a nice letter from the Commodore who said that he was going to ignore the incident and praised our skipper for doing the right thing in protecting our visit to Hong Kong. The entire crew of the ship felt the same way.

The Birds of Midway

I was standing the afternoon watch on our return journey to San Diego on the tail end of our 1960 WestPac deployment. We were enroute to Midway Island for a refueling stop, then on to Pearl Harbor and finally to San Diego. It was late November, and I was enjoying the warm afternoon sun. Just after 1300, Shipfitter (Pipe) second class Sedlak reported to me that all was "sound and secure." Sedlak had the sounding and security watch, which entailed roving the ship, checking all spaces and sounding tanks and voids to ensure that there was no undetected flooding. I was Sedlak's division officer, as I had assumed the position of Damage Control Assistant and was the Repair Division Officer. We stood together watching the sea and the birds flying along with the ship and attacking the garbage from our noon meal, which the mess cook had just dumped from the fantail.

"I have been watching that large bird for the last three days" I remarked, "it never lands on the water or the ship, but keeps gliding on the breeze and just stays with us—it is almost effortless in its flight. What do you think it is?"

Sedlak was quick to reply, "That's a Laysan Albatross; it's also called a Gooney Bird, probably on its way to Midway."

"How did you know that?" I asked.

"Gooney Birds live on Midway Island, and I was stationed there for three years. There's not much to do on Midway, so I got to know the birds." Sedlak responded. "Did you know that 70 per-cent of the world's population of Laysan Albatrosses live on Midway, and that there are over 100,000 nesting pairs on the island? They all return in November for the mating season"

Well, I didn't know that…and over the next several days, Sedlak proceeded to tell me a lot more about the birds of Midway. He was literally a walking encyclopedia with an incredible amount of knowledge about the types of birds on Midway, their nesting and mating habits and their range of flight throughout the Pacific. Sedlak had completed two years of high school before he joined the Navy during World War II. He had sixteen years of service and had not been able to pass the exam for first class petty officer, and would likely be forced to retire at twenty years of service. He maintained all the plumbing pipes on the ship; was an excellent welder and he would likely become a plumber when he left the service. What he lacked in formal education, he made up for in skills developed in the Navy and his remarkable knowledge about the birds of Midway.

I learned from my High School English class about the albatross in The Rime of the Ancient Mariner by Samuel Coleridge. An albatross following a ship is a sign of good fortune, but the ancient mariner killed the albatross and his ship was doomed; his shipmates forced him to wear the dead albatross around his neck. Now we had an albatross following our ship and we were going to Midway Island, the largest nesting place in the world for albatross. I wanted to learn more and my teacher was Petty Officer Sedlak.

The albatross is large bird, weighing 5 to 6 pounds with a wingspan of nearly 7 feet. The albatross has a life span of 40 years. It leaves Midway after its first year and does not return for 4 or 5 years, when it finds a mate. The selection of a mate can take many weeks, but once determined they mate for life. They build their nest on the ground and return to the same nest every year. The female lays one egg a year, and the male and the female both share in the feeding and raising of the chick. A week after the egg has hatched, the chick is on its own, as both parents go out to sea in search of food and may be gone for several days, before returning with nourishment that is regurgitated from the parent to the chick. They have earned their reputation as Gooney birds because of the difficulty they have attaining flight from the land, with many crashes before a successful takeoff. The albatross spends about half of the year at sea and ranges throughout the Pacific Ocean. It is a graceful bird in the air and will follow a ship for several days as it journeys across the ocean.

Our brief stop in Midway for refueling was my only opportunity to see this remarkable bird in its natural habitat. Petty Officer Sedlak took me in tow; we spent two hours wandering among thousands of nesting, and mating birds. They ignored us unless we got too close to their nest and then would peck at our legs, and some would vomit on our shoes, so I quickly learned to keep my distance. We also saw many other species of birds that called Midway Island home.

The Navy no longer has a Naval Station on Midway Island. It is now a National Wildlife Refuge and can only be visited by special permission. I feel very fortunate to have had an opportunity to see Midway and its Gooney Birds and a tour by a shipmate who was also an expert.

Gooney Birds

The Reserve Fleet

When the Navy retires a ship from service, it places that ship in the Reserve Fleet, popularly referred to as the "mothball" fleet. The ships are preserved and carefully laid up so that they can be returned to service if needed. I found out that there was another use for these retired ships while I was serving on the USS Wedderburn (DD 684).

Most Navy ships during the late fifties used steam power to drive the main engines (turbines). After the steam goes through the turbines, it condenses to liquid water and the water is pumped back to the boiler where it is heated up again to make steam to drive the turbines. The steam is condensed in the main condenser, which uses seawater flowing through tubes in the condenser to cool and condense the steam. The seawater is forced to flow through the condenser tubes by one of two means. Normally at sea, the seawater enters a scoop at the condenser inlet and flows through the condenser tubes because of the ship's motion through the water. When the ship's speed is less than five knots or it is anticipated that it will be stopped, then a special seawater circulating pump is started to pump seawater through the condenser. If there is no sea water flow through the condenser, then the steam stops condensing and the pressure rapidly builds up in the condenser. The turbines will then overheat and must be shut down.

Upon returning to port in San Diego in December 1960, we had a casualty to our port main condenser. As the ship slowed down, the port seawater circulating pump was started, but it was obvious that there was no flow through the port condenser as the pressure in the condenser started to increase causing the turbine to overheat. As long as the ship stayed above five knots, and we relied on the scoop flow, the condenser continued to operate. We shut down the port main engine and we made it into port and alongside the pier using the starboard engine.

Once alongside the pier and after the engine room was shut down, we took the inspection covers off the seawater side of the main condenser to find out what was wrong. I thought that we would find the inlet to the seawater-circulating pump plugged with barnacles and other sea growth, but it was clean as a whistle. It turned out that the problem was a corroded flapper valve that is designed to prevent back flow through the seawater scoop. The flapper valve was so badly corroded that it had come loose from its foundation and was lying in the bottom of the sea chest. This valve is made of bronze and is essentially a large disc about four feet in diameter. Finding a replacement was going to be a challenge.

We were scheduled to have an overhaul at Long Beach Naval Shipyard about 100 miles up the coast from San Diego starting in January. The shipyard said that they could cast a new valve in their foundry as part of our overhaul work package, but we would have to get along on one main engine until then. The captain was not pleased with this solution, so I was looking for an alternative. Senior Chief Petty Officer Flowers, who was the senior man in the engineering department said that there were a lot of flapper valves sitting unused in the reserve fleet and that maybe we could get one there. What a great idea! We found out that three of the destroyers in the reserve fleet were scheduled to be scrapped in about four months, and one of them was built in the same shipyard as our ship.

It took about three days along with several messages and long distance phone calls to Washington to get permission from the Bureau of Navy Ships to remove the flapper valve from one of the reserve ships. The next day I accompanied Chief Flowers and his engine room team to the reserve fleet area and we went aboard a destroyer that had been laid up in mothballs in 1946. The ship had seen action during World War II, had participated in the landings at Leyte Gulf, Iwo Jima and Okinawa. It had been badly damaged by a Kamikaze attack off Okinawa. Going aboard this veteran ship was a truly moving experience for all of us. It was almost as if we could sense the spirits of the men who served on her 15 years before.

The port engine room was lit with extension lights, as there was no power on the ship. It took us about three hours to open the seawater side of the main condenser and inspect the flapper valve. It appeared in good condition and our measurements confirmed that it was an exact fit for our damaged valve. We removed the valve and manhandled it topside (it weighed about 200 pounds).

The next day we installed the flapper valve in our port main condenser, started up the engine room and tested the seawater circulating system. It worked perfectly and we were ready for sea, thanks to an assist from a veteran ship that still had something to give to the active duty Navy.

The Reserve Fleet

High and Dry with Sand Crabs and a Roach Coach

About every three years, each Navy ship enters a shipyard in order to conduct a routine dry-docking to sandblast and paint the under-hull and to conduct additional repairs and routine maintenance. USS Wedderburn left San Diego in late January 1961 for Long Beach Naval Shipyard for a scheduled four-month shipyard overhaul. As the assistant engineering officer, I had prepared all the work requests for the overhaul and worked closely with the Chief Engineer in planning our overhaul period.

Once we arrived at the shipyard, we entered the dry dock. The shipyard-docking officer aligns the ship in the dock, the dry dock caisson (gate) is lowered in place and the dock is pumped dry. The ship settles onto blocks and, after about three hours of pumping, is high and dry; a most unnatural state for a ship. As soon as the dock was reasonably dry, I assisted in a thorough inspection of the under-hull and the sea chests (intakes) for all our salt water systems. The two propellers were inspected and it was determined that one would be removed for refurbishment. In addition to the propeller work, three sea chests had significant corrosion and would be cut out and replaced. Sand blasting and painting would begin in a few days.

Because of all the major industrial work, the ship was declared uninhabitable and the crew was moved off to reside in berthing at the Naval Station. There was insufficient berthing for the officers, and we received an extra $75 per month to find a place to live ashore. Seven bachelor officers pooled our money and we rented an apartment overlooking the Pacific Ocean. In Navy lingo, a bachelor "pad" is called a "Snake Ranch."

About one month into the overhaul, the engineering officer was unexpectedly transferred and I took over as the Chief Engineer. I had been well prepared for this position by the schooling that I had attended a year earlier and by working closely with the previous Chief Engineer in the preparation and conduct of the overhaul. Nevertheless, this was a significant added responsibility. I had been in the Navy for one and half years and now had 120 men working for me and was responsible for all the details involved in a complex and expensive shipyard overhaul. Larry Wilder, my Commanding Officer, placed great trust and confidence in me during this period, which helped tremendously.

I had planned to spend more time at the Snake Ranch, but found that there were a lot of details involved in the day-to-day managing of an overhaul and I could only find time to get ashore a few days a week and on the week-ends. The Chief Engineer's stateroom was also my office, so I had a place to sleep when I stayed aboard. Getting something to eat during these long days was another problem however. The shipyard provided a mobile food truck to service the ships during overhaul. affectionately called the "Roach Coach" it provided sandwiches, coffee and soda pop.

The shipyard work was significant. All four boilers had been disassembled for cleaning and repairs. The fireboxes for the boilers were being rebricked. One of the stacks was removed from the ship to allow access to the top of the boilers to replace banks of tubing. The starboard main engine high-pressure turbine casing was lifted to replace the bearings. Main Feed pumps and lubricating oil pumps were overhauled or replaced. Ship's force, particularly the engineering department, had a great deal of hard and dirty work during this period. I don't know of a Sailor who likes a shipyard overhaul. The ship is torn apart, the shipyard workers are not members of ship's company; they don't view the ship as their "home" and have little interest in maintaining the cleanliness of the work site. Sailors have a nickname for shipyard workers: Sand Crabs. This seems to fit pretty well, as Sand Crabs live on the beach and they swarm over any object that is placed on the beach looking for food.

By the end of March, our dry dock work was complete. Our ship was once again afloat and we were moved alongside a pier for the remainder of the overhaul. The boiler and engine room work was finished in early May and we started to light off the boilers and test the safety valves. Bringing steam into the engine room and testing out the steam plant took a few weeks because of deficiencies that had to be corrected. By the third week in May, we were ready for sea trials, during which we uncovered more problems that the shipyard had to correct. Finally, by the end of May, we steamed out of Long Beach and said good-bye to our Snake Ranch, to the Roach Coach and to the Sand Crabs of Long Beach Naval Shipyard.

Our next step, once we returned to San Diego, was Refresher Training.

Sand Crabs at work in drydock

General Quarters—Man Your Battle Stations

"General Quarters. Man your Battle Stations. All Hands, man your Battle Stations." blared the announcement over the 1MC followed by the sounding of the General Alarm. Everyone on the ship was moving at once. Those with topside Battle Station assignments were donning life jackets and helmets. As Chief Engineer my station was in Main Control, which was in the forward engine room.

Climbing down the ladder into the engine room, the 1MC came alive again; "Enemy aircraft have been sighted on the port beam, closing. The ship will be taking evasive maneuvers." We had four boilers on the line ready for flank speed. The bridge rang up Full Speed on the engine order telegraph; the throttleman responded by increasing the steam flow to the main turbines. The ship heeled over as we commenced evasive maneuvers. The 40mm anti-aircraft batteries came to life with their sharp "Crack-crack-crack." Tension mounted, as we could not see what was happening topside.

An explosion was reported aft of the bridge. We were hit! I asked the phone talker for a damage report from all spaces. The throttleman reported steam pressure dropping. The phone talker could not establish contact with the forward fire room. The bridge reported that it appeared that the bomb had struck the main deck near the forward fire room. Steam pressure continued to fall. I ordered the starboard main engines secured. The forward ship's service turbine generator tripped on low frequency. We restored power by paralleling with the after switchboard. I then ordered the forward bulkhead steam-stops shut.

The bridge asked for the status of the propulsion plant. I advised them that at present we had two boilers on the line with one main engine and could make 20 knots. We were in the process of cross-connecting main steam so that we would have two main engines on the line. The bridge advised that electrical power to the forward part of the ship was out and I ordered the damage control team to evaluate rigging casualty power cables forward. I also asked for a report on the condition of the forward fire room.

The damage control team reported that the forward fire room was filled with steam and smoke and they were entering the space with men wearing oxygen-breathing apparatuses. The bridge reported a loss of steering and had shifted to emergency steering aft. The forward engine room started to receive steam from the after fire-room and began to start up the steam plant. Ten minutes later I was able to report to the bridge that we had successfully cross connected the steam plants, and had both main engines on the line with two boilers operational capable of making 27 knots.

Damage Control reported a significant fire in the forward fire room and several casualties from the bomb explosion. The corpsman was on the scene and the wounded were being evacuated. The ship was still under attack from aircraft and was conducting evasive maneuvers. Casualty power cables were being connected to provide power to essential equipment in the forward part of the ship.

Another explosion was reported near the after engine room. Reports indicated that a bomb had missed the ship but the subsequent underwater explosion had tripped the after turbine generator. Electrical power was restored by using the forward turbine generator. The port main engine had considerable vibration and within a few minutes, two bearings had overheated and seized. The port shaft was locked in place. I advised the bridge that we now had two boilers and one main engine on the line and because we had locked the shaft on the port main engine, our maximum sustained speed was 12 knots. The Captain asked how much more damage we could sustain and I told him that we had very little reserve left.

A few minutes later we heard the word passed on the 1MC "Secure from exercise, secure from General Quarters, restore all casualties." I glanced over at the Fleet Training Group observer to get some idea of his evaluation of how we did. He was non-committal and said that we would find out at the critique. For the last two days, we had been involved in the final exam phase of our refresher training scheduled after our shipyard overhaul. Earlier in the day, we had conducted a shore bombardment exercise with our main battery of 5-inch guns. The day before, we had tracked a submarine and conducted a simulated depth charge attack. We knew that during the final exercise, we would sustain a great deal of simulated damage and our ability to keep the ship operating would be closely evaluated. In other words, the Engineering Department was "center stage."

Once we got the engineering plant back to normal operation, the ship headed "toward the barn" at full speed and we were back in San Diego before sunset. The next day we attended the critique of our refresher training operations. We were somewhat apprehensive about the final exercise, as we had come very close to losing all our propulsion plant capabilities. But the refresher training team was very complimentary about this part of the exercise. They pointed out that my early decision to cross connect the steam plant and the crew's ability to quickly restore the forward engine room was critical to our success. Other ships with the same scenario who failed to restore the forward engine room, lost all power and were dead in the water when the second bomb hit near the after engine room. In all categories, we were evaluated as above average.

USS Wedderburn conducting a shore bombardment

San Diego—A Navy Town

I have always treasured this picture painted by artist Walter Brightwell for the Navy Combat Art Collection in the early 1960s. It portrays the Navy that I remember when I first reported to the USS Wedderburn (DD 684). The destroyer tender in the picture is the USS Prairie (AD 15) a venerable old ship commissioned in 1940 that saw all of World War II, first in the Atlantic and then the Pacific, repairing and patching up battle damaged destroyers and sending them back to fight another day. After World War II, the Prairie made 25 deployments to the western Pacific during the Cold War supporting operations in Korea and Vietnam. She became the oldest active commissioned ship in the Navy in 1982, and was decommissioned in 1993 after 53 years of service.

In the picture, the Prairie is moored to Buoy 23 in the middle of San Diego harbor; her usual spot. She is providing repair services to five Fletcher class destroyers, four of which make up the destroyer division that USS Wedderburn (DD 684) was part of; USS Boyd (DD 544), USS Bradford (DD 545) and USS McDermut (DD 677). The other destroyer in the picture is USS Ingersoll (DD 652). We would be assigned a two or three week tender availability on a quarterly basis—an opportunity to get repair work done that was beyond the capability of ship's force. The tender also provided electrical power and other services that allowed us to shut down our engineering plant. There was very little pier space available in San Diego, so destroyers spent a lot of time nested together and tied to a buoy in the middle of the harbor. One of the destroyers would keep its engineering plant on the line and provide power and steam to the other destroyers in the nest.

The picture is looking south with the city of San Diego on the left and Coronado, an upscale beach community, out of view on the right. Also on the Coronado peninsula is the North Island Naval Air Station. Navy seaplanes were stationed at North Island and they used the harbor for landing and take-off. Today there is a bridge to Coronado, but in the early 60s the Coronado ferries were shuttling back forth across the harbor. The San Diego harbor was a busy place and dodging the ferries and seaplanes was always a challenge.

The final element of the picture that really brings back memories is the funny looking craft just passing the bow of the Wedderburn. This is a water taxi, which was the common mode of transportation between the destroyers moored at the buoys and ashore. Destroyer Sailors were young (18-21) and single and nearly all lived aboard the ship. Liberty was granted every day and most Sailors returned to the ship at night.

As one of the junior officers, I was assigned as an in-port Officer of the Deck and was expected to be present on the quarterdeck for the arrival of all ship's launches and water taxis. The main reason for this requirement was to maintain "good order and discipline" when the late evening water taxis arrived with their usual load of slightly intoxicated Sailors. They would arrive singing bawdy ballads and were generally in a very happy mood. The first order of business as they came aboard was to be sure that they got off at the right stop, as all destroyers look the same at night. If they were going to another ship moored in the same nest, we had to make sure they got across our quarterdeck and on to the next ship in the nest. Finally, with the aid of the duty Chief Petty Officer, we would make sure that the members of our crew returning to the ship were able to make it down the ladder into their berthing compartment. There were occasional confrontations with a few who had far too much to drink, but they were rare.

San Diego was a Navy town. The majority of the destroyers in the Pacific Fleet were home ported in San Diego along with many cruisers and submarines. There were always a few aircraft carriers present as well. The view from the waterfront was impressive with dozens of Navy ships in view on any single day. Sailors on liberty in their uniforms were everywhere. Fleet landing, where the liberty launches and water taxis boarded and discharged their passengers, was literally in the middle of the waterfront and just off the main street in the center of the city. Although there are other cities with large Navy concentrations such as Norfolk and Honolulu, none had the intimacy and sense of belonging that all Sailors felt with San Diego.

Decision Time

After refresher training during the summer of 1961, USS Wedderburn conducted a series of local operations and training evolutions as we worked up for another Western Pacific deployment scheduled for the summer of 1962. I would complete my obligated service requirement in June 1962 and was facing a difficult decision regarding my future. I truly enjoyed my first tour in the Navy. I had been given a great deal of early responsibility and had thrived on it. When I had graduated from college, I had an interest in attending graduate school, but had not decided on a field of study. Although I was still interested in submarines, I did not feel that my grades in my engineering courses would qualify me for the Nuclear Power Training Program. I was facing an uncertain future. The Navy came to my rescue!

In January 1962, I received a set of orders directing me to detach in March and proceed to the U.S. Naval Postgraduate School in Monterey, California to enroll in the Advanced Science Curriculum. These orders were contingent on my agreeing to remain on active duty for two additional years for each year I spent in graduate school. So if I executed the orders, I was in effect making a decision to stay in the Navy for at least a few more years. I thought long and hard about this decision and got a great deal of advice from various senior officers. The Navy knew what it was doing of course by offering me this opportunity for graduate school just at the time that I was making a career decision. I took the bait and was detached from the ship in March to make my way up the coast to the Monterey peninsula and the Navy Postgraduate School.

Before I left the ship, the Engineering Department presented me with a very meaningful plaque that I have cherished over the years. It is a gear wheel with the inscription "LTJG Hank McKinney, Chief Engineer, USS Wedderburn (DD 684), March 1961-March 1962, Fair Winds and Following Seas." I don't have a picture of this presentation ceremony, but I do have one of a similar ceremony (follows on the next page) when First Class Machinists Mate "Pappy" Summers detached. In the pictures is the forward engine room gang, led by Senior Chief Petty Officer Flowers making a presentation to Petty Officer Summers sometime in early 1962. I remember most of the individuals in this picture, and as you can see, most are very young, 18-21 years old.

Engine room gang presenting award to Pappy Summers

As I reflect on this picture, I realize once again how important people are to our Navy and our ships. The special bonding that occurs in the Navy is truly unique. I was only a few years older than most of the young sailors in the picture, yet we had a mutual respect for each other that is still with each of us today. Senior Chief Flowers has five "hash-marks" on his sleeve, each mark standing for 4 years of service. He had been serving in the Navy since 1940 and had seen a lot of action in destroyers in World War II. He was old enough to be my father and he was one of my early mentors, and oddly enough was also my subordinate. The Navy has always had a tradition of the Chiefs teaching the junior officers during their first tour. My case was no different and I am indebted to Senior Chief Flowers, Chiefs Saxon, Mellner, Sullivan and Sykes for their patience and skill in helping me set my course.

When I left the ship, I left behind many good friends and shipmates. I thought that I would never see them again, but I was wrong. USS

Wedderburn remained on active duty until 1969. She earned seven battle stars for World War II service, four battle stars for Korean War service and six battle stars for service in the Vietnam conflict. Literally thousands of individuals served aboard the Wedderburn during her 25 years of service. Many of these veterans have bonded together to form a ship reunion group and I have been fortunate to attend a few of these reunions in the past. These reunions are a great opportunity to renew friendships with old shipmates and to tell and retell some of the sea stories that I have been able to recall in this book.

Chapter III - Submarine Training

A New Start

After completion of my first shipboard tour in the Navy, I was transferred to the Navy Postgraduate School in Monterey, California in March 1962 and enrolled in the Advanced Science Curriculum. As it turned out, this was a smart move for the Navy and for me. The Navy clearly was not sure what area of graduate study I was qualified for, nor was I certain what field of study that I wanted to pursue. The Advanced Science Curriculum was largely review material in Mathematics, Physics and general engineering, and my performance in these courses would determine what field of advanced study I would qualify for. I realized that this was an opportunity to overcome my mediocre academic performance in my engineering courses in college. I applied a maximum effort in these courses and it paid off. I qualified for virtually all of the advanced fields of study offered at the school. I selected a relatively new field, called Operations Analysis.

In the summer of 1962, the remainder of the class of students enrolled in the Operation Analysis Curriculum. The new students had been transferred from various shipboard assignments; many were Lieutenant Commanders and had just completed a command tour on a small ship. I was by far, the greenest and most junior officer in the class. The review courses that I had taken in the spring allowed me to get a jump on the class when we started the formal course. I remember particularly a course in advanced mathematics taught by a young professor named Borelli who had just received his PhD from the University of California at Berkeley. The entire class was completely lost in this course. I understood some of what he was covering, at least enough to ask a few questions. After about a week, several of the more senior officers came to me for help and asked if I would hold some tutoring sessions. I was more than happy to help and this occasion created a lasting friendship among us. Because of their experience in the Navy, they were my mentors and role models and because of my academic background, I became their tutors. Talk about symbiosis! Just as the Chief Petty Officers on my first ship helped me set my initial course in the Navy, these senior officers; Joe Metcalf, Wayne Hughes, Tom Meeks, Curt Anderson and Tom Harper all provided much needed advice on my future career choices in the Navy

I finished the first year of the Operations Analysis curriculum, but rather than continue for a second year, I was encouraged to apply to Stanford University for an advanced degree in mathematics (statistics) under the sponsorship of the Office of Naval Research. Accepted into the program that summer (1963), I took a course in Russian at the Army Language School in order to meet the language requirements for a PhD program at Stanford. Because of the opportunity provided by the Navy at the Navy Postgraduate School, I had overcome my concerns about my poor academic performance in college and I was on track for a PhD from one of the most prestigious universities in America. Little did I realize at that time, the Bureau of Naval Personnel had also noted my academic performance and had other plans for me; but I would find this out by the end of the summer.

In late August, I received orders to report to Washington, DC for an interview with Admiral Rickover, the head of the Navy's Nuclear Power Program. The Navy was rapidly expanding the nuclear submarine force and more officers were needed to man these new ships. Admiral Rickover personally interviewed and selected each officer for this program. The standards were very high. Up until the summer of 1963, only volunteers were selected for this program, but that was to change. The Bureau of Naval Personnel screened all the professional and academic records of Lieutenant Commanders and junior, and selected about 500 to be interviewed by Admiral Rickover. If you were selected by the Admiral, you did not have the option to decline and you received orders for nuclear power training.

Naval Post-Graduate School

An Interview with Admiral Rickover

In early September 1963, I flew to Washington, DC on a Friday and reported at 0730 Saturday morning to the Bureau of Naval Personnel (BUPERS). Vice Admiral Smedberg, the Chief of Naval Personnel met with about forty nuclear power candidates. He explained that we were all academically and professionally qualified for entry into the Nuclear Power program and we would be interviewed by Admiral Rickover. Even though none of us had requested this program, he made it clear that if Admiral Rickover found that we were suitable candidates, then we would receive orders to commence the one-year Nuclear Power training program. There were many questions and some very unhappy naval officers whose careers were about to be seriously disrupted.

The reason for this extraordinary action by the Navy was the result of the Cold War and the rapid build-up of nuclear submarines. Forty-one Polaris missile submarines would be commissioned by 1967. Each of these submarines had two crews and there simply had not been enough officer volunteers to meet these requirements. A principal question from our group was would we be drafted into the submarine force or would it remain a voluntary force. Admiral Smedberg told us that he hoped that there would be sufficient volunteers for submarines and that there was still a need for officers to man the growing nuclear surface ship Navy. At 0900, we were bussed across the Potomac River to the Main Navy building near the reflecting pool in Washington, DC. During this bus trip, I considered my options. Although I had always been interested in serving in submarines, I really enjoyed my first tour on a destroyer, and I decided that, if asked, I would say that I was not a volunteer for submarines and wanted to serve in the nuclear surface Navy.

The Main Navy building was a rundown temporary office building built during World War I, and Naval Reactors, Admiral Rickover's section of the building, was anything but luxurious. Grey linoleum covered decks with old metal desks and chairs that had been there since the 40s was our first impression. Even though it was Saturday, the offices seemed to be fully manned and very busy; in the passageways, everybody was in a hurry. Everybody was also in civilian clothes so you had no idea of their rank or position. We were briefed and told that we would be interviewed individually by different sections of the organization, and then later on in the afternoon by

Admiral Rickover.

Three individuals conducted my first session and they probed my academic background and understanding of fundamental principles in mathematics, physics, chemistry and thermodynamics. The second session probed my professional background particularly focused on my tour as Chief Engineer of a destroyer. I felt very confident that in both of these sessions I had done very well. I was asked about my interest in submarines and I stuck to my decision that I was not a volunteer.

Later on, I was called out of the waiting area to report to Admiral Rickover's office. A Captain who said that he would be with me during the interview briefed me. He told me to listen closely to the Admiral's questions and answer them honestly. The Admiral would probably ask some questions that would be direct and sometimes difficult to answer because of their personal nature, but that he was looking for an honest answer. His last bit of advice was simple: don't lie.

I went into his office and took a seat on a chair immediately in front of his desk, as I had been instructed to do. The Admiral did not acknowledge my presence. In a few minutes, he looked up from the paper he was reading and asked, "Why didn't you get better grades in college?" I was ready for this question.

"I didn't work hard enough."

"You were lazy?"

After a slight pause, I responded. "Yes sir, I was."

"Did the Navy pay your way to college?"

"Yes sir. I had an NROTC Scholarship"

"Did you feel any obligation to the Navy to work harder?"

I was now beginning to squirm.

"Yes sir."

"Have you considered paying the Navy back because you did not meet your obligation?"

Another pause, "Yes sir. I feel that I am paying the Navy back with my time in service."

The Admiral gave me a hard look and banged his hand on his desk "I'm not talking about time in service, I'm talking about money!"

"No sir, I never considered that."

"Well you should. Dismissed."

The Captain sitting behind me grabbed my elbow and hustled me out of the office. I was in state of shock. My interview had lasted less than a minute, and I had been essentially tossed out on my ear. Oh well, I told myself, I didn't really want the program anyway.

I Volunteer for Submarine Duty

After I left Admiral Rickover's office, I was directed to another room where several other candidates were gathered. They also had finished their interviews and the consensus was that we all failed the interview. After another hour or so, the room filled up with the rest of the candidates. The Captain came into the room and read off about ten names and they were asked to leave the room; we all thought that they were the ones who had been selected, and most of us breathed a sigh of relief. The Captain then congratulated us on our selection for the Nuclear Power Program.

We were told that we needed to go back to the Bureau of Naval Personnel (BUPERS) to discuss our future assignments. I agreed with several others to share a taxi to BUPERS, but as I was leaving the building, I was intercepted by one of the individuals who had interviewed me that morning and he offered me a ride. I suggested that he might want to include a few others in his car, but he said no, he couldn't take everyone. During the trip across the Potomac, he asked me about my interview with the Admiral, and when I told him the details, he just smiled and said that was "par for the course." He asked me about my interest in submarines and I made it clear that I was not a volunteer. He encouraged me to reconsider, as he thought that there was a great opportunity for me in submarines. I felt that our meeting was not a coincidence, but I wasn't sure why.

I arrived at BUPERS about 1600. I was directed to the submarine assignment office and as I entered, I could see all the desks were occupied and they were waiting for the candidates to show up. I was the first one. "Who are you?" I was asked. "McKinney" I replied. One of the officers announced, "Captain, Lieutenant McKinney has arrived." and a Captain from the back office came out to greet me and asked me to come into his office and sit down. He congratulated me on my selection for the Nuclear Power program and asked about my interview with Admiral Rickover. He then surprised me by saying that he had received a call from the Admiral who said that I was not a volunteer for the submarine program, and that he wanted the Captain to "change my mind." At that point, it dawned on me, that even though I had no choice about being ordered into the Nuclear Power Program, I still had a card to play regarding my decision about volunteering for submarines. I decided to hold this card for the time being and see what the stakes were. I also became convinced that the chance meeting and the car ride had been planned. Could it be that even though the Admiral had essentially thrown me out of his office, he really did think that I had a future?

We discussed my status in graduate education. The Captain told me that all those just starting graduate school would be transferred directly to nuclear power training. Since I had already completed a year of graduate study, he would let me complete my work at Stanford. When I told him that I would need at least three years to obtain a Ph.D., he said that he could not give me that much time. We compromised on one year at Stanford to complete a master's degree. He then told me that I did not have to make a commitment to volunteer for submarines until I was enrolled in Nuclear Power School.

I received my master's degree from Stanford in June 1964 and commenced nuclear power training in August. This training is conducted in two phases. The first six months is a graduate level course in nuclear reactor theory and nuclear engineering. The second six months is a practical hands-on experience at an operating nuclear reactor prototype in either Idaho or up-state New York near Saratoga Springs. The schoolhouse phase was at Mare Island Naval Shipyard in Vallejo, California. I was asked about my decision to volunteer for submarines, and told them that I had not decided. I would have to decide by the end of the schoolhouse phase.

Nearing completion of this phase, we were told that we would all be going to the prototype phase in Idaho. I was disappointed with this news. I knew that after the training program, I would be heavily involved in the most advanced ships in the Navy and on the "front line" of the Cold War at sea. At this point in my life, I was single, 27, hoping to find "the right girl" but with no prospects on the horizon. I was anxious to meet the right girl before I went back to sea, and something told me that I would not meet her in Idaho. But in up-state New York, there was a fine women's college, Skidmore in Saratoga Springs and I had a feeling that I would find her there. This was my last chance and I was determined. I asked about the opportunity to go to New York for training and was told that the reactor prototypes were shut down for maintenance and only a few students could be accommodated. I asked to be one of those students. What about my decision regarding submarines? I decided it was time to play my trump card, and volunteered for submarine duty. I was transferred to the Nuclear Power Training Unit in New York in February 1965. Had I made the right decision? I was about to find out.

He volunteered for SUBMARINE SERVICE

My Qualification as a Nuc and as a Bridegroom

After Nuclear Power School, I drove across country from California to New York in early February with a brief stop in Chicago to see my parents. I arrived in Saratoga Springs on Friday, 12 February. My first stop was a realtor to see if I could find a rental unit.

"What are you looking for?" I was asked.

"A one bedroom furnished apartment or flat close to Skidmore College." I replied.

"We have a second floor flat on Union Avenue in the middle of the campus."

"Let's take a look."

The flat was in a lovely Victorian house within easy walking distance of the town and many of the surrounding Victorian houses were in fact dormitories for Skidmore college students. We signed the papers a half hour later. This was probably the quickest deal that they had made that week. I could move in on Monday.

I called my good friends Chuck and Betsy Smith to see if their offer of a spare bed was still open. Chuck was a classmate Lieutenant from the Monterey Naval Post Graduate School and was in the class three months ahead of mine at the prototype. The offer was not only still open, but they had planned a welcome aboard party for me for Saturday night with other classmates from Monterey. We had quite a reunion Saturday night that I paid for Sunday morning. By noon, I decided I would probably survive, but I was still a little shaky. Chuck and Betsy told me that they wanted me to meet their baby sitter who was a senior at Skidmore and had invited her over for Sunday afternoon dinner. After our Saturday night celebrations, I was certainly not in my top form, but I would give it my best shot.

Chuck picked her up at school, and when he walked through the front door and introduced me to Mary Phinney, I knew that I was meeting a very special person. It had been a long time since I had talked with a college senior and my slightly buzzing headache did not make it any easier to carry on an intelligent conversation. Mary later told me that she thought I was very intellectual and thoughtful because it took me a long time to respond to her questions. Little did she know that I was struggling to keep my head above water. We had a nice dinner, played some cards (whist I think) and I took Mary back to her dorm and asked if she was free next Saturday and we made a date. I am not sure that I believe in love at first sight, but something definitely clicked between us. It was not until sometime later that I realized that we had met on Valentine's Day!

I was involved in a very rigorous training program that required 12-hour days at the Nuclear Power Training Unit, and of course, Mary was very busy completing her senior year at Skidmore with graduation in June. We saw each other on the weekends and on some weeknights for a late dinner during the next month or so. Then I started shift work seven days a week, 12 hours a day, with a few days off when we rotated the shift. Somehow or other during this hectic schedule, we fell in love and I proposed marriage to her in April. Her family came out from Cincinnati for her graduation in June and we set the date for our wedding for September 4, 1965.

The training schedule at the Nuclear Power Training Unit was very demanding. All of the work was "in hull" which meant that we were studying the actual reactor plant that was built in the hull of a land based submarine mock-up. Once you entered the hull, for all practical purposes, you were inside of the engine room of a nuclear powered submarine. This was not a simulator, but a real nuclear power plant that was the prototype plant for the nuclear submarine USS Triton. We were expected to trace all the piping systems, study all the electrical systems, and learn all the normal and emergency operating procedures. When we felt we had mastered the material in a specific area, we then asked one of the instructors for a checkout interview, which lasted several hours and included both oral and written exams. Officer students were also expected to qualify on all the operating watch stations, with our final qualification as Engineering Officer of the Watch. I completed my qualification in July and spent the month of August standing watch, which allowed the instructors to help other students complete their qualification.

I transferred at the end of August and headed toward Cincinnati. I would have two weeks off between prototype training and the start of submarine school and we decided that we could fit the wedding and a honeymoon into this period. The schedule was a little tight, but we had a glorious honeymoon in a cabin on an island in Maine, and we made it to submarine school on time for another six months of training.

Had I made the right decision to volunteer for submarine duty and go to New York rather than Idaho? You bet I did! Mary and I look back on the last forty-five years with a great deal of happiness, all made possible by a phone call from Admiral Rickover to the submarine assignment officer. Thanks Admiral.

Mary and I just after our engagement

Submarine School

Submarine School was six months long, and the last leg in my training program before I went back to sea. It was also a time for Mary and I to adjust to our new life together, as the previous six months had been a whirlwind of courtship, college graduation and nuclear power training with very little time for anything else. We found a nice apartment in Groton, Connecticut near the submarine base and I started school on Monday after our honeymoon in Maine.

Our submarine force was in a period of transition in the early sixties. Diesel submarines were gradually being retired and replaced by nuclear submarines. The submarine's principal role during World War II was the sinking of surface ships, but that was changing and the primary mission of the nuclear submarine was becoming open ocean anti-submarine warfare to meet the threat of the rapidly expanding Soviet submarine force. The Navy was rapidly developing new sonar systems, weapons and computers to support this new mission. The curriculum of the submarine school was trying to keep up with this changing tactical environment.

One thing wasn't changing however, that was the basic operating procedures of a submarine, and that was drilled into us from day one. We studied how to analyze the trim or neutral buoyancy of a submarine and to adjust the trim. We learned the functions of the main ballast tanks, variable ballast tanks, safety and negative tank and the trim tanks. We studied the air and hydraulic systems necessary for submarine operations. We studied the atmosphere control systems so necessary to life support. We studied the physics of sound propagation in water. How sound waves are attenuated, bent and deflected by temperature gradients and reflected off the bottom of the ocean. We learned that radio communications from a submarine at sea was very difficult primarily due to antenna difficulties. Submarines could reliably receive radio messages however via very low frequency (VLF) transmission from high-powered shore based transmitters. We studied the characteristics and performance of torpedoes, steam driven and electric.

We spent many hours on various simulators to gain proficiency before going to sea. The diving simulator was a full-scale mock-up of the diving controls of a diesel submarine. We would be going to sea on diesel submarines to gain practical experience. The simulator was mounted on gimbals and was able to take an angle up or down, as would a real submarine. The depth gages and other instruments reflected the effect of actions taken by the diving party. We learned to operate a Torpedo Data Computer (TDC) which was developed before World War II and used throughout the war with great success and still in service on most diesel boats 20 years later. Finally, we learned how to use a periscope for observations of a target. We learned to call the angle on bow (AOB) of the target, which was the angle that the target made as measured from its bow to our line of sight. If the target was headed directly at us for example, then the AOB was zero. If we saw the target on the beam, the AOB was port 90 or starboard 90. We practiced on the simulator until we were able to call an AOB within 5 degrees of actual. We also learned how to establish the range of the target using the periscope. I used these skills for the rest of my career in submarines.

I have often been asked if there was a special screening test for submarine volunteers to check for claustrophobia or adverse reaction to stress. There was not a special test that I was aware of, but one of the exercises that we had to pass early in our training was a submarine escape from a depth of 50 feet underwater.

The escape training tower is 100 feet tall and full of water. We entered a chamber at the 50-foot level. Six students and an instructor jammed together in a small compartment. The compartment was then flooded up to our necks and then air pressure was increased to equalize with 50 feet of water pressure (about 38 psi). A hatch was then opened into the escape tower and one at a time, the students exited to begin their ascent to the surface. It was important that you continuously blew air out as you ascended to protect your lungs from becoming damaged because of air expansion as the water pressure decreased. SCUBA divers were stationed in the water column to ensure the safety of the students. After completing this exercise, I became convinced that if you passed, then it was unlikely that you would suffer from claustrophobia.

New London – Submarine Escape Training Tower

Submarine School—A Close Call

During the six months of submarine school, there were two underway training periods, each one-week long. The first was devoted to learning how to dive and control the depth of the submarine, analyze out of trim conditions and make adjustments using variable ballast. The second phase was devoted to conducting periscope approaches on a target and firing exercise torpedoes. Diesel submarines were utilized as school ships and the USS Tench (SS 417) was the ship that I was aboard for both periods.

As opposed to a nuclear submarine, a diesel submarine is a surface ship designed to submerge for short periods to remain undetected. Most of the time, the submarine is on the surface running its diesel engines. When it submerges, the diesel engines are shut down and a large battery provides power to electric motors that turn the propellers of the submarine. Because the submarine is vulnerable to detection and attack while on the surface, a well-trained crew is able to submerge the ship quite rapidly: less than a minute. As students, this was the standard that we were expected to achieve.

We would assume the watch on the bridge on the surface. The instructor would pass the word to the student officer of the deck, "Submerge the ship." The OOD would order, "Clear the Bridge", sound two blasts on the diving alarm and announce on the 1MC "Dive, Dive." The two lookouts, both officer students, would leap down the hatch into the conning tower, grabbing the ladder's handrail to slow their descent, then down another hatch into the control room. The OOD followed down the hatch into the conning tower pulling on the lanyard that pulls the bridge hatch shut behind him. After the Quartermaster dogged the hatch securely shut, he would report, "Last man down, hatch secured." He would then follow down the hatch into the control room and take control of the dive and submerged control of the ship. The two lookouts would operate the two wheels controlling the bow and stern planes.

On the second blast of the diving alarm, the chief of the watch in the control room would open all the main ballast tank vents, which allows seawater to rapidly fill these tanks causing the submarine to submerge. Less than a minute after these vents opened, the submarine is submerged. The Chief of the Watch has been monitoring a board of red and green lights, called the "Christmas Tree" which indicates all the critical openings in the ship through which flooding could occur. Two of these openings are the bridge hatch, which was just shut and the Main Induction Valve through which the diesel engines receive air when operating on the surface. When all are shut, all the lights are green and he reports "Green Board." If he reports a red board, then the submarine is immediately surfaced.

The submarine is negatively buoyant at this point, which decreases the amount of time it takes to submerge. This is accomplished by having a special tank, called "negative" tank filled with water. As the submarine passes fifty feet, the diving officer orders "Blow negative tank to the mark." which should make the submarine neutrally buoyant. Once the diving officer reaches the depth ordered by the Officer of the Deck, he commences to trim the boat to achieve neutral buoyancy. As we became more confident in this procedure, the instructor would give us problems in which the submarine was significantly out of trim and in which various casualties were imposed to impede the dive.

On our last night at sea, the senior instructor, who was a relatively senior commander and a previous commanding officer of a diesel submarine, asked the commanding officer of the Tench if he could conduct a one-man dive as a demonstration. The captain approved the request. A one-man dive is one in which only one person performs all the functions normally carried out by a team of watch standers. This would have to be a shallow dive as we were in Long Island sound and the depth of water was 110 feet.

The commander sounded the diving alarm from the bridge, shut and secured the bridge hatch, came down the ladder from the conning tower and opened the Main Ballast Tank vents. We were going down like a rock. At fifty feet, he blew negative tank, which slowed our descent, but we still had a 5 degree down angle and were still going down. We watched the commander try to get control of the angle with the stern planes, but he had forgotten to go to dive first in order to release the stops, and as a result, he could not get the stern planes to rise and reduce the angle of the ship. We watched transfixed as the depth gauge indicated that the ship was headed toward the bottom. At 80 feet, the captain came in control and started issuing orders and his crew responded: "Blow bow buoyancy. Blow the forward group. Blow all main ballast. Surface the ship!" We leveled off at 100 feet and then went to the surface. A red-faced commander and an angry captain went forward to the wardroom for a discussion, and diving evolutions for the evening were terminated.

My next underway period on USS Tench would prove to be even more interesting.

USS Tench (SS 417)

Submarine School—A Flooded Conning Tower

In late January, we had our second underway training period, and I was again embarked in USS Tench (SS417). This period was devoted to giving us some at-sea practical experience making periscope approaches on surface targets and firing exercise torpedoes. The weather did not cooperate and the sea was too rough to recover the exercise torpedoes on most days. We did get in some valuable time conducting practice periscope approaches and learning how to control submarine depth in rough seas. The submarines participating in this exercise would trade off acting as surface targets while others conducted submerged approaches.

It was particularly rough on the day we were on the surface and the waves were breaking over the bridge making it very cold and uncomfortable for the bridge watch standers. If the Officer of the Deck noted a large swell that might swamp the bridge, he would order the bridge hatch shut, and the Quartermaster in the conning tower would pull on the lanyard, slamming the bridge hatch shut. This went on most of the day. In the late afternoon, the periscope approaches were terminated because of the rough weather and impending darkness, and we prepared to conduct more practice dives.

On the first practice dive, the Chief of the Watch, observing the "Christmas Tree," called a "Red Board" and the ship was immediately surfaced. A red light indicated that the bridge hatch was not shut. Further examination revealed that although the hatch was shut and securely dogged, the shut indicator was faulty. As it turned out, the frequent slamming of the hatch during the earlier period on the surface in rough seas had damaged it. The ship attempted to repair the indicator with no success. In order to continue our training period, the captain approved diving with a "red board" indication for the bridge hatch as long as there was a positive verification that it was shut and securely dogged.

Later on that evening, I was assigned to the conning tower to observe the dive from this location. The conning tower is actually an eight-foot diameter cylinder about fourteen feet long. It sits above the control room where the diving party is stationed. In the center of the conning tower are two periscopes; also located in this compartment is the helm, the sonar receiver, the torpedo data computer and torpedo firing panels. During battle stations, about ten individuals are also crammed in this space. Since it is above the pressure hull, and vulnerable to flooding in a collision or depth charge attack, it can be sealed off from the rest of the submarine. The submarine has a special tank, called the Safety Tank that contains 23 tons of water. If the conning tower is flooded, safety tank is blown dry to restore the submarine to neutral buoyancy.

It was a dark and stormy night; the ship was rolling twenty degrees. There were four of us in the conning tower, the ship's officer of the deck, the helmsman, the quartermaster and myself. To preserve night vision, the conning tower had only dim red lights for illumination. The officer of the deck directed the student officer on the bridge to submerge the ship, we heard two blasts on the diving alarm, the lookouts came crashing down the ladder and continued down to the control room. The student officer was hanging onto the lanyard pulling the bridge hatch shut and the quartermaster was having trouble with the dogging mechanism that secures the hatch, but he finally said that the hatch was dogged shut and the student officer disappeared down the hatch into the control room.

The next thing I knew a torrent of water was flooding into the ship from the bridge hatch, almost knocking over the helmsman and pouring down into the control room below. The officer of the deck took prompt immediate action: "Shut the lower hatch." "Blow Safety" "Emergency Surface." and sounded the collision alarm. With the lower hatch to the control room shut, the conning tower was rapidly filling with water. There were blue sparks coming from the electrical equipment. Electrical power to the conning tower was secured from the control room. By the time the ship was again on the surface, we were standing in three feet of very cold North Atlantic water. We evacuated up through the bridge hatch and huddled together for warmth on the open bridge. Because of the rough seas, it was not possible to open a deck hatch to get us below. It took two hours to pump out the conning tower and to open the lower hatch. Once we got down into the warmth of the ship, the corpsman checked us over, prescribed some medicinal brandy and a hot shower, both of which were very welcome.

Subsequent review of the casualty revealed that not only was the hatch indicator light faulty, but the interlock mechanism that prevents dogging the hatch in an open position was damaged and the quartermaster had dogged the hatch open, which caused the flooding. Not only did I get my "baptism" in submarine diving operations, but we all learned a valuable lesson that cutting corners in submarine safety can lead to disaster.

The picture is looking forward on the port side of the conning tower. The man in the picture is standing above the hatch leading to the control room. The helm is on his left and just out of the picture to the right is the ladder leading up to the bridge hatch.

Chapter IV - USS Shark (SSN 591)

USS Shark (SSN 591), my first submarine assignment

USS Shark (SSN 591)

Toward the end of submarine school in February 1966, we chose our submarine assignments. The order of choice was based upon our class standing and I pretty much had the "pick of the litter." I chose the USS Shark (SSN 591) which was a relatively new nuclear attack submarine home ported in Norfolk, Virginia. The next week, I was notified by the commanding officer of the school that the Shark was about to deploy and if I wanted to make the deployment, I would have to miss the last week of school in order to transfer to the ship in time. I asked about where the ship was going and how long we would be gone. The commanding officer of the school told me that information was classified and he did not know. He did know that in general, these deployments were of a short duration, less than three months, and we would not be making any port calls. He also encouraged me to make this deployment as he thought that I would gain a great deal of experience.

I went home that afternoon to discuss the options with my wife Mary. We had been married less than six months and the Navy was a new experience to her. The honeymoon was over and we were learning the hard way that planning for the future would be a challenge in the Navy. Mary was wonderful and very understanding that my career choices were very important, particularly at this point as I started out in submarines. We drove down to Norfolk the next weekend to find an apartment in advance of our transfer. We found a very nice townhouse just off Little Creek Boulevard about ten miles from the Naval Station.

We arranged for the shipment of our household goods in early March and drove down to Norfolk and I reported aboard USS Shark. As it turned out, I knew the Navigator/Operations Officer from our time together at Nuclear Power School: Lieutenant Commander Bob Montrose and due to a health problem he would not be making the deployment. Bob and his wife very graciously offered to take Mary under their wing until she was settled in our new home. Two days later Shark left on deployment. All I could tell Mary when we left was that we would return in about three months. Since we would not make a port call, there would be no mail. In case of a family emergency, the Navy would contact the ship. I still had no idea where we were going or what our mission would be. I found out what the "Silent" in the Silent Service really means.

After we left Norfolk and were still on the surface, I stood watch on the bridge with J.D. Williams, the ship's engineer. I asked JD where we were going. He seemed surprised that I did not know. I told him that all I knew was that it was classified and I would find out when I got to the ship. When he told me that we were headed north to the Norwegian Sea, and then around North Cape to the Barents Sea north of Murmansk to observe Soviet Navy operations, I was dumbfounded. I knew that when I went into the submarine force that I would be involved in Cold War operations; I just did not expect to be involved the day after I reported to my first submarine.

Later on that afternoon, we submerged to continue our transit and we would not surface again for about two months. I met with the Captain, Bob Kelsey and the Executive Officer, John Deveraux and they told me that my principal task for the next two months was to qualify as Engineering Officer of the Watch on the nuclear propulsion plant and to stand watch as a Junior Officer of the Deck in the control room supervising the plotting party. Although I had not been part of the work-up training for this operation, they felt that my recent training at sub school would allow me to quickly assimilate into the watch section. They also assured me that we would have many contacts to keep track of once we reached our patrol area.

Even though I had seven year's experience in the Navy, I was next to the most junior officer on board. The officer staterooms were assigned to officers that are more senior and my bunk was in the torpedo room in a section called the "hanging gardens." This was a small berthing compartment for six people above the area where the torpedoes are stored amidst hydraulic valves and high-pressure air lines. A bunk and a small locker in this intimate setting would be my "home" for the next three months.

Homecoming

We had been gone on patrol for about two and half months, which is not the standard six-month deployment that most Navy ships undertake, but without any mail or contact with our families throughout this period, we were all anxious to get home. We had been confined in a submerged submarine and living together in cramped quarters for the entire period. The nature of our operations during this period created a lot of tension. The captain rarely slept more than a few hours at a stretch and the entire crew had been operating at peak efficiency, but under a great deal of stress. I found that submariners are able to endure these conditions with little complaint during the patrol, but once the end is in sight, we all tended to be somewhat edgy and anxious. We looked forward to a warm reunion with family and loved ones. We had not had fresh milk in two months or fresh vegetables and we craved a fresh salad and a cold glass of fresh milk. In fact, the principal reason that a submarine must return to port after a sustained period at sea is that it runs out of food. By careful planning and loading, a submarine can carry about 90 days of food for the crew; we had not reached that limit, but we had run out of several items and the cooks were struggling to maintain a diverse and interesting menu. We were having a lot of canned green beans, powdered mashed potatoes, and some type of "mystery meat" as I recall.

My goal for this patrol had been to complete my qualifications as Engineering Officer of the Watch. I was able to run the required engineering casualty drills on our return transit, complete the written exam and have a qualification board before we returned to port. In order to complete the qualification I would have to stand a few in-port watches "under-instruction" with the nuclear power plant shutdown, as I had never seen the plant in a shutdown condition since I had been aboard.

I looked forward with great anticipation to seeing my wife Mary again, but I realized that for the last three months, I had not seen her, and had no idea what she had been doing; did she have a job, had she moved into our townhouse all right, was the car still running, any financial problems? All these questions and more were going through my mind as we continued our return transit. I had been so caught up in the Shark's mission and operation that it was not until the last week that I realized that almost three months ago I had just dropped her off in Norfolk with people she hardly knew and in a town, she had never seen. We had been married for just six months, and I suddenly realized that I had just assumed that she would adapt to being a Navy wife. What if I was wrong?

We arrived in Norfolk in mid-May on a glorious sunny morning. As we turned into the pier to make our landing everyone not on watch was crowding into the attack center to get a look through the periscope to see if we could spot our loved ones on the pier. We were like schoolboys anticipating the final bell before summer recess begins and I was no exception. When I got my turn on the periscope, I had no trouble spotting Mary. There she was, a vision of loveliness, wearing the same green outfit that she wore on our wedding day when we left the wedding reception to depart on our honeymoon.

When we finally got the brow over to the pier and we were able to go ashore, there was Mary with open arms and a warm embrace. We were both so overcome with emotion that we couldn't talk, so we just held on to each other and savored the moment. Later on as we drove home, I asked all the questions that had so concerned me earlier, and I should never have worried. Mary had met all the challenges of our first deployment separation with flying colors. She had qualified as an operating room nurse at a local hospital, moved into our new townhouse and decorated it beautifully, kept the car running, paid all the bills and had even adopted a dog, an older cocker spaniel named Brandy. The other wives had gone out of their way to help her as she settled in, and she had made many friends. Just as I had completed my first qualification goals in Shark, Mary had completed her qualification as a Navy wife: "The toughest job in the Navy."

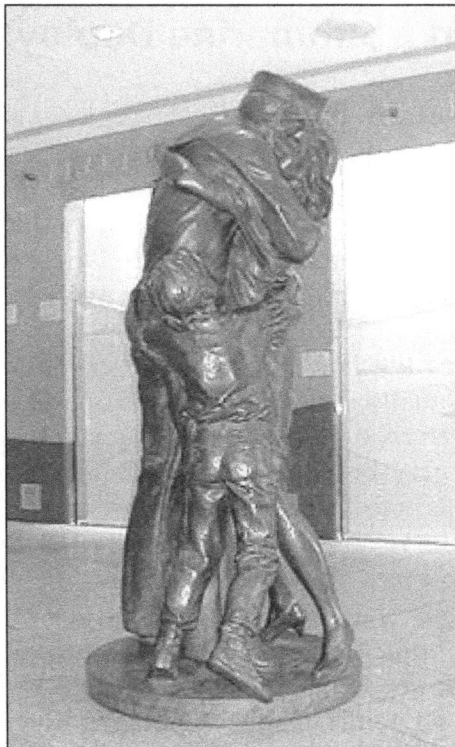

The bronze sculpture in the picture created by Stanley Bleifeld for the Navy Memorial, titled "Homecoming", portrays the joyous reunion of a Sailor, wife and child. Most families endure short separations, but in the military, these separations are six to twelve months long. The reunion depicted here evokes release from awesome loneliness and fear—for all the participants. The reunion is as much a celebration of success as it is liberation from hardship. The "Homecoming" attests to a shared sense of accomplishment, recognition by sailor, wife and child that each has done the duty set before them.

Reflections on a Submarine Deployment

After I had been home a few days and had gotten used to the joy and wonder of being reunited with Mary, I began to reflect on what my experiences were during the last few months underwater in a nuclear submarine. I had easily adapted to the environment of the ship and had learned a great deal about submarine operations during the Cold War that would become the principal focus of my submarine career for the next twenty years.

But there was another aspect of my experience that I gradually became aware of. Actually, I first noticed this on our drive home from the ship on the day we returned. Mary was driving and I watched the road, the buildings and the scenery, but something didn't look right, and I couldn't put my finger on what was bothering me. Finally, I realized that I was focused on people and objects at a relatively long distance (fifty feet, fifty yards, etc.) and I had not been able to do this for the last three months. On a submarine, in an enclosed environment, everything that you can see is within about ten feet. You cannot see something fifty feet away, much less fifty yards. The only time that you can see something at a distance is by looking through the periscope at a ship or shoreline in the distance. But when looking through the periscope, you do not have the same sensory experience that you would have if you were observing the same object or scene directly. You cannot hear the waves breaking on the ocean, feel the wind in your face or taste the saltiness of the ocean spray. In short, you are deprived of all your senses except sight when looking through a periscope and even then, the image is generally somewhat blurred. The more I thought about it, the more I realized that this sensory deprivation is present in many other aspects of submarine life.

With the exception of the periscope, a submarine is blind. When we are operating deep, we must rely upon sonar to "see" for us. Submariners want to remain covert and undetected, so we do not use active sonar, that is we do not send out an active ping and look for a returning echo. We rely exclusively on passive sonar and depend upon what we hear to tell us what is in the ocean near us. For instance, we spent weeks tracking submarine contacts. These contacts are detected by an array of hydrophones located in the bow of the submarine. The watch standers in Sonar would detect an unusual noise; generally, the sound of a ship's propeller in the water but it could also be the sound of a particularly noisy piece of a ship's machinery, such as a diesel engine. This would be reported to the Officer of the Deck

(OOD) and further analysis of the noise would be made in Sonar. In the mid-1960s, this analysis was principally subjective and was based upon the experience and training of the sonar operator. Later on, we would have sophisticated computers to assist in contact classification, but on this patrol, we relied exclusively on the ears of the sonar operator. By listening to countless training tapes of actual sonar contacts, the sonar operators were trained to distinguish the unique sounds of Soviet submarine contacts, which were our principal concern on patrol. They would use terms like "flutter," "compressed cavitation" and "sheet cavitation" to describe what they were hearing. If they were unsure that we were tracking a submarine, or whether or not it was submerged, we would make a brief excursion to periscope depth and look with the periscope in the direction of the contact; if no visual contact was seen, then it was likely that we were tracking a submarine.

Once the contact was confirmed to be a submerged submarine, then the hard work would commence. Sonar would use the hydrophone array to determine the exact direction, or bearing, to the contact. The bearing was transmitted to the fire control computer and was plotted manually. We would make several course and speed maneuvers, all in an attempt to determine the contact's course, speed and, most importantly, range. All of this tracking was done without the use of active sonar. Since range was always uncertain, we also chose a depth to operate different from that of the contact to avoid a collision. The problem was, however, that we were never certain of the contact's depth. Soviet submarines generally operated at even 50 and 100 meter depths, so we would chose depths in between, e.g. 75 or 125 meters.

For one period, we spent nearly two weeks tracking a single submerged contact conducting a missile patrol. During the entire period, we were dependent upon Sonar's "ears" to maintain contact and to provide bearings to our plotting and tracking system. We were able to determine the contact's patrol area and patrol routine, which was of significant intelligence value. During a few of the contact's periscope depth excursions, we were close enough to come to periscope depth as well and get pictures of the periscope and antenna configuration, which were used to confirm the class of submarine we were tracking. Other than these brief glimpses of a periscope and a few antennas, we never saw the contact, and only the sonar operators heard the contact.

Because of the lack of normal sensory inputs, this entire period had an "unreality" to it that I found to be one of the most unusual aspects of a submarine patrol.

USS Shark on the surface

Life Aboard a Submarine

After my initial Navy experiences aboard a destroyer, I found that I had a lot to get used to living aboard a submarine. The first and most obvious change was the fact that you simply could not walk out on deck, stand by the railing, watch the waves, the birds, the clouds, and smell the fresh ocean air. These were the experiences that I cherished during my time on destroyers and I knew that I would miss them during my submarine career. I loved the opportunity to be on the bridge of a submarine as we departed port for sea and returned to port, but these were the only occasions that the ship was on the surface and they were limited to a few hours every month or so.

The watch rotation is considerably different from that on surface ships. Submarines have adopted a six-hour watch rather the traditional four hour watch on surface ships. Most personnel are assigned to a three-section watch, which means that they are on watch for six hours then off watch for twelve hours and then back on watch for another six hours. If you do not get any sleep during the twelve hour "off watch" period, then you are awake for twenty-four hours or more, and it is not possible to sustain this regimen. As a result, the submariner's day becomes 18 hours long rather than 24 and one's sleep cycle rotates around the clock. As an example, if you have the 0600-1200 watch, then you might do normal ship's work from 1200 to 1700, have dinner and sleep from 1800 to 2300, stand watch from 0000 to 0600 and sleep again from 1200 to 1700 and so on. Sleeping 4 or 5 hours every 18 hours works for most people and after a few weeks, one gets quite used to this cycle. Four meals are served every day at 0500, 1100, 1700 and 2300 to accommodate this watch rotation. The 2300 meal is a light fare of sandwiches and soup and is referred to as midnight rations or "Mid-Rats."

Because some of the crew is always asleep, all berthing compartments are kept dark and quiet 24 hours a day. When the ship holds emergency drills, an almost daily event during normal at-sea operations, all hands respond, but after securing from the drill, the berthing compartments are again darkened. Because of the lack of space in a submarine for any type of recreational activity, only the crew's mess (dining area) and the wardroom (officer's dining area) are available, and off watch personnel are encouraged to sleep in order to provide room for others. Most submarines do not have bunks for the entire crew, which results in some of the crew "hot bunking" which essentially means that two men in different watch sections use the same bunk; termed a hot bunk because it never "cools off." Generally, about 20 out of a 130-man crew are assigned to hot bunk. They are the junior members of the crew and are issued individual sleeping bags for their use.

The crew quickly becomes used to the routine of standing watch, sleeping and eating. The variety and quality of meals becomes an important factor in breaking up the monotony of the routine. Just as the U.S. Marines are looking for "a few good men," U.S. Submarines are looking for a few good cooks. Submarines are authorized specialty items on the menu such as steak and lobster, crab legs, frog legs and rabbit. After a few weeks at sea, there is no fresh milk, fresh eggs or fresh vegetables, so a creative chef who can work his magic with these specialty items is worth his weight in gold.

Submarines today are encouraged to send their cooks to "Cordon Bleu" school and to specialize in gourmet cooking. This effort has enhanced the quality of life on board the ship but has also increased the need for physical exercise for the crew. Given the limited space aboard a submarine, this requires some unique solutions. It may seem out place to find an exercise bike and a rowing machine in the engine room and a set of weights and a treadmill in the torpedo room, but submariners place a special emphasis on physical fitness and these exercise machines are an essential element. After all, it is difficult to go out and run a few miles, although that is possible on our Trident submarines, but more about that later.

Neutral Buoyancy--Test Depth--Angles and Dangles

USS Shark is back at sea for two weeks of independent operations and crew training. We had about four weeks of stand-down after the deployment. The run from Norfolk out to the continental shelf where the Atlantic Ocean is deep enough for us to dive safely is about four hours. Shortly after lunch, the captain orders the officer of the deck to rig the bridge for dive and lay below. This takes about fifteen minutes as the bridge communications system or suitcase has to be disconnected and a protective plug installed in the cable connector to prevent it from flooding. The bridge clamshell doors are shut to streamline the top of the sail and then the Officer of the Deck shuts and dogs the upper and lower bridge access hatches and proceeds to the control room and reports, "Last man down, hatch secured, Sir." This deliberate procedure is quite a bit different from the rapid dives I had experienced on diesel submarines.

The captain takes a final look through the periscope, asks for a fathometer sounding to check the depth of water and then directs the diving officer to submerge the ship and proceed to 150 feet. "Dive, Dive" is announced on the 1MC followed by two blasts on the diving alarm. The diving officer rings up 2/3 speed, or 10 knots on the engine order telegraph. The Chief of the Watch opens the Main Ballast Tank vents and the Shark gradually submerges; it takes about seven minutes to fully submerge. The diving officer directs the planesmen to level off at 100 feet. The captain tells the diving officer to obtain a three-knot trim. The variable ballast tanks have been compensated for various weight changes, which occurred in port such as off-loading torpedoes, loading food stores, etc., but there remain some adjustments that can only be accomplished once the ship is at sea. The object is to obtain a condition of neutral buoyancy. As the ship's speed drops from 10 knots to three knots, the planesmen have to use an up angle to control the ship's depth, indicating that the ship is heavy and the diving officer directs the Chief of the Watch to pump 5,000 pounds of water from the auxiliary tank to sea. Further adjustments are made between the after and forward trim tank to correct fore and aft trim, and the diving officer announces "3 knot trim satisfactory." The captain turns over the watch to the Officer of the Deck and directs that the ship proceed to test depth. In addition to establishing neutral buoyancy, there are a few other checks every submarine does when returning to sea after a long in-port period.

"Rig ship for deep submergence" is passed on the 1MC. Rigging for deep submergence requires the closure of various valves and securing of unnecessary sea water systems in order to decrease the likelihood of flooding at test depth. Reports start flowing into control from all the compartments in the ship that they are rigged for deep submergence. When all reports have been received, the diving officer orders 2/3 speed, 10 knots, and a ten-degree down angle and directs the planesmen to level off at test depth. At test depth, the word is passed to check for abnormal conditions. All compartments then report the results of their inspections.

After the completion of our test depth excursion, the word is passed "The ship will be taking large angles." Submariners know these maneuvers as "Angles and Dangles." This is not only an exercise for the planesmen and diving officer, but is also a test of the proper stowage of the ship and get the crew accustomed to submarine operations in three dimensions. We increase speed to 18 knots and then change depth using 10 degree up and down angles. These angles are increased to 20 degrees and finally to 30 degrees. There are many clunks and clatters heard throughout the ship as improperly stowed items come loose. When taking a 30-degree angle, everyone simply hangs on to whatever is near, as it is very difficult to move. The planesmen and diving officer are buckled into their seats. Then the Officer of the Deck orders left full rudder, and the ship "snap rolls" 25 degrees to port as we go into a very rapid turn. The reason for the "snap roll" is the high sail on Shark. Due to its momentum, the ship continues in its original direction, even though the heading of the ship is altered 90 degrees. This motion of the ship sideways creates a force on the sail (a projection above the hull) which forces the ship to roll to port. Because of the heel of the ship, the rudder is also acting as a stern plane forcing the ship into a down angle that is compensated by the planesmen. Aviators who have observed these submarine maneuvers have often commented on their similarity to flight operations.

Having established neutral buoyancy completed a test depth dive and run through a series of "Angles and Dangles," the commanding officer is satisfied with the operation of the ship and we are now ready to conduct routine submarine training operations.

Reactor Scram

On our second day at sea, I had just assumed the morning watch (0600-1200) as Engineering Officer of the Watch (EOOW); my first watch as a newly qualified EOOW. A siren got my immediate attention and the reactor operator reported "Reactor Scram" and shifted the main coolant pumps to slow speed. I reported to the Officer of the Deck, "Reactor Scram, request rig ship for reduced electrical power." Meanwhile, the throttleman had shut the main engine throttle, and the electrical operator was shifting electrical loads to the battery. The ship was at 300 feet and doing twelve knots when the reactor shut down.

The OOD announced on the 1MC, "Reactor Scram, Rig ship for reduced Electrical Power" and I could feel the ship take a 10 degree up angle as we proceeded to 100 feet in preparation for coming to periscope depth. Although the throttle for the main engines was shut, we still had sufficient residual speed for some early maneuvering. The Engineering Watch Supervisor and the Reactor Control Technician both reported that there was no apparent cause for the reactor scram, and I requested the Engineering Casualty Assistance team from the OOD. My immediate concern was to get the engineering plant into a stable condition and then to worry about the troubleshooting to find the cause of the reactor scram.

The electrical operator had shifted as much of the electrical load to the battery as possible, but we still had too much electrical power being drawn from the turbine generators. Steam is used to power these generators and the use of this steam was causing the reactor plant to lose temperature since the reactor was shut down. We had to get the cool-down rate under control. I requested that the OOD expedite the rig for reduced electrical power. Gradually the electrical load was reduced and the electrical operator reported that the battery discharge rate was satisfactory and that we had one hour left before the battery was discharged. I reported the same to the OOD, and recommended that we snorkel and use the diesel generator to carry the electrical loads. We were still at 100 feet, but the ship had slowed to 3 knots and the OOD ordered "Shift propulsion to the EPM." The Emergency Propulsion Motor is a separate electrical motor that drives the propeller in place of the main turbines. We used a clutch to disconnect the main turbines from the propeller shaft.

With propulsion shifted to the EPM, we proceeded to periscope depth and the word was passed "Prepare to snorkel." We were about fifteen minutes into this casualty and it felt like an hour. The air conditioning plants had been secured and temperatures in the engineering spaces were 90 degrees and rising. The Casualty Assistance Team reported that they had found a malfunction in the reactor control system that had caused the scram and they were in the process of changing out a module, which would then require some testing before we could restart the reactor. Fifteen minutes later the diesel engine was running and carrying the electrical load. The reactor cool-down rate was under control, and the battery discharge rate was essentially zero. The engineering plant was stable, and the circuit failure was being repaired.

The engineering officer reported to me that he was satisfied with the drill and we should consider the casualty repaired. I reported to the OOD that the casualty was repaired and that we were commencing a fast scram recovery. I directed the reactor operator to latch rods and commence a fast reactor startup. This procedure allows a nuclear reactor, which has been shut down for a brief period to regain criticality in a safe, but rapid manner so that the reactor can once again power the engineering plant to provide electrical power to the ship and steam for the main turbines. In about ten minutes, I was able to report that the reactor was critical and about fifteen minutes later, the engineering plant was self- sustaining and the diesel engine was secured.

This particular drill is run often on nuclear submarines. The nuclear reactor is the primary source of power to the ship and its loss is a major casualty that requires instant action. This was my first experience in handling this casualty (on my first qualified watch too) and I would see this drill many times in the future as an EOOW, later as an executive officer and as a commanding officer evaluating the crew. *It is important to note, that in submarines, casualties, whether fire, flooding or reactor casualties are never preannounced as drills, but are treated by all hands as an actual casualty.* In the case of a reactor scram, it really is a casualty because the control rods are inserted into the core, the reactor is shut down, and all the actions I just described must be carried out to restart the reactor and restore the engineering plant. I was a rookie Engineering Officer of the Watch and all of the actions carried out by the watch-standers would have happened whether I was there or not. They were well qualified and I would learn to rely on my shipmates in many future crises.

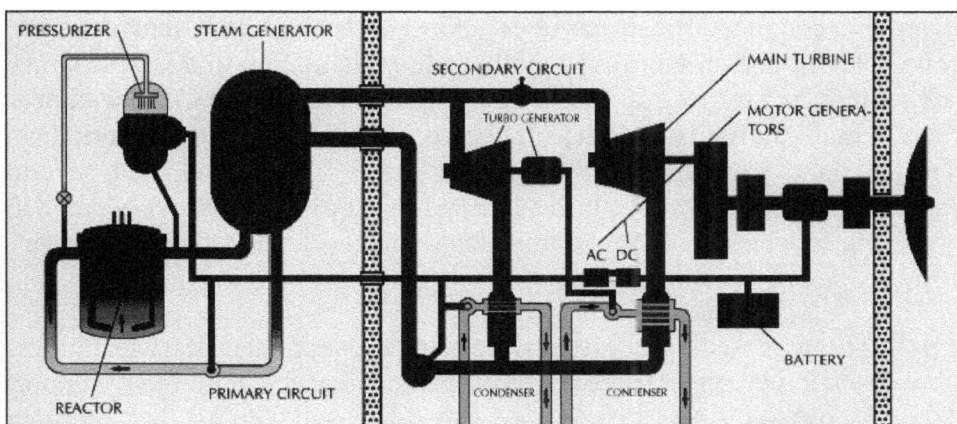

PRESSURIZER   STEAM GENERATOR   SECONDARY CIRCUIT   MAIN TURBINE   MOTOR GENERATORS   TURBO GENERATOR   AC DC   BATTERY   REACTOR   PRIMARY CIRCUIT   CONDENSER   CONDENSER

Submarine Nuclear Power Plant

Caribbean Mishap

In order to conduct torpedo exercises against other ships and submarines, the Navy uses an underwater range that has instrumentation to track the ships, submarines and torpedoes. These ranges are located in the Caribbean near Nassau and Andros Island and off the coast of Saint Croix, an American Virgin Island southeast of Puerto Rico. USS Shark conducted several exercises in the Caribbean in the summer and fall of 1966. We were also preparing for another North Atlantic deployment scheduled for late January 1967.

Our trips to the Caribbean were not Carnival Cruise line vacations as we worked long hours during exercises on the range and at the Navy support base at Roosevelt Roads, Puerto Rico. We did get some time off for liberty in Puerto Rico and in Saint Croix. One of the advantages of a visit to Saint Croix was that you were allowed to bring back a gallon of alcoholic beverages duty free. Most of the crew over 21 took advantage of this opportunity. The problem was where to store the alcohol on board the submarine in a secure and safe location, as use of alcohol on Navy ships is forbidden. Josephus Daniels was the Secretary of the Navy under President Wilson, and in July 1914, he signed General Order 99, which strictly prohibited the use of Alcoholic beverages on board any naval vessel. Ever since then, Sailors have referred to a cup of coffee as a "Cup of Joe."

In the past, the ship had stored the alcohol in a locked and empty torpedo tube, but as we were still firing exercise torpedoes, an alternative location was needed. Shark had two variable ballast tanks amidships, designated Auxiliary Tank #1 and #2. These tanks are designed to hold variable amounts of seawater in order establish neutral buoyancy of the ship while submerged. As we found from experience, #2 Auxiliary tank was sufficient to meet our requirements, and #1 Auxiliary tank was maintained dry at all times and used as a storage space for various items. Entry into the tank was difficult through a small hatch that was maintained bolted shut normally. It could also be locked shut and the Executive Officer determined that this dry tank would be suitable for the secure storage of the alcohol.

On our last day in Saint Croix, the vendor delivered the alcohol to the ship. Each of us, who had ordered a gallon, claimed our alcohol on the pier and paid the vendor. As I recall, a bottle of Chivas Regal scotch cost about three dollars. Many bought local rum for a dollar a bottle. Each of us had five fifths of alcohol packaged in a convenient cardboard carrying case which we carried on board and delivered to the Chief of the Boat who insured that it was properly stored in #1 Auxiliary tank, then the hatch was bolted shut and locked and the key delivered to the Executive Officer.

After we completed our exercises on the range at Saint Croix, we commenced our return transit to Norfolk. Several ship casualty drills were run during this transit. One of the drills was a fire in the deep fat fryer in the galley. In order to pressurize the fire hose to combat this fire, #2 Auxiliary tank was pressurized with 400 pounds per square inch air pressure. At the conclusion of the drill, the air pressure was vented into the ship. It did not take long for all hands to realize that there had been a mix up in the valve line up, as we could all smell the alcohol. As we later determined, both Auxiliary tanks #1 and #2 had been pressurized. The vapors were so strong, that the ship surfaced and commenced emergency ventilation to reduce the effect.

The Chief of the Boat asked volunteers to enter the Auxiliary tank to assess the damage and clean up the mess. He did not lack for volunteers, but it was hard work done in emergency airline breathing masks because of the volatile fumes encountered. Many of the bottles had imploded and the alcohol had soaked the cardboard containers, turning them to mush. The labels on the bottles had also come off, so it became very difficult to determine which bottles belonged to whom. Another odd phenomenon was noted and that was that several bottles were half-full or a third full, but the cap and seal was still in place. We could only surmise that the air pressure got into the bottle and then forced some of the alcohol out around the cap and seal.

Since we could not identify most of the bottles, we split up the remaining bottles equally between all who had purchased alcohol in Saint Croix and after we cleared customs upon arrival in Norfolk, we went home with about two and a half bottles of unknown alcohol and a good story to remember from our Caribbean Cruise.

Submariners and Dolphins

Throughout the summer and fall of 1966, I worked very hard to complete my qualification in submarines. The chest insignia for a qualified submariner is two dolphins on the bow planes of a submarine, and this device is commonly referred to as a submariner's "Dolphins." Gold dolphins for officers and silver for enlisted personnel. Unlike aviator "wings" which are presented upon completion of flight school, submarine dolphins are earned after one has been aboard a submarine for about a year and has been evaluated by most of the experienced members of the crew through individual qualification check-outs, and for officers, an at-sea evaluation by the squadron commander or another commanding officer.

During our Caribbean cruise, I had completed my qualification as Officer of the Deck. I was well on my way to earning my "Dolphins" and I couldn't wait to tell Mary the news. But she had even more important news for me. We were going to have a baby! Wow, was that great but unexpected news. Somehow, I had missed the morning sickness and other early symptoms since the Shark had been away conducting training exercises in the Caribbean. Mary said that the expected delivery date was February or early March. It dawned on both of us at that point that our homecoming reunion in May after my first deployment with the Shark had been more important than we had realized. That was the good news. The bad news was that the Shark was scheduled for another special operations deployment in January and I would most likely be gone for the birth of our first child. It was clear that the old Navy maxim was true. There are two important events when a husband and wife have a child: the keel laying and the launching. It is important that the husband be present for the keel laying, but his presence at the launching is optional.

The Shark went through an extensive refit and training period in preparation for our deployment. I had been assigned as the Communications Officer and Electronics Material Officer and was also responsible for the classified material on the ship. The impending deployment greatly increased the complexity of my responsibilities. The Captain told me that I would have to postpone my submarine qualification effort until after we departed in January, and he would ensure that I would have my final qualification exam when the ship returned in March or April. This was something of a letdown for me, but Mary set my thinking straight on this issue. She reminded me that although I might be slightly delayed in earning my submarine dolphins, she was not going to be delayed in delivering our "baby dolphin" even if I wasn't going to be there. What a girl!

The crew worked very hard through the fall to get the ship ready for deployment. We were all exhausted by the time the Christmas holidays arrived, but we were essentially ready to go on patrol. The Captain authorized a liberal leave policy and Mary and I went home to visit her family in Cincinnati and mine in LaGrange, Illinois. Both families were concerned about my being gone when Mary delivered and agreed to help her through this period. Mary did not want to leave Norfolk as she had been working in the hospital as a nurse and knew the delivery team very well.

It was a cold and wet day in early January when Mary drove me down to the pier and we had our last embrace before I left her. This was much more difficult farewell for both of us than the previous year on my first deployment on Shark. She told me not to worry about her, as she was certain that she would have all the help she needed from our families and from the other officer wives and that the doctor, the hospital and the delivery team were there for her. When I got back from patrol, she said that she was looking forward to presenting me with my "baby dolphin."

After we departed Norfolk, I was glum. I had come to the realization that family separation in the Navy goes both ways. Those that remain at home and those that go to sea both go through a period of intense loneliness. It is probably easier for the men at sea, as we can immerse ourselves in the day-to-day routine of the ship and focus on the upcoming mission.

After a brief stop in Holy Loch, Scotland, we arrived on station and commenced another submarine patrol off the shores of the Soviet Union. We were north of the Arctic Circle and saw daylight less than six hours a day. The weather was cloudy and stormy most of the time with heavy snow obscuring our visibility. The weather reflected our mood and we were all looking forward to some good news. For me, that good news arrived in the form of a radio message February 21. Our "baby dolphin" William weighing 6 pounds 9 ounces had arrived. I was a long way from home, but this was the news that I had been waiting for. I would have to wait another six weeks to get home.

NAVAL MESSAGE									
OPNAV FORM 2110-28 (REV. 3-61) S/N 0107-705-4000

RELEASED BY			DRAFTED BY			PHONE EXT NR		PAGE	P
DATE 21 FEB 67		TOR/TOD 210001Z		ROUTED BY	CHECKED BY			OF	

MESSAGE NR	DATE/TIME GROUP (GCT) 201931Z		PRECE-DENCE	FLASH	EMERGENCY	OPERATIONAL IMMEDIATE	PRIORITY	ROUTINE	DE
			ACTION						
			INFO						

```
FROM: COMSUBLANT

TO  : SHARK

FOR CO ONLY: REQUEST YOU INFORM LT MCKINNEY THAT WIFE GAVE BIRTH

TO WILLIAM CLAYTON MCKINNEY AT 0900 ON 18 FEB.  MOTHER AND SON DOING

FINE.  WEIGHT 6 LBS 9 OZ.  CAPT H. E. RICE SENDS CONGRATULATIONS.
```

Bill's birth announcement

The Haircut

USS Shark completed her surveillance patrol in early March. The weather had been miserable, but typical for this time of year north of the Arctic Circle and we were looking forward to returning to warmer waters, but first we had a port call in the Holy Loch, Scotland where the U.S. Navy had a Ballistic Missile Submarine refit and support operation. In addition to a visit to Scotland, the officers had been invited to meet with the Admiral in charge of the Royal Navy's Submarine Force in London. His official title is Flag Officer Submarines, but he is known by the abbreviation FOSM (pronounced Fosim).

We had been at sea for about sixty days and I needed a haircut. In fact, the Executive Officer (XO) had remarked about how scruffy I looked, and he told me that I would not be going ashore in Holy Loch until I had a haircut. The crew had held a contest for the best beard and my red beard had won "the most colorful" award. The XO had won the scruffiest beard award, and I think that he was still smarting from this recognition, and as a result was giving me a hard time about my haircut. I asked him if he was planning to shave his beard off before going ashore. He was not amused.

I told him that I planned to get my haircut in Holy Loch by a barber in the town of Dunoon. He allowed how that was a good idea, but I wasn't leaving the ship until I had a haircut. As there was not a barber on the ship, I didn't see how that would be possible. My haircut plans and the good-natured dispute with the executive officer became a source of some amusement for the rest of the officers in the wardroom. Some siding with me and some with the XO. Bets were placed as to the outcome of the dispute. I really wanted to make the trip to London, and a haircut stood in my way.

You could tell that the tensions of the last month while on patrol were starting to ease on this return transit to Holy Loch. The rest of the crew had also heard about my haircut dilemma and most were rooting for me. As I walked around the ship, they would greet me with sayings like "Damn the haircut, full speed ahead" and "Give me liberty or give me a haircut." The day before we were to arrive in Holy Loch, Jim Cossey who was a good friend came to my rescue. He assured me that he had great tonsorial skills, having cut hair to earn his way through college. I didn't believe a word, but I also realized that at this point, I had very little choice. Jim proposed to cut my hair that afternoon in the officer's head and all the officers were invited to witness the event. I wasn't sure whether this public display was necessary, but Jim felt that it was the best way to convince the XO that he had won his point. I reluctantly agreed.

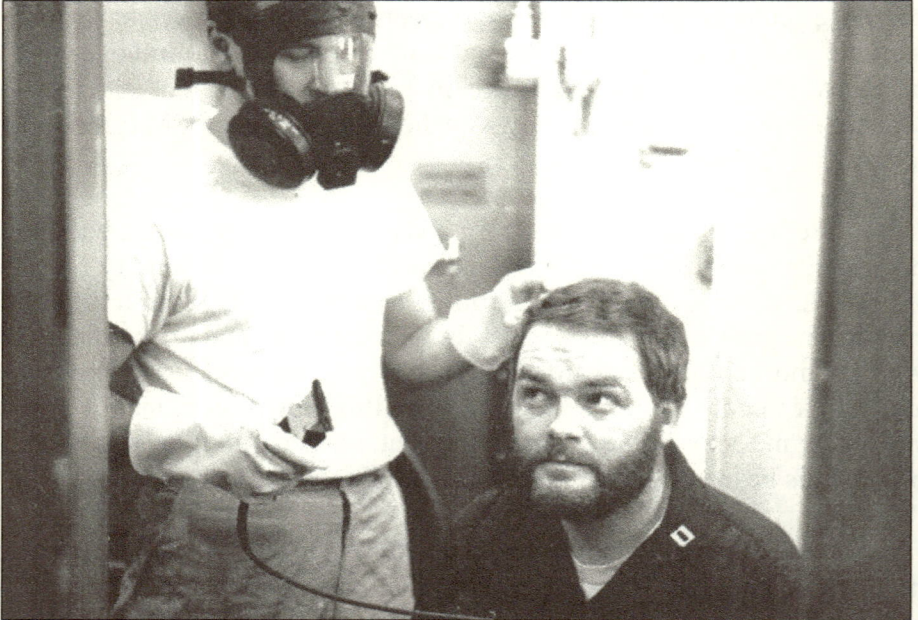

Jim was not taking any chances with contamination from any "critters" which may have taken up residence in my hair. He was wearing rubber gloves and a Mark 5 gas mask. And, you will note the look of apprehension on my face.

Next, the outcome...

But all's well that ends well, and Jim gave me a great haircut. I was happy to buy him a few beers in the local pub in Dunoon.

Our trip to London to meet FOSM was a great experience for us all. He was very aware of our success during our previous patrol and very interested in our impressions on this our second patrol in a less than a year. While in London, I was also able to purchase a linen infant christening gown for my newborn son, William. Back in Dunoon, I was pleased to find a beautiful plaid kilt/skirt for Mary. After five days in Holy Loch, we were all anxious to set sail for Norfolk.

Garbagecicles

USS Shark left Holy Loch, Scotland in late March 1967 for a return transit to our home port of Norfolk, Virginia. It was another short but successful deployment and we were all anxious to get home. I was particularly anxious, as I would be meeting my newborn son, William, for the first time. Our first night out of Holy Loch, we had a casualty to our Trash Disposal Unit (TDU) that was to plague us for the rest of the transit home.

Disposing of trash and wet garbage at sea has always been a challenge for submarines. There is no room to store it on board for the long term, so it must be disposed of every day. In World War II, our diesel submarines would carry bags of garbage topside when the submarine was on the surface and heave the garbage over the side. The bags would be weighted with whatever was available and the hope was that they would sink. In fact, many did not sink, and the Japanese Navy would alert their fishing boats to pick up these bags so that they could identify the submarines operating in their home waters.

Since nuclear submarines do not surface routinely, another method of trash and garbage disposal needed to be developed. The solution was the TDU, which is similar to a miniature torpedo tube, only mounted vertically in the submarine. The diameter of the tube is about eight inches and the length of the tube is about ten feet. Like a torpedo tube, it has an outer door at the hull of the ship (bottom of the tube) and an inner door at the top of the tube. With the outer door closed, the inner door can be opened and the TDU is loaded with the wet garbage and other trash such as tin cans and bottles. Then the inner door is closed and the tube is flooded with seawater and the pressure equalized with sea pressure, which allows the outer door to be opened. The two doors are interlocked so that they cannot both be opened at the same time. With the outer door open, seawater is flushed through the TDU to force the garbage and trash out of the tube into the ocean.

The wet garbage is collected in mesh bags, about three feet long and the diameter of the TDU. Two garbage weights (disks weighing about 4 pounds each) are placed in the bottom of each bag. The bags are each weighed before they are loaded in the TDU to insure that they will sink to the bottom of the ocean. Trash such as tin cans and bottles are compacted in a trash compactor and loaded in a metal trash can designed to fit in the TDU.

When the ship is at periscope depth to copy a radio broadcast certain routine housekeeping chores are also accomplished; one of these chores is "shooting the TDU."

Shortly after leaving Holy Loch, while "shooting the TDU" the outer door jammed in the open position. Every effort was made to free the door by flushing water through the TDU, but nothing worked and the TDU was placed in an out of commission (OOC) status. We still had to eat and as a result, we had to find somewhere to store our wet garbage. This was not a new problem for the old hands who had served on other nuclear submarines with a jammed TDU. The solution was to freeze the wet garbage in the frozen food storage box. Fortunately, as we were on our way back to home port after about sixty days at sea, our frozen food had been considerably reduced and there was ample room for our garbage. As we filled up the three feet long eight-inch diameter bags, they were tied off and hung in the freeze locker for the duration of the run to Norfolk. It did not take long for the crew to start calling these frozen bags "garbagecicles." By the time we were ready to surface off Norfolk, we had nearly one hundred "garbagecicles" in the freeze locker.

The Executive Officer decided that we should dispose of the wet (frozen) garbage after we surfaced and before we arrived in Norfolk. This made sense as the whole crew would be available for a working party and the job could be quickly accomplished. We surfaced about 0200 just before we reached the shallow water of the continental shelf, and we still had a four hour run before we reached the Thimble Shoals channel and the entrance to the Chesapeake Bay. Although 0300 might seem a little early for an all hands working party, this was the morning that we were returning from deployment and very few of us could sleep anyway.

We formed a human chain from the freeze box, up a ladder, through the crew's mess, down a passageway up another ladder through the control room and up a vertical ladder into the sail area just below the bridge cockpit. Each "garbagecicle" was passed from one man to the next all the way to the sail where it was thrown over the side. The front end of the chain was passing frozen garbage, but by the time the "garbagecicle" reached the end of the chain going up the ladder into the sail, it had become pretty soggy and drippy from all the handling. Some of the more experienced members of the crew had anticipated this outcome and they were all at the front end of the chain. Many of the officers, including me were at the end of the chain and after handling one hundred semi-frozen bags of garbage, we all needed a shower and a fresh uniform. This was of little concern to me as I was about to meet my son for the first time.

A Busy Spring 1967

USS Shark returned to Norfolk on Good Friday, March 24 after our January/February Special Operation. We moored alongside our submarine support ship, the USS Orion (AS-18) on a hazy and rainy morning. Waiting on the Orion was Mary with William cradled in her arms. I was five weeks late for the launching, but he was certainly worth waiting for. I am not sure what I expected, but somehow or other, I thought that after five weeks, he would have grown much larger than he was and would probably be starting to talk. Well obviously, I knew very little about babies, but then I was going to learn… Oh boy, did I learn!

Easter Sunday was celebrated with Mary's youngest sister Bea, and then later in the week we flew to Chicago and drove with my parents to Goshen, Indiana for the marriage of my younger brother Steve to Cinda Shrock on April 1, 1967. I was back on board Shark on April 3; a very short leave period, but we were preparing for pre-overhaul engineering trials scheduled for later in the week. The Captain had recommended me for qualification in submarines and I would have my underway evaluation during this period at sea.

My underway examination was conducted by a Captain W. Masek who was assigned to the staff of the Commander of the Atlantic Fleet Submarine Force. I was to demonstrate to his satisfaction my ability to handle the ship surfaced and submerged, to compensate and obtain a satisfactory trim, to navigate and conduct a submerged torpedo approach and attack. Because of the nature of our engineering trials, we were not able to conduct a torpedo approach and attack, but Captain Masek quizzed me extensively in this area to his satisfaction. At the end of our two-day trials, he recommended me for qualification in submarines. The second phase of my qualification would be an in port exam by the commanding officer of our sister ship, the USS Scorpion (SSN 589).

Scorpion was in the shipyard and the Captain, Commander Dick Lewis asked me to send over my submarine qualification notebook in advance of our meeting. This notebook was completed during our January/February deployment and I did not have a lot of time to devote to it. The notebook consisted of about 35 pages with a series of questions about submarine systems and operations, and the officer filling it out is expected to draw systems diagrams and explain fundamental submarine operations. I had not built an elaborate notebook as many of my contemporaries had done. When I reported to the ship for my interview, Commander Lewis spent an hour or so going over my notebook. He seemed very interested in the brevity of the notebook and said that it was the slimmest notebook that he had ever seen from an officer seeking submarine qualification. I felt that I was not doing well in my interview and possibly, he would send me back to Shark with a recommendation that I write a new and more complete notebook. After our interview, he invited me to stay for lunch with his wardroom officers and I accepted.

During lunch, Commander Lewis discussed my submarine qualification notebook and told his executive officer to distribute it among the qualifying officers as an example of what he would like to see in the future from his officers. I was dumbfounded! Here I thought that I had failed my interview and just the opposite was true. I left the Scorpion floating on "Cloud 9" and made it back to the Shark. My captain, Bob Kelsey, had already received a call from Commander Lewis, and he wanted me to share my notebook with the other officers in our wardroom. This experience left a lasting impression on me and many years later, I was in a position to change the basic submarine officer qualification process and reduce the cumbersome paperwork involved.

On April 14, after an interview with our division commander, Captain "Bo" Coppedge, I reported to the Squadron Commodore, Captain H. E. Rice, and he presented me with my submarine dolphins. I couldn't wait to get home to see Mary and our baby dolphin, William. This capped off an extraordinary three weeks; meeting my son for the first time, being part of my brother's wedding, and going back to sea to complete my submarine qualification.

Next, we are off to Halifax, Nova Scotia!

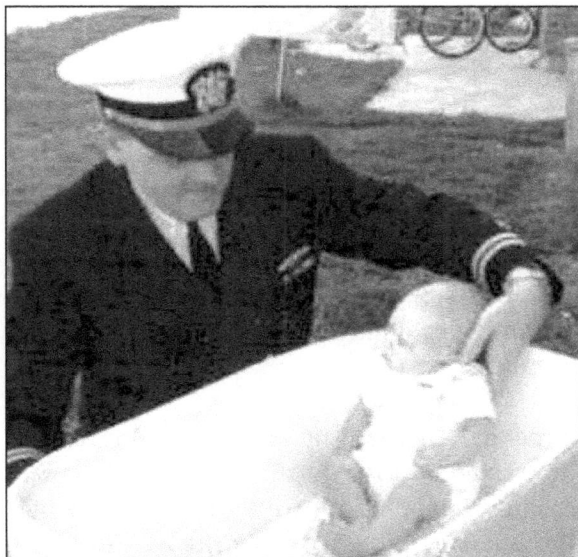

Qualified in submarines

Halifax, Nova Scotia

In the late spring of 1967, USS Shark made an historic port visit to Halifax, Nova Scotia. This was historic because it was the first visit of a U.S. nuclear submarine to a Canadian port. Today, we take for granted the visits of U.S. nuclear powered ships to foreign ports, but in the early days of our nuclear Navy, these port visits were the subject of carefully worked out diplomatic and technical agreements between the nations involved. The unblemished safety record of our nuclear ships has been instrumental in gaining access to foreign ports around the world.

The Commander of the Atlantic Submarine Force, Vice Admiral Arnold F. Schade was aboard for our transit from Norfolk to Halifax. This was the first occasion of many that I would have during my service to meet the heroes of the submarine force from World War II. In 1943, Schade was the Executive Officer of the USS Growler with Howard Gilmore as Commanding Officer. In February 1943, the Growler was on the surface attempting a night torpedo attack, when the Japanese warship it was trying to attack tried to ram the Growler. Gilmore was on the bridge and was mortally wounded by enemy gunfire. His last words to Schade from the bridge were "Take her down" which have become a submarine legend. Schade had to make the difficult choice to attempt to save his captain or follow the captain's orders and save the ship. He ordered the bridge hatch shut and the ship submerged. A badly damaged Growler limped into port two weeks later. Gilmore was posthumously awarded the Medal of Honor for sacrificing his life to save his ship. He was the first of five submariners to receive the Medal of Honor in World War II.

We entered Halifax on a cold and foggy May morning. Even though the weather was dismal, our reception by the Canadian Navy and the citizens of Halifax was warm and heartfelt. The city leaders went out of their way to make us feel welcome and we had several official receptions. The Canadian Navy had a diesel submarine, the HMCS Ojibwa, which was a British Oberon class submarine newly commissioned in 1965, and she was our host ship during this port visit. As in the Royal Navy, alcoholic beverages are served aboard Canadian Navy ships, and the officers of the Ojibwa invited the officers of the Shark to a welcome aboard cocktail party, which turned out to be quite an event.

Fifty guests were crammed into the control room and wardroom of the Ojibwa which is a space about the size of a greyhound bus and full of operating equipment such as radar and sonar, periscopes, pipes, valves and various air and hydraulic manifolds. After a few drinks, everyone felt a little more comfortable in the confined space and as you can imagine, we all got to know each other very well. There were a few problems however. One of our officers had a few too many drinks and he decided that he could operate some of the equipment on the submarine. Our captain asked if I would assist in helping my inebriated shipmate off the ship, as the Canadians were a little nervous. Before we could get him up the ladder topside however, we had to disentangle the Chief of the Royal Canadian Mounted Police from the ladder. The Chief had come to the cocktail party in full dress uniform that included spurs. You did not want to stand too close to him in the crowded control room. He had left the party early and when he tried to go up the ladder, he slipped and got his spurs caught in one of the metal ladder rungs.

We finally had to take off the Chief's boots; he had a badly sprained ankle and we had to carry him up the ladder where we met his driver and he was taken home. We then got our shipmate into a taxi and headed back to the Shark. When we returned aboard, the party was winding down, and the captain of the Ojibwa thanked us for our assistance. The next few days in Halifax were spent planning an at sea exercise with Ojibwa which culminated our port visit, and we made our return transit to Norfolk.

Our next stop was Fort Lauderdale.

HMCS Ojibwa in Halifax

Rock Hudson in Fort Lauderdale

In June of 1967, USS Shark was scheduled to conduct test firings of the new Mark 48 torpedo shape to ensure compatibility with the torpedo tube configuration in the Skipjack class submarine. These test firings were to take place off Fort Lauderdale, Florida where the Navy had a torpedo test facility. I arranged for Mary and our newborn son William to spend some time in Fort Lauderdale during the period that we would be in port. I received a great deal of support from the Navy League, a civilian Navy support organization and the Fort Lauderdale chapter that went out of its way to support submarine port visits to Fort Lauderdale. I was able to arrange a hotel room for Mary and rent a car through our Navy League hosts.

Our first night in port we got a babysitter and decided to have dinner at the Coral Ridge Yacht Club, where we had guest membership privileges courtesy of the Navy League. As we were signing in at the front desk, the familiar voice of my captain, Commander Bob Kelsey said, "Hank and Mary. What a surprise to see you here. Have you met Rock Hudson?" We turned around and were almost speechless as we came face to face with the most popular movie star in the country. He was tall and handsome just like he is on the screen. We were quite taken with him. The captain invited us to join his party for cocktails before they went out to dinner and naturally, we accepted. The captain and the executive officer, the submarine force public affairs officer, a studio representative, Rock Hudson, Mary and I all went into the cocktail lounge for a drink.

During cocktails, we found out that Paramount Studios was going to produce the film, "Ice Station Zebra" based upon the novel of the same name by Alistair MacLean. Rock Hudson was to have the role of the commanding officer of a nuclear submarine, and since Shark was going to conduct daily operations from Fort Lauderdale, this would be a perfect opportunity for Hudson to get a feel for the role of captain. We were quite taken with Rock during our brief cocktail hour. He was very friendly, easy to talk to and a very genuine person. Not at all like the stereotypes of the Hollywood stars that we had heard about.

After they left, Mary and I went in for dinner. Mary asked me if I really thought that Rock Hudson was as handsome in person as he was in the movies. I said absolutely, he really is a good-looking man. I wondered why she asked, as she was seated right across the table from him. She replied that she couldn't see very well as she wasn't wearing her glasses.

"Why not?" I asked.

She replied, "You don't think that I would wear glasses in front of Rock Hudson, do you?"

"Sure, why not? I did." I responded.

"You're a guy. It doesn't matter for you, but it does for me."

We had been married for almost two years, and I thought that I understood my wife, but I found out that I still had a lot to learn. We have now been married over forty-five years, and I am still learning and loving every minute of it!

The next morning we were underway at 0730 for torpedo testing. Rock Hudson came aboard at about 0725 and when we had secured the maneuvering watch after leaving port we were asked to maintain quiet around the wardroom as our guest was asleep in the Captain's cabin. Apparently, they had had quite a night on the town the night before. He finally got up just before 1200, had lunch with the officers, and then spent the afternoon observing ship operations and torpedo launchings. We returned to port that evening and went through the same routine the next day. Rock Hudson went out of his way to spend time with the crew and we were all very impressed by his friendly outgoing manner.

The movie "Ice Station Zebra" came out the next year and was a critical success, nominated for two Oscars. Mary and I have continued to enjoy all of Rock Hudson's movies.

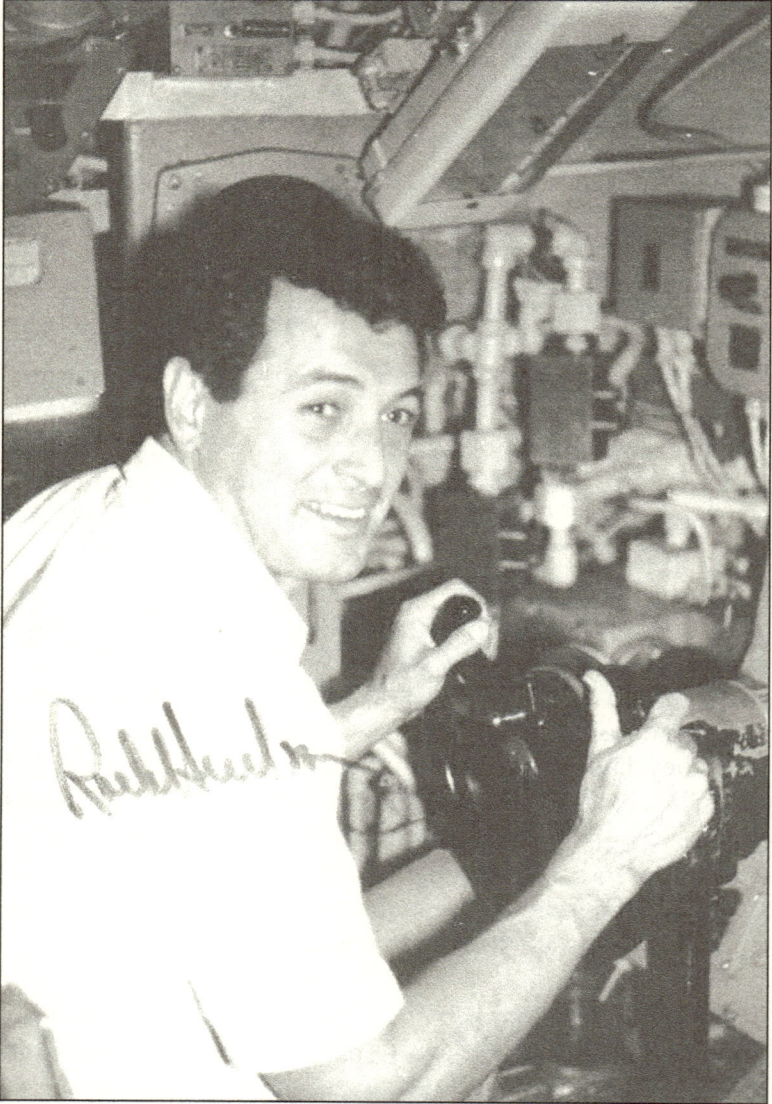

Rock Hudson operating the stern planes on USS Shark

Christmas Leave Plans are Cancelled

In late June 1967, USS Shark entered Norfolk Naval Shipyard for a restricted availability to replace the spent fuel in the reactor core and to install a new submarine electronics surveillance system. The original reactor core had lasted for approximately five years and the new core that replaced it was of an advanced design and would last about ten years. Nuclear power plant technology has continued to advance so that today's nuclear submarines have reactor cores that will last the life of the ship or about 30 years.

Shark entered drydock No. 2 in the shipyard and after the dock was pumped dry, the shipyard workers started to install scaffolding that surrounded the ship. Within a few days, the ship had been transformed into what appeared to be an extension of the shipyard buildings surrounding the drydock. A large building was erected on top of the ship and it was connected to an adjacent shipyard building. The building on top of the ship was called the Reactor Access House and it would become the work area for the shipyard to conduct our reactor refueling.A 7-foot diameter hole was then cut into the top of the pressure hull above the reactor compartment, then the pressure vessel head was removed and a vertical extension to the pressure vessel was installed and filled with water. The reactor core was then visible from the reactor access house through about 8 feet of water on the top of the core. The spent core is highly radioactive and the water served as a shield for much of this radiation.

The actual replacement of the spent fuel modules and the installation of the new reactor core was accomplished by highly skilled shipyard technicians. The submarine crew was responsible for the operations of ship systems that maintained the water level above the core and since the core was still generating radioactive decay heat, we maintained a flow of cooling water through the core to prevent the core from overheating.

It took about two months of work and various procedures before the actual refueling process was started, then about six weeks for the refueling and another three months to restore nuclear power plant systems. Extensive testing was accomplished to ensure that the nuclear power plant met all the required specifications for safe and reliable operation.

Admiral Rickover had complete oversight of all aspects of the Navy's nuclear propulsion program and the refueling of a nuclear reactor was no exception. There was a Naval Reactors Office in the shipyard and the personnel in this office carefully monitored all operations of the shipyard's refueling team and our submarine crew. During this period in the shipyard, the nuclear power plant operators in the submarine's crew were expected to conduct an extensive retraining program to re-qualify all hands on their respective nuclear watchstations. Prior to commencing nuclear reactor plant testing and operations, the crew was required to undergo a special examination and evaluation by the members of Admiral Rickover's staff from Washington, DC. This examination is commonly referred to as a crew quiz and it takes place approximately two weeks before commencing nuclear power plant operations.

Fallen asleep sitting at the wardroom table after an 8 hour shift during refueling

Our crew quiz was scheduled for the middle of December 1967. Admiral Rickover decided to visit the shipyard at the completion of our crew quiz. He arrived late in the afternoon after we had completed our oral exams with his staff. We had been on three-section shift work for a few months and we were all tired and ready for a Christmas holiday break. I had gone home for dinner with my wife and the phone rang at about 2100 (9:00PM). We were all directed back aboard by 2200. I still have a vivid memory of that night sitting in the crew's dining hall on our support barge with the Christmas tree lights blinking in the background as the captain briefed us on his meeting with Admiral Rickover.

It wasn't good news. We failed the crew quiz and had three weeks to prepare for a re-examination. Christmas leave plans were cancelled and we were back on shift work. As I left the meeting, I was reminded of that old Navy maxim: "Liberty for the crew is cancelled until morale improves."

We passed the re-examination in January and prepared for initial criticality and reactor plant start-up.

A Nuclear Reactor Comes to Life

In early January 1968, the shipyard removed all the scaffolding from around the ship and completed the remaining hull work so that ship could be refloated and moved from the drydock to alongside a pier. The work continued around the clock on the reactor plant in preparation for reactor plant start-up in about four weeks. The Naval Reactors crew quiz was completed satisfactorily and we started into our final testing of reactor plant systems.

Initial start-up of a new reactor plant core is very much like breathing new life into an inanimate object. The core has been fabricated in various pieces that have never before been assembled as a whole until it has been loaded into the reactor vessel. The uranium in the core is the energy source about to be unleashed. This energy will come from the splitting of the Uranium atom (more correctly, the nucleus of the atom). But it takes a neutron to make this happen. When Uranium absorbs a neutron, the nucleus is in an excited state and it fissions or splits into two other atoms and a certain amount of energy is released. The energy released is absorbed in the reactor core and if enough fissions occur every second, then the temperature of the core will increase. In addition to the energy released, two or three neutrons are also released in each fission. Other material in the core absorbs some of these neutrons, some leak out of the core and some are absorbed by Uranium atoms to cause additional fissions. If one of the neutrons born in each fission is absorbed by another Uranium atom, causing another fission, then we have a self-sustaining chain reaction, and the reactor is said to be "Critical." The design engineers have done all their calculations and the manufacturer has built the reactor core to their specifications. But the reactor will not come to life until the control rods are pulled from the core. The control rods are made of Hafnium, an element that absorbs neutrons. As the control rods are pulled out of the core, fewer neutrons are absorbed by the Hafnium and they are thus more likely to be absorbed by the Uranium to cause another fission.

The initial approach to criticality is a very special event and I was fortunate enough to be in charge of the engineering watch section in Shark that conducted this evolution in February 1968. There is always a very low level of neutrons present in a reactor core, and as the control rods are removed from the core these neutrons cause fissions that start multiplying, creating additional fissions and additional neutrons. There are some very sensitive neutron detectors placed near the core and these detectors measure the power level of the reactor core. The more neutrons that they detect, the higher the power level in the reactor. The initial level of neutrons in a new reactor is considerably less than the threshold of the neutron detectors, and thus they are not able to detect reactor power. If the control rods were pulled out continuously past the point of criticality, the neutron multiplication would lag behind considerably and there would not be enough neutrons for the detectors to measure. In this situation, it would be possible for the reactor to become "supercritical" with a power excursion that would do considerable damage to the reactor core. To prevent this possibility from happening, a "pull and wait" procedure is prescribed in which the control rods are pulled for three seconds and then the reactor operator waits for 57 seconds before pulling again for three seconds. By the time that the neutron levels in the core have built up to a level where they are detected by the neutron detectors, the reactor has not reached criticality.

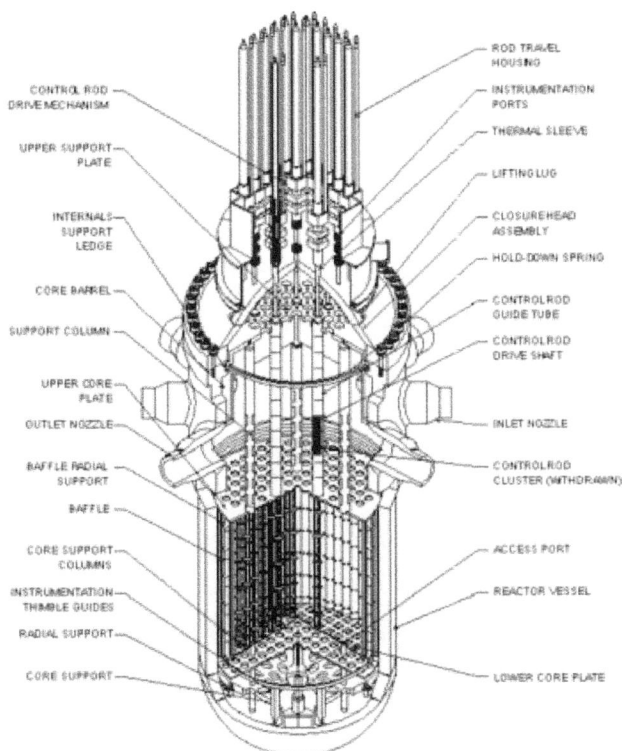

Pressurized Water Reactor

This is precisely what happened during our reactor plant start-up. We had been in the "Pull and Wait" procedure for hours and had not been able to detect any indication from the neutron detectors. Finally, we saw a slight motion in the needle as it "came off the peg." After the next "pull and wait" cycle, there was definite movement and a few moments later we had solid indication. We continued pulling rods until the reactor operator reported that the "Reactor is critical." Success! There was no alarm or increase in noise level, only an indication on a few meters on the reactor control panel. But we all knew that we had just witnessed the coming to life of a nuclear reactor that had been an inert lump of metal buried inside of the reactor vessel. This newly energized nuclear reactor would power our submarine for another ten years. It was quite a remarkable experience for us all.

An Unexpected Trip to Charleston

March 1968 saw the end of our time in the shipyard. We had a successful sea trial and then commenced a training cycle to prepare for our next deployment, scheduled that summer for the Mediterranean. We had a change of command with Commander Dave Self relieving Bob Kelsey. I had been on Shark for just two years and had witnessed a complete turnover of the officers on the ship. When I had reported aboard, I was next to the most junior officer aboard and now I was the Operations Officer and Navigator and the most senior officer next to the Executive Officer and the Captain. The submarine force was going through a rapid expansion at this time and we were typical of the inexperience on most of the ships. We only had three officers qualified as underway officers of the deck.

After we completed an at-sea training period, we had returned to port and were moored at the end of the pier with our bow pointed out. This was a rather unusual position, but it was to provide more room on the remainder of the pier to accommodate a ballistic missile submarine, the USS Woodrow Wilson due to moor later in that afternoon. As I was leaving the ship, I paused on the pier with the captain to observe the Woodrow Wilson making its landing astern of us. The Wilson had two tugs mate up to it to push it into the pier. As it passed by the Shark, the captain remarked that he thought that it was going to be a tight fit to moor her astern of Shark. He was right.

The Wilson was stopped near her intended berth at the pier and the tugs started to push her into her berth. From where we stood by the Shark's stern, it was obvious that the Wilson was not far enough along the pier and that she was going collide with our stern. The captain ran down the pier to advise the people on the Wilson's bridge of the problem and I told the Shark's topside watch to sound the collision alarm. It was too late to stop the Wilson and her propeller and stern planes smashed into our propeller and stern planes before the tugs could pull her back. We went back aboard the Shark to inspect for damage, but other than the shock of the collision among the crew, we could find no obvious damage inside the ship or above the waterline. We would have to await the diver's inspection of the stern planes, rudder and propeller.

The next morning the divers from the repair ship, USS Orion, conducted their inspection and the results were as we had feared. The propeller had been damaged with two of the seven blades bent over and a third blade badly scored on the leading edge. The rudder was not hit in the collision but the stern planes were questionable. The Wilson's propeller was still turning at the time of the collision and had hit the stern plane bearing housing several times. Even though the stern planes appeared to operate normally, the bearing would have to be disassembled and the alignment of the stern plane operating shaft would have to be checked. This procedure required the ship to be in drydock. There was no drydock available in the Norfolk area, but there was a floating drydock available at the Naval Weapons Station in Charleston, South Carolina. COMSUBLANT made the decision to send us to Charleston. We had a new propeller installed by the Orion's repair crew and we were underway for Charleston two days later on May 27, 1968. Because of the stern plane damage, we were not allowed to dive, so this would be a surfaced transit.

We left Norfolk with a full gale blowing. The winds were gusting to fifty knots with significantly reduced visibility. I headed up the navigation party in the control room. We were still in the channel proceeding toward the cut at the Chesapeake Bay Bridge tunnel. Radio called on the 21MC: "Conn—Radio. Squadron has called and asked if we see the Scorpion. She is due back today from a Mediterranean deployment. They are unable to raise her on the radio." The USS Scorpion was a sister ship of the USS Shark. I responded: "Radio—Conn. I have not seen her. I will ask the bridge."
The bridge had not seen her. Squadron asked us to try and contact Scorpion on the radio. We continued calling her for the next two hours with no luck. COMSUBLANT declared a SUBMISS/SUBSUNK emergency and directed all ships at sea to rendezvous at the Norfolk harbor entrance and start a search back along her intended track.

It was clear that we would be of little assistance in this search effort, as we could not operate submerged. An hour later, COMSUBLANT released us and directed us to continue to Charleston. With heavy heart, we turned south toward Cape Hatteras. Our immediate thoughts were about our sister ship and her crew, but soon, we were fighting a severe storm as we rounded Cape Hatteras. The Captain made the decision that it was too dangerous to man the bridge, so the officer of the deck maintained a watch on the periscope in the control room. A nuclear submarine on the surface in a big storm is not a pleasant experience. We were rolling 30 to 40 degrees and submerging to 50 feet as big waves washed over us. Almost the entire crew was seasick and each of us was just hanging on to whatever support we could find. I was one of the fortunate few who did not get seasick.

The Loss of USS Scorpion (SSN 589)

USS Shark arrived in Charleston, South Carolina two days after we had left Norfolk. It seemed as if the entire Atlantic Fleet was searching for the USS Scorpion. We all felt that we should have been part of that search effort, but our potentially damaged stern planes prevented us from conducting submerged operations and it was essential that we get into drydock to find out the extent of damage. The trip up the Cooper River to the Naval Weapons Station was uneventful and we entered the drydock in the morning and were "high and dry" that afternoon. That evening I had the opportunity to call home and assure Mary that our trip to Charleston had gone well and that we were all safe and very worried about the crew and the families of Scorpion. She said that it had been a rough couple of days for all the submarine families in Norfolk.

The Scorpion families had all been gathered on the pier awaiting the arrival of the Scorpion at 1000. The weather was miserable, raining and very windy. Very little information was provided to the families until about noon when it was clear that the ship was not going to arrive. By the afternoon, the Navy declared that the ship was overdue and that a search effort was underway. Many of the families stayed on the pier through the afternoon hoping against hope that the ship would arrive. The submarine squadron staff and the submarines in Norfolk assigned personnel to each of the Scorpion families as liaison and support.

The disassembly and inspection of our stern planes took a few days, and after all the data was collected it was determined that our stern planes had not been damaged and we were no longer restricted from submerged operations. We left the drydock and Charleston and returned to Norfolk in early June. By the time we had returned, the Navy had officially declared the Scorpion missing and presumed lost. The loss of a sister ship was extremely difficult for all of us to accept. Just a year ago, I had been aboard the Scorpion for my in-port submarine qualification and had lunch in the wardroom with many of the officers who were now presumed lost at sea. Nobody had any idea why the ship was lost. USS Thresher had been lost in 1963, but she was on sea trials after a shipyard period and was making her initial test dive with an escort ship in contact with her at the time. It was clear that her loss was due to catastrophic flooding. But the loss of Scorpion was a mystery. There would be no chance of solving this mystery until the Navy located the remains of the Scorpion somewhere in the Atlantic Ocean.

USS Scorpion (SSN 589) at sea

In late October 1968, the USS Scorpion was found 400 miles southwest of the Azores in 10,000 feet of water and photographed by an underwater search vehicle towed by a hydrographic research ship. Additional deep diving vessels were sent to analyze the wreckage. The Navy had developed a broad ocean area listening capability and from the data analyzed, it was determined that the Scorpion was lost on May 22, five days before she was scheduled to arrive in Norfolk. Submarines do not routinely send radio messages while at sea, so the Navy was not unduly concerned about not hearing from the ship until the day she was to arrive home. The Navy board of inquiry concluded that the most likely cause of the loss was a torpedo explosion from an on-board Mark-37 torpedo caused by an electrical fault and a battery explosion in the torpedo. There are several other alternative theories, including faulty stern planes, which was the concern we had on Shark. None of the theories has been conclusive.

We attended a very moving memorial service for the crew of the USS Scorpion and the next day the Captain was at the submarine force headquarters for a pre-deployment briefing. When he returned, he met with the Executive Officer and me. He told us that the Mediterranean deployment was off and that we would be picking up the deployment planned for Scorpion. This deployment would take us to the Pacific. We were expected at SUBLANT headquarters for pre-deployment briefings that afternoon, and I was to pick up a package of Pacific Ocean charts. I could not figure out why we would be going to the Pacific Ocean.

Our briefings at SUBLANT headquarters solved the mystery. The French were conducting nuclear weapons testing at a remote atoll in the South Pacific and the U.S. was monitoring these tests. The U.S. Air Force would over-fly the tests to sample the upper atmosphere for fallout. A submarine with suitable electronics equipment installed would observe the test from international waters near the atoll. There was already a Pacific submarine on station and we were to be her relief. We were to complete all preparations, including the special electronics equipment installation as quickly as possible and depart for the Panama Canal with a subsequent transit to Pearl Harbor, Hawaii. Aloha!

Norfolk to Pearl Harbor via the Panama Canal

We made a high-speed transit to Pearl Harbor via the Panama Canal. As navigator, I worked up all the charts needed for the transit, and was truly surprised at the distance we would have to go to get to Pearl Harbor. Norfolk to the Panama Canal is 1820 miles and it is another 4688 miles from the Panama Canal to Pearl Harbor. Although nuclear submarines are capable of higher speeds, 18 to 20 knots is usually the maximum speed for a long-term transit. This means that it would take us 5 days to reach the canal and an additional 11 days to reach Pearl Harbor. With a day to transit the canal, we would take 17 days to get to Pearl Harbor.

I was due to be transferred from the Shark in August, but the captain persuaded the Bureau of Naval Personnel to delay my transfer until after this deployment. My relief had already reported aboard which gave us an additional qualified watchstander for the deployment. I expected to be transferred to another submarine to serve as navigator for an additional two years, and I was happy to stay aboard Shark for this deployment.

A principal concern of mine for this deployment would be the navigation problems that we would face in remote areas of the south pacific. In 1968, the Navy had a navigation satellite system, but it was available only to ballistic missile submarines. There was no GPS, which is in use today worldwide. In the south pacific there were no electronic navigation aids, the atolls were low-lying reefs with few navigational lights and were not easily seen visually, particularly from a submarine periscope. The waters were not well-charted and there was limited sounding data. In short, we were heading toward unknown and potentially dangerous waters. On the plus side, we had installed a new type-15 periscope that incorporated a periscope sextant, which would allow me to take star sights for celestial navigation. In discussions with other submarine navigators, I found that most thought that the periscope sextant was unreliable, providing very poor results. I did find an article in a submarine journal that emphasized that the periscope sextant had some inherent errors, but once properly calibrated these errors could be minimized. The principal problem was that the barrel of the periscope would bend or flex...the amount dependent on the speed and depth of the submarine. This bending would introduce an error in the angle measured between the star and the horizon. By choosing the same depth and speed each time a star sight was obtained and developing an error curve that plotted the error against the relative bearing of the periscope, it was possible to greatly improve the accuracy of the star sight. Quartermaster First Class Caruthers was my assistant navigator, and we were able to improve our techniques during sea trials off Norfolk and during our transit to Hawaii. As a result, I was confident that we would not have a problem with navigation in the south pacific.

Passage through the Panama Canal was a first for me. There are two situations when the safe navigation of the ship is no longer the responsibility of the Commanding Officer. The first is when the ship enters a drydock and the other is in the Panama Canal. The pilot of the Panama Canal Company is responsible for the safety of the ship. As a result, the captain and I were observers as we spent a day going through the canal. The other unusual aspect is that nuclear submarines are provided a priority transit through the canal. All other shipping is stopped and the submarine does not have to wait at any of the locks in the canal. The locks are enormous and can accommodate a battleship. A Skipjack class submarine, which is only 250 feet long, is dwarfed by the size of the lock.

Skipjack class in Panama canal

The trip to Pearl Harbor was uneventful and we arrived in early July. The submarine base had anticipated many repairs would be needed, but we had no special needs and would be ready to sail in three or four days. The

Chief Engineer, Al More, had reported to the ship just prior to our departure from Norfolk. He had previously been stationed on a submarine in Pearl Harbor and was anxious to see his girlfriend, Pua. The next morning, Al came into the wardroom and invited all of us to his wedding, which would be the next day in the submarine base chapel. We were all taken by surprise, but he and his bride had planned to be married after the deployment and they thought why wait? So the next day the crew of the Shark and the family and friends of Al and Pua attended a lovely wedding in the historic submarine base chapel where submarine crews attended church services before going on war patrols in World War II. Al and Pua had a one-night honeymoon and we were underway for French Polynesia in the south pacific the next morning.

Sub Base Chapel

South to Mururoa and Fangataufa

In mid-July 1968, we departed Pearl Harbor for the remote atolls of Mururoa and Fangataufa in French Polynesia where the French were conducting their second annual nuclear weapons testing program. A Pacific Fleet nuclear submarine had been covering the first half of the testing period and the French had already conducted two nuclear weapons tests. They had announced that this year they would conduct a thermonuclear test (Hydrogen bomb) and that was the principal reason that the U.S. was monitoring these tests. It appeared that this would occur on our watch.

Fangataufa

Mururoa

Mururoa is at latitude 22 degrees South and about 1,000 miles east of Tahiti, the major population center of French Polynesia. Fangataufa is another 25 miles south of Mururoa. We had another long transit to Mururoa, nearly 3,000 miles from Pearl Harbor. Before we got there however, we had another important evolution to conduct and that was a "crossing the line ceremony" when we crossed the equator. The Navy has maintained the tradition of crossing the line ceremonies for over two hundred years, and it is still in place today. Those who have previously crossed the equator are known as (trusty) shellbacks and those who have not, are (slimy) Pollywogs. The shellbacks have the responsibility of indoctrinating the pollywogs into the mysteries of the deep in an appropriate ceremony. I had previously been in one of these ceremonies ten years earlier aboard the USS Ranger, an aircraft carrier, when over 4,000 pollywogs were indoctrinated by about 800 shellbacks. The odds were not as favorable this time however, as there were only 8 shellbacks and over 110 pollywogs. Only one other officer was a shellback and that was the captain, who by tradition does not participate in the ceremony. I was the senior shellback and we had already held some planning meetings before arriving in Pearl Harbor. We had laid in some supplies that we would need for the ceremony during our stop in Pearl Harbor.

Our principal concern was that there were so few shellbacks and that if the pollywogs had a revolt, as was rumored, then we would have a difficult time holding a ceremony. The assistant navigator, petty officer Carruthers was also a shellback and we came up with a plan. Navigation and determining the ship's position was only by star sights using the periscope sextant and he and I were the only ones involved in this evolution. We could keep two sets of charts, one with our actual position and one with a fictitious position that was available for the crew to see. Using the bogus chart, we would advise the crew that the ship was scheduled to cross the equator at 1500 and that the ceremony would be in the afternoon. In reality, we would cross the equator about twelve hours earlier at 0300, when most of the crew was asleep. I had to get the captain's approval of our plan and after I explained our expectations of a pollywog revolt, he approved.

As navigator, I had scheduled a routine excursion to periscope depth at 0300 to copy our radio traffic from the submarine broadcast. Carruthers and I were in the control room for navigation with the remainder of the shellbacks gathered in the crew's mess. We announced the arrival of Davy Jones on the 1MC and a few minutes later sounded the general alarm in order to get all the crew out of their bunks. We had planned on indoctrinating several of the chief petty officers first, and then using these new shellbacks to control the rest of the crew.

Our plan went off without a hitch. The pollywogs had indeed been planning some type of revolt, but they were still trying to wake up when we started the ceremonies in the mess decks. They were slow to get organized and they never had a chance as they were rounded up by the new shellbacks. I was King Neptune, Carruthers was Davy Jones, and we enjoyed watching the entire crew of USS Shark participate in this traditional ceremony. We completed the ceremonies by 0530, and the entire crew enjoyed an early breakfast as we continued our transit to Mururoa.

Nuclear Weapons Testing in French Polynesia

Author's note: The pictures and descriptions of the French nuclear weapons testing conducted on Mururoa and Fangataufa atolls in French Polynesia are unclassified and were obtained from the Atomic Forum website (www.atomicforum.org). My shipmates and I aboard USS Shark were fortunate to be on hand as observers of these historic events.

Nuclear Explosion over Mururoa

When we arrived in the waters off Mururoa, we carefully observed the French Navy ships moored in the lagoon of the atoll and we remained well clear of the atoll in international waters. A barrage balloon was in place over Mururoa with a gondola suspended from the balloon. We calculated that the altitude of the gondola was 1500 feet. We were able to copy a television signal transmitted from Mururoa that displayed several scenes including the gondola, a blockhouse that was the command center and additional views of the atoll. On 2 August, all the ships in the lagoon departed and we watched a countdown on television that terminated with a detonation of a nuclear weapon on 3 August. This was a 150-kiloton explosion and not the hydrogen bomb that we were expecting. Note: a kiloton is the equivalent of one thousand tons of conventional explosive material or TNT. The bomb dropped on Hiroshima was a 20-kiloton weapon. Because the weapon was suspended from a balloon at 1500 feet, this was an airburst, which minimizes nuclear fallout because the fireball created by the explosion does not touch the earth or the waters of the lagoon. The French ships returned the next day, and it was apparent that the radiation fallout was minimal allowing the immediate occupation of the atoll.

The French then turned their attention to the placement of another barrage balloon over Fangataufa, an atoll about 25 miles south of Mururoa. The gondola below this balloon seemed considerably larger than the previous one and it was at an altitude of 1800 feet. Maybe this would be the hydrogen bomb test that we were expecting. The ships all departed the Mururoa lagoon on 21 August and we were left alone for the next three days monitoring the countdown on television. There were several delays due to unfavorable winds, which would affect the fallout from the explosion. On 24 August, we witnessed a considerably stronger explosion that we thought was probably a thermonuclear or hydrogen bomb test. As it turned out this test was code-named Canopus and in fact it was announced by France the next day that they had successfully tested a thermonuclear device. Canopus was a 2.6-megaton explosion, almost 200 times more powerful than the first explosion we witnessed.

Barrage Balloon over Fangataufa

The ships returned to Mururoa two days later. Our visual inspection of the Fangataufa atoll from our periscope revealed considerable damage to the structures that we had previously seen on the atoll. A blockhouse near where the barrage balloon was moored was gone. We could see no palm trees, where previously they were in abundance. It was apparent that the fireball had touched down on the atoll and there was probably considerable radioactive contamination present. The French did not send any ships into the Fangataufa lagoon. The Atomic Forum website reports that there was considerable radioactive contamination on Fangtaufa and parts of the atoll could not be occupied for over six years.

The French erected another barrage balloon over the Mururoa atoll and the gondola was at 2250 feet. On September 8, they detonated their second thermonuclear device, which was code named Procyon. This was a 1.3-megaton explosion. This was apparently their last nuclear weapons test as the ships did not return to Mururoa but departed for their home port of Papeete, Tahiti.

Two days later, COMSUBPAC terminated our operation and directed our return to Pearl Harbor. We had conducted a very successful intelligence collection mission. Using a specially designed high-speed movie camera adapted to our periscope, we had obtained high-resolution photographs of the fireballs in each of the three tests and with sophisticated electronics equipment, had recorded the electromagnetic signature of each explosion. This information would prove of great value to our scientific community.

Since France had withdrawn from the military alliance of NATO in the late 1950s and was not sharing information about its nuclear testing and development program with the United States, the data we collected was of importance to our national security. As current events unfold today in Iran and North Korea, the U.S. has much the same interest in evaluating the capability of emerging nuclear powers.

Farewell to USS Shark

In September 1968, USS Shark completed its mission in French Polynesia and was returning to Pearl Harbor, Hawaii. I expected reassignment to another submarine, but I had not yet seen my orders. On 12 September, we received the following message from the Bureau of Naval Personnel (BUPERS): "UNCLAS BUPERS ORDER NR 144370. LCDR HENRY C MCKINNEY 593206/1100. DIRDET IN SEP OR OCT PROREP NAVNUCPWRSCOL NTC BAIN DUTY. DELREP 21 OCT." Translated, these orders read, "When directed, detached duty indicated in September or October 1968. Proceed to U.S. Naval Nuclear Power School, U.S. Naval Training Center, Bainbridge, Maryland and report for duty. Provided no excess leave involved, authorized delay until 21 October 1968, in reporting, to count as leave." These orders were a real surprise to me. Everyone that I knew was being reassigned to sea duty as the submarine force was critically short of officers, and I was going to shore duty. What had I done wrong, I wondered. The captain, Commander Dave Self assured me that he was sure that this was a top-notch assignment, and one that was carefully screened. He would make some inquiries on my behalf as soon as we arrived in Pearl Harbor.

My relief, Terry Camilleri, was already on board, so for the remainder of our trip to Hawaii, we turned over the Operations Department and he relieved me as navigator. We arrived in Pearl Harbor on 18 September and we all felt it was a little strange that there were no families to meet us, as they were all in Norfolk, Virginia. I found out from my telephone call home to Mary that afternoon that the Navy had notified our families of our safe return from patrol. She had heard something about my orders and wanted more details, as did I, but that would have to wait until the skipper called BUPERS. We were just happy to have a few minutes to talk together for the first time since June. I would be home in a few days, but the rest of the crew would have to wait for another month before the ship got back to Norfolk.

The phone call to BUPERS cleared up the mystery. After reporting to Nuclear Power School, Bainbridge, MD, I would relieve the Director of the Officer Department and be responsible for the training of all the officer students attending the school. The submarine assignment officer told the skipper that this was a carefully screened assignment and that Admiral

Rickover had to personally approve my assignment to this position. Although I had my heart set on another sea tour as I felt that I needed more experience at sea, I was relieved to hear that this assignment was career enhancing.

Leaving a ship is always a bittersweet experience. The Shark had been my principal focus for the last two and half years. Three deployments including a most unusual inter-fleet deployment, a nuclear refueling, port calls throughout the Caribbean, Halifax, and Bermuda. The loss of a sister ship, USS Scorpion with many friends aboard. You never forget your first submarine as the one you completed your submarine qualification on. It was hard to leave good friends and shipmates, and because the ship still had a return transit to Norfolk to complete, there was a sense that I was leaving with unfinished business still to be done.

The officers held a nice dinner in my honor at the historic Pearl Harbor submarine base officer's club. I had reported on board in March 1966 and was next to the most junior officer in a wardroom of twelve officers. Two and a half years later, I was leaving as the third most senior officer and the longest serving officer on board. It was hard for me to believe that so much had happened in such a short time span. I hoped that all the officers remaining on Shark would have the same success and experiences that I had.

The next day, 21 September, my assistant Navigator, Petty Officer First Class Carruthers, drove me to the MAC terminal on Hickam Air Force base and I departed Hawaii on a MAC fight to Travis Air Force base. Mary and our son William were waiting for me at the Baltimore airport when I arrived on 23 September. It was great to be home, and we had almost a month before I had to report to my next duty station. First, we had to find out where Bainbridge, Maryland is.

Chapter V - Nuclear Power School Bainbridge

Leaders and Mentors

I relieved as Director of the Officer Department at Nuclear Power School Bainbridge in early December 1968. After class graduation in mid-December, the school observed a two-week Christmas leave period, Mary, and I drove to Cincinnati and the Chicago area to be with our families for Christmas. We had missed that opportunity the previous year because of the Shark's nuclear refueling.

When we returned to Bainbridge, we discovered that the roof of our temporary apartment had collapsed due to ice accumulation and we had suffered some water damage to our personal belongings. Our permanent quarters were ready for us, so we moved the next weekend. We moved into a small older house, with three bedrooms and one bath. We had a nice yard with room for a vegetable garden and an apple orchard out back. On the other side of the chain link fence in the front yard was the highway leading into the front gate of the Naval Training Center. Not the best view, certainly, but we were very happy to have a nice home for the next few years.

Mary and I were very fortunate to have this time together on shore duty and to share in the joys and wonders of watching our son grow through the terrible twos and tumultuous threes. This was also a terrible and tumultuous time for our country with the agony of the Vietnam War resulting in protests and unrest sweeping the nation. We were relatively isolated from much of this because of the remote location of Bainbridge. Anti-war protesters did not show up at the front gate of Bainbridge, probably because they couldn't find it. The officer students were serious engineering students and their workload did not allow for much time off. For the most part, they would all be assigned to nuclear submarines that were not involved in Vietnam. But even though Bainbridge was not in the center of the anti-war maelstrom, most of the students were recent college graduates and they had all been profoundly affected by what was happening on our college campuses. In retrospect, it could have been that Bainbridge served as a sanctuary and safe haven for them.

I was also influenced by two remarkable Navy leaders during this period, one directly and the other indirectly. The first was Commander Frank Kelso who took over as the Commanding Officer of the Nuclear Power School in January 1969. Frank had a wealth of submarine experience, having qualified on a diesel submarine and then served as a junior officer on the nuclear submarine USS Pollock, engineering officer of the ballistic missile submarine USS Daniel Webster and Executive Officer of the USS Sculpin, which was the same class as my only submarine USS Shark. Frank is the same age as my older brother Pete and we quickly fell into a senior-junior mentoring relationship that would last throughout the rest of my career in the Navy, during which Frank rose to the rank of four-star admiral and the Chief of Naval Operations. When compared to my one submarine tour, Frank Kelso's submarine experience allowed me to tap into the wealth of his accumulated wisdom and advice that was invaluable at this stage in my career. Frank was a role model for me and as well, his wife Landess was the Navy wife that Mary aspired to become. Both Frank and Landess gave of their time and energy selflessly to the Navy family and community. As our paths crossed over the ensuing years, Mary and I became evermore enriched by their friendship and support.

Admiral Frank B. Kelso

The other Navy leader who had great influence on me during this period was Admiral Elmo Zumwalt who became the Chief of Naval Operations in July 1970. Admiral Zumwalt was a transformational leader who changed the culture of our Navy. The unrest and turmoil in our nation was reflected in our Navy as well. To address these problems, Admiral Zumwalt made some monumental changes in a remarkably short time after he became the CNO. He used the Navy's communication system to issue a series of messages to "all hands." These messages were called "Z Grams" and they were not sent via the chain of command to be interpreted by intervening layers of the bureaucracy, but rather were posted on bulletin boards on all ships and stations to be read by all hands. One had only to stand in the background and observe the reactions of sailors and junior officers reading these missives to realize that Admiral Zumwalt was striking a responsive chord. Admiral Zumwalt's leadership initiatives had a profound influence on my Navy career and this will be the subject of another story.

Admiral Elmo R. Zumwalt, Jr.

Although I did not know Admiral Zumwalt at the time, twenty-six years later, after I retired from the Navy, I became the President and CEO of the Navy Memorial Foundation. Admiral Zumwalt was the Chairman of the Board of Directors who hired me and Admiral Frank Kelso was a member of the board.

Nuclear Engineering in a 1941 Mess Hall

NTC Bainbridge

I reported to Nuclear Power School, at Naval Training Center, Bainbridge, Maryland in late October 1968. I was to relieve as the Director of the Officer Department. Admiral Rickover was well known for his Spartan life style. I remember well his office in Washington with grey metal desks that had been around for twenty years and grey linoleum floors that had been there even longer. The Nuclear Power School that I had attended four years earlier had been located in an old wooden building at the Mare Island Naval Shipyard in California. Even with this previous experience, I wasn't prepared for what I would find in Bainbridge.

The Bainbridge Naval Training Center had been built in the early 1940s as a recruit training center. It had been abandoned in 1947, reopened in 1951 and had been in a state of gradual decline ever since. By 1968, the majority of the buildings of the training center had been abandoned and was badly deteriorated. The Nuclear Power School had taken over a recruit classroom and administration building and this served as the enlisted department training area. The officer department was located in an adjacent recruit mess hall. This cavernous building would feed 4,000 recruits at one sitting. Half the building was walled off and not occupied. The other half of the mess hall was partitioned into six classrooms and office space for a staff of 20 instructors. My office was the scullery for the mess hall. The sinks had been removed, but the piping had not. Pipes were simply capped off and protruded through the walls. The storage area for our classified textbooks was the old refrigerated space. A large oak door led into a galvanized steel lined freezer and chill box. Bookshelves lined the walls and were filled with the classified material relating to our Navy's nuclear submarine propulsion systems. A padlock secured the oak door. Steam pipes from a central boiler provided heat to the building. Every fall when the heating system was turned on, the rusty pipes developed leaks, and we had repairs going on through most of November. There was no air conditioning.

Bachelor officer students were provided small rooms in what had once been the nurse's quarters for the base hospital. Married officer students were provided apartments, if available, in a substandard family housing area. The enlisted students were provided substandard berthing in the original recruit barracks. In summary, the classroom facilities were makeshift and badly run down and the living facilities were inadequate. No one would ever suggest that Admiral Rickover was wasting the taxpayer's money on training facilities.

The course of instruction for the officer students was six months long with six to seven hours of lectures each day, five days a week. The level of instruction was at the graduate level and by the end of six months, the student had essentially completed the requirements for a master's degree in nuclear engineering. The students were expected to put in an hour of study for each hour of classroom instruction. I had been through the course four years earlier, and had never studied harder in my life, so I knew what was required and made sure that the officer students understood what I expected of them.

The instructors were an interesting group of individuals. Each had been selected by Admiral Rickover based upon their academic standing and field of study when they graduated from college in the NROTC program. They each had agreed to serve an extra year beyond their minimum obligated service of three years. Most were pursuing advanced degrees in their field of expertise. We also had a few officer instructors who had served at sea on submarines.

In my position as Director of the Officer Department, I was both the academic dean and the dean of students. I was expected to regularly monitor the classroom instruction, I approved all examinations and I advised the

Commanding Officer of the school regarding student progress. Admiral Rickover also monitored the progress of officer students through a letter that I wrote to him on a regular basis. Students who fell behind in their studies or who had failing grades were counseled and placed on mandatory study hours. We had four six-month long classes in a year and the average class size was 55 officer students, most of who had just graduated from the Naval Academy or a college with an NROTC program. I really enjoyed my role as counselor and mentor to these newly commissioned officers.

Seafood Bounty

Bainbridge Naval Training Center was located at the northern end of the Chesapeake Bay and living there, we were anxious to sample all the seafood that is available from this remarkable body of water. Striped bass, cherrystone clams, oysters and blue point crabs were all high on our list. We had grown quite fond of cherrystone clams on the half shell during our time in Norfolk. We would buy them for $1.00 a dozen from Henry's Clam Shack on Lynnhaven inlet in Virginia Beach, then take them home, shuck them and serve with a seafood cocktail sauce with extra horseradish added. This was a real treat.

Cherrystone Clams

In Bainbridge, we determined that on our trips to Baltimore we could find clams on the half shell in the harbor area. Baltimore Harbor today is very "up-scale" with a world-class aquarium, science museum and trendy seafood restaurants, but in the late 1960s, the harbor area was still a rough neighborhood. I took my three-year son, William into a "raw bar" one Saturday morning. All the customers were men who appeared to be longshoremen taking a mid-morning break. I found a place at the bar and hoisted William up so that he could sit on the bar and watch the clams and oysters being shucked.

I ordered a dozen clams and we watched as they were shucked. The man behind the counter asked what my son would like and I replied that we were here to eat clams. Well, that got the attention of the other men around the bar and they all watched with great interest as William downed three clams right off the half shell without so much as batting an eye. That performance received a small round of applause and I was asked how long he had been enjoying clams on the half shell. I replied that he had his first clam at his first birthday party and has been enjoying them ever since. When we were ready to leave, I asked for my bill. The man behind the counter charged me for the clams I had eaten, but said that William's clams were "on the house."

Chesapeake Bay blue point crabs are delicious but learning how to prepare them properly is important and then how to eat them is a challenge. The crabs are small, about five to six inches in diameter. The male crab is called a jimmy and is preferred for eating as it is larger and has more meat. They are quite aggressive and handling them can be a challenge as their bite is painful. Usually sold by the bushel and as I recall a bushel in 1970 cost $10. A bushel today will run $75, which is still a bargain.

A jimmy

Blue crabs are steamed in a large pot and covered with a special seasoning consisting of a pound kosher salt, 5 ounces of crushed red pepper, 3 ounces of dried mustard, ginger, black pepper and 8 other spices. This is a very spicy hot seasoning. The crabs are layered into the pot and liberal seasoning is added to each layer (two pounds of seasoning for six dozen crabs). The pot is covered and the crabs are steamed for about 25 minutes and served hot. Crabs are generally eaten outdoors on a picnic table covered with several layers of newspaper with a mallet and paring knife handy as well some liquid refreshments.

Getting the meat out of the crabs is termed "picking." Techniques for picking the meat from a steamed crab vary. Some people go at the crab with a mallet, which is not the preferred method. Others take their time, watch how their neighbors extract large juicy chunks of crabmeat and develop their own technique. The masters of picking steamed crabs rarely talk…they eat!

The preferred method is to split off the back shell of the crab, remove the legs and claws and then start working on the lower section of the body as seen in the picture of the "jimmy" which contains all the meat. All this is done with your hands and by the time you get to the meat, your fingers are covered with the spicy seasoning that covers the crab. You eat the crabmeat with your fingers and enjoy the seasoning. Cracking open the claws with a mallet allows you to enjoy the claw meat, which has a special flavor. The "back fin" crabmeat is connected to the swimming "paddle", the two lower appendages. This is the sweetest meat in the crab and is easily removed by holding on to the "paddle" as you open the crab. About 18 crabs will produce a pound of crab meat, which is more than enough for most people and it will take the average "picker" about thirty or forty minutes to pick this many crabs.

The best part of the meal is the cleanup. Just roll up the newspaper with all the "remains" of the crabs inside and dispose in a plastic bag for the garbage. Now that's what I call "doing the dishes."

Tomato Plants

One of the interesting aspects of living on an old military base is exploring buildings, long abandoned, and imagining what it was like twenty-five years earlier when the base was teeming with raw recruits preparing to go to war. My three year-old, William along with our dog, a cocker spaniel named Sam would spend a Saturday or Sunday morning on long walks exploring history. One morning in the summer of 1970, we happened upon the Bainbridge Naval Training Center sewage treatment plant. I had never really understood how these plants functioned so we looked around without much comprehension when I spotted an older gentleman pushing a wheelbarrow. He came toward us and asked what we were doing. I introduced us and Sam sniffed the man's shoes with some interest. He introduced himself as Charlie, told us that he was in charge of the plant, and asked if we would like a tour. I accepted his offer and we set off to examine the three tanks that were used in the treatment of sewage. William lost interest quickly, but I could see that the smells held Sam's attention.

Charlie had been in charge of operations here since the base was built in 1944 and it was clear that he knew a lot about his job. He gave a very informative tour and I learned a good deal more than I had bargained for. As we came to the last holding tank, Charlie explained that there was great deal of chemical and biological action going on in this tank and he pointed out the bubbles of gas coming to the surface. He said that the gas was a combination of hydrogen sulfide and methane.

"See that pipe over there," said Charlie pointing to his left. "The gas is directed up that pipe and is discharged up into the air."

I nodded and added that I had sometimes smelled the gas over at my house.

"We used to burn the gas," Charlie said "and that reduced the odor quite a bit."

"Why don't you burn the gas now?" I asked.

"Can't now." he responded "Not enough gas to light a flame."
"That's too bad." I said.

"Yeah," Charlie went on "back in 1945 there were 55,000 people on this base and we generated a lot of gas back then. The flame from that pipe was thirty feet high and it lit up the whole countryside. Burned day and night. It was quite a sight!"

Then Charlie sighed. "Don't expect that we'll ever see that sight again."

After a few moments of silence remembering the good old days, Charlie pointed to his wheelbarrow and asked if I would like to take home some tomato plants for my garden. I then noted that there were small tomato plants growing in the black dirt in his wheelbarrow.

"Do you grow a garden here?" I asked.

"Nope," Charlie said, "they grow naturally all around here."

"Why?" I wondered.

"Well, you see," he explained, "when you eat tomatoes, the seeds go right through your system and they end up here. They also survive the treatment here and end up in this black dirt, the sludge that I remove from the last tank. After a few weeks, they sprout into new tomato plants. I take a few home with me every week and plant them in my garden. They make good eating, and you are welcome to take as many as you want." He went on to say, "The only problem is that you are never sure what type of tomato you are growing as there are hundreds of varieties." Then he added, with what had to be his favorite joke: "You might say that growing tomatoes this way, to use a gambler's phrase, is something of a crap shoot."

I thanked Charlie for his generous offer, but told him that we had already planted our garden, and that we had quite a few tomato plants already. "Suit yourself," he said "but you are welcome to have all you want any time in the future." I thanked Charlie for an interesting tour and William, Sam and I headed home for lunch. I hoped that Mary wasn't serving BLT's, as I wasn't ready to eat a tomato just yet.

Zebra Skin Shoes, a new Navy fashion trend

In the summer of 1970, The Bainbridge Naval Training Center had a visit from Mrs. Pat Nixon, wife of the President. Apparently, the White House had heard of the Navy's efforts to provide support to inner-city children. At Bainbridge, the Navy sponsored Camp Concern, a special day camp that had been set up for inner-city kids from Baltimore, and the White House felt that this would be a perfect opportunity for a photo op for Mrs. Nixon. Commander Frank Kelso, the commanding officer of the Nuclear Power School had a meeting with the Director of the Enlisted Department and me to discuss this visit. She would not be anywhere near the Nuclear Power School and he expected business as usual, but the Commander, Bainbridge Naval Training Center had directed that the uniform of the day for all hands would be Tropical Whites. I knew that this was going to be a problem for the officers as their uniform during the summer was khakis and I wondered how many had a white uniform.

I put out this word to the Officer Department and was not surprised when the officer instructors, as well as many of the officer students, came to me to express their concern that they did not have summer whites. The officer instructors had been specially selected from the NROTC program by Admiral Rickover to serve five years as instructors at Nuclear Power School. They never expected to go to sea and so had made no effort to have a complete set of uniforms when they were commissioned. The officer students did not think that they would need summer whites for their six-month course of instruction and many did not have these uniforms with them. As I recall, I discussed their concerns with Commander Kelso and he was firm that we would follow the direction of the Center Commander. I told my staff and students that I expected to see them all in the designated uniform of the day and I encouraged them to share extra uniforms with each other and to be creative where necessary.

The big day arrived and as I walked through the offices and classrooms, I was pleased to see all the officers splendidly turned out in summer whites. I did note a few uniform problems such as slightly yellowed whites, some that looked like they had just come out of suitcase where they had been packed for three years, and a few non-regulation white trousers with cuffs. By-and-large it was a reasonable turnout, and since we knew that Mrs. Nixon would not be coming within half a mile of the Nuclear Power School, we could continue with our primary mission of teaching the finer points of nuclear reactor theory to future nuclear submariners.

Mid-morning, I received a call from the captain's office advising me that he would be monitoring one of our classes at 1100. I stopped by the Physics class, being taught by Lieutenant (junior grade) Mike Bozoian and noted that the skipper was in the back row listening to his discussion of nuclear binding energy. As I was leaving the classroom, I noticed that Mike was teaching in his stocking feet--white socks, but no shoes. I was sure that the skipper had noticed as well, and I was "eagerly" anticipating his comments after class. He did not disappoint me, as he made a beeline for my office after class and asked what in the world Mike Bozoian was thinking about teaching his class in his socks. I said that I was sure that there was a reasonable explanation, and that Mike was on his way to my office.

Mike knocked on the door, and came in, still in his socks, but no shoes.

"Mike, where are your shoes." I asked.

"In the Physics office." He responded.

"Why aren't you wearing them? Do you have a foot problem? Blisters?" I asked.

"No sir" He responded. "It's just that the shoes don't look right."

"Why don't you bring them here, so that we can see for ourselves?" I said.

Mike returned, a little flustered, and presented a pair of black and white striped shoes. He said that he had taken to heart my advice to be creative, and since he did not own any white shoes, he thought that he could paint his black shoes white, and that would work for one day. He said that they looked great this morning, until he put them on, and then the white paint started to come off at the creases in the shoes. By the time, he had arrived at the office they looked like zebra skin and he realized that he would look ridiculous wearing these shoes in the classroom, so he opted to wear just his socks instead. He apologized to both of us, but by that time, we were laughing so hard, that no apologies were necessary.

Fast Attacks and Boomers

My projected rotation date (PRD) from Bainbridge was in the spring of 1971 and I was looking forward to my next assignment as executive officer of a nuclear submarine. There are two different types of nuclear submarines, fast attack submarines (SSNs), such as the USS Shark to which I had previously been assigned, and ballistic missile submarines (SSBNs), affectionately called "Boomers." The fast attack submarine conducts surveillance missions, hunts other submarines and surface ships and carries torpedoes as its main armament. The main mission of ballistic missile submarines is strategic defense. They carry long-range ballistic missiles with nuclear warheads and will retaliate with nuclear weapons if our nation is attacked by an adversary using nuclear weapons. They also carry torpedoes to be used for self-defense if necessary.

SSNs are tasked with many different missions as I discovered during my tour on USS Shark. These ships deploy worldwide to the North Atlantic, Western Pacific and the Mediterranean and make port calls to many different countries. SSBNs were forward deployed to advanced bases in Guam, Holy Loch, Scotland and Rota, Spain. They are "at sea" conducting strategic deterrent patrols about 65% of the time. In order to maintain this operational tempo, each SSBN is manned with two crews designated Gold and Blue. The crews relieve each other every three months. The "off-crew" spends its time in the homeports of New London, Connecticut, Charleston, South Carolina and Pearl Harbor, Hawaii conducting training before flying out to Holy Loch, Rota or Guam to relieve their counterpart crew as they complete a two-month patrol.

SSBNs do not have a variety of missions. When conducting a strategic deterrent patrol, they have two principal concerns: (1) maintain the communication, missile and navigation systems in a fully alert condition able to launch a retaliatory attack within 15 minutes and (2) remain undetected 100% of the time. The first requirement means that the SSBN must be able to continuously monitor communications from the national command authority. This is accomplished with a long floating wire antenna that is deployed with the submarine at a depth of 150 to 400 feet. The floating wire antenna is on the surface and picks up a worldwide submarine Very Low Frequency (VLF) radio transmission. An alternative is a buoy antenna that is connected to the submarine by a cable and is controlled by the submarine so that it remains just below the surface and is designed to receive VLF signals. In both cases, the SSBN operates at relatively slow speeds (4 knots) and at relatively shallow depths to maintain continuous reception. The second requirement means that the SSBN operates in remote areas of the ocean away from normal shipping lanes and away from known naval operating areas. If a ship or submarine is detected by sonar, the SSBN will change course to avoid closing any closer to the contact if possible.

An advantage to SSBN duty is the certainty of the operating schedule as one could determine two years in advance when you would be home and when you would be deployed and in addition, when you are home in an off-crew status, your training duties are relatively light and you are home every night. On the other hand, the patrols on SSBNs are long and tedious (some would say boring). Operating a ship at four knots at 150 feet for day after day, week after week just did not appeal to me. I had strongly indicated my desire for my next assignment as executive officer to be on an SSN. But I was to find out that the odds were against me.

I received a call from the submarine "detailer" (the officer at the Bureau of Naval Personnel responsible for my next assignment) in the late fall of 1970. We discussed my next assignment options, and although I strongly wanted an SSN he told me he had very few available in the period that I was to rotate and that he felt an assignment to an SSBN would provide me with a more balanced submarine background for future assignments. This sounded like so much BUPERS double-talk to me (detailers are known to talk with forked tongues!) and I told him that I would get back to him after I had a talk with my Commanding Officer.

My CO, Frank Kelso, called BUPERS on my behalf and then told me that he agreed with the detailer. He pointed out that there were 41 SSBNs, with two crews for each ship for a total of 82 crews, and at that time, there were only 35 SSNs. Thus, the detailer had a much larger SSBN requirement than an SSN requirement. He then asked me what type of submarine I would like to have for my command tour. I told him an SSN without a doubt. He then told me that one of the balanced tour requirements that the detailer had to consider was experience in both types of submarines. If I had an executive officer tour on an SSBN, he felt that my chances for a command tour on an SSN would be enhanced. Well, that convinced me, not that I had much choice anyway. I received orders to report in July 1971 as Executive Officer of the Blue Crew of the USS Daniel Webster (SSBN 626) homeported in Pearl Harbor, Hawaii.

USS Daniel Webster (SSBN 626)

Chapter VI - USS Daniel Webster (SSBN 626)

Cold Turkey and Boomer Training

With orders in hand to report to the Blue Crew of the USS Daniel Webster(SSBN 626) in Pearl Harbor in July 1971, Mary and I left Nuclear Power School, Bainbridge in April and relocated to Virginia Beach, VA where I would attend a six week course to prepare me for assignment as Executive Officer of a ballistic missile submarine. We found a lovely furnished duplex about one block from the Atlantic Ocean that would be our home for the next six weeks of "Boomer" training. First, I had to face a problem that wouldn't go away

I had been a smoker since I was 18 and was now smoking two and a half packs a day. In short, I was addicted to nicotine and was anxious to break the habit. Mary and I both felt that this would be an opportune time to quit smoking, as I would be in transition for the next three months and not in an established routine. On a Saturday morning, our son William and I took a walk on the beach. It was a cool early spring morning and our dog Sam was enjoying chasing the birds on the beach. I decided that it was time to "join the unhooked generation." William and I dug a hole in the sand and buried my half-empty pack of cigarettes and then I gave William my Zippo lighter and asked him to throw it into the ocean, which he did. We went home and told Mary my decision and I found out that was the easy part!

Quitting smoking "cold turkey" was extremely difficult, probably one of the hardest things that I have ever done. I chewed a lot of gum, sucked on a lot of hard candies, tried smoking a pipe, chewed on toothpicks, but I never smoked another cigarette. I couldn't stand a pipe and that only lasted a few weeks. I went through all the typical withdrawal symptoms, but by the time we got to Hawaii in July, I was over the worst of it. I wouldn't have been able to quit if it hadn't been for Mary's support and understanding during some very black moments in the early summer of 1971.

The "Boomer" training was very well done and I learned a lot. The first thing that you need to grasp is that an SSBN is a mobile platform, which makes it considerably more complicated to launch ballistic missiles when compared to an Air Force silo in North Dakota. The accuracy of the ballistic missile depends upon knowing precisely where you are when you launch the missile, which is not a problem in a silo in North Dakota, but is a considerable problem for a submarine in the middle of the Pacific Ocean. The ballistic missile submarines of the early seventies depended on a Ship's Inertial Navigation System or SINS to provide location data. The SINS is a complex of Gyroscopes and accelerometers that updates the ship's position as the submarine maneuvers underwater. But the SINS needs periodic updates of actual ship's position in order to maintain its accuracy. Navigation satellites or NAVSATs were developed in the early 60s to provide the navigational accuracy needed by missile submarines. Every ninety minutes or so, a NAVSAT would pass overhead and the submarine could copy its signal and use it to determine its position. The NAVSAT system has evolved today into the Global Positioning System (GPS), which is a complex of navigation satellites that provide continuous navigation information. GPS was developed to provide accurate navigation information to our ballistic missile submarines, but it is in use around the world by both civilians and the military.

We learned how a submarine launched ballistic missile functions, how the launcher works and most importantly, we spent a considerable amount of time learning the safeguards built into our command and control system for nuclear weapons. There are a series of keys that must be inserted into the launching circuit of an SSBN. Different individuals, principally the Captain, the Executive Officer and the Weapons Officer, control these keys. When an SSBN receives a message that may be a launch order, the ship goes to general quarters. The Executive Officer proceeds to the radio room to evaluate the message. If the message appears valid, then the Executive Officer and another officer proceed to a two man controlled safe and each opens his half of the combination, they remove a sealed authenticator code and the captain's firing panel key and then proceed to the control room where the Captain awaits. The message is again reviewed and if all agree that it appears valid, then the sealed authenticator is opened and if this authenticator code matches the one in the message, then it is a valid and authenticated message. The Captain's firing panel key is given to the Captain and the Captain gives his launcher keys to the weapons officer. This is an abbreviated description of the command and control system, but it has been in place for over forty years and it has withstood the test of time. Little did I expect that I would be involved in the actual launch of ballistic missiles within the next six months.

Sailing to Hawaii in Style

SS President Wilson

I completed my introductory course in ballistic missile submariners, "Boomer School," in late May 1971. I had applied for "surface transit" to Hawaii, which means traveling by passenger ship rather than air. It seems that there were still a few passenger ships sailing under the American flag and the military was providing subsidized support of these ships in case they would be required as troop transports. We had been approved for transit to Hawaii aboard the SS President Wilson of the American President Lines sailing from Oakland, California on June 25. I had also made reservations for a week's stay at the Stanford Sierra Camp that is near Lake Tahoe. Having attended graduate school at Stanford, I was eligible to stay at this camp, which is reserved for Stanford alumni. After obligatory stops at our parents' homes in Cincinnati and Chicago, we had two weeks left to travel across country.

Wall Drug, the South Dakota badlands, Mount Rushmore, Yellowstone, Jackson Hole, the Grand Tetons were all highlights of this abbreviated tour. We camped out all the way and enjoyed beautiful weather and some spectacular scenery. The Stanford Sierra Camp allowed us to catch our breath and relax. Our son William, who was four, was taken under the wings of the camp counselors, which allowed Mary and me to enjoy hiking, and some of the adult activities offered. We left the camp in time to drive to Oakland, turn in our car for shipment to Hawaii, and make the afternoon sailing of the SS President Wilson.

We had no idea what to expect when we got to the passenger terminal in Oakland. Would we have a stateroom or would we sleep in some special berthing area for military families? In other words, were we going first class or steerage? After boarding the ship, we checked in at reception and yes our names were on the manifest and we were escorted to our stateroom. The steward showed up to help us get settled in. He told me that I should report to the chief steward on the boat deck to make a table reservation for the dining room. I left Mary to do some unpacking and William and I went in search of the chief steward. We found him with a long line in front of his table. While standing in line I was able to observe my fellow passengers, and I concluded that most appeared to be young married couples with children, and judging from their haircuts, the men all seemed to be in the military.

When I got to the head of the line, the chief steward, noting my four-year-old son, told me that families with children were seated for early dinner at 1830. I asked if there was a later seating, and he said yes at 2000 (8:00PM) but children were not allowed at this seating. He then said that if I preferred, my son could eat at a special table for unaccompanied children at the early seating and that my wife and I could enjoy the second seating. The ship provided a nursery for children while their parents had dinner. I wasn't sure if Mary would be pleased with this option, but after noting that the line behind me was now twice as long as earlier, I threw caution to the wind and opted for the second dinner seating. The chief steward then said that unless I had a special table preference, he would recommend that we sit at the purser's table. At that point, I sensed that he was steering me toward a good deal, and I accepted his offer with pleasure.

As I expected, Mary was a little concerned about William eating all by himself, but after taking him down to the dining room and meeting his waiter, Jimmy, she felt that he would do all right. When we went to pick him up after dinner, he was all smiles. He had been able to order whatever he wanted to eat, and as I recall, he had a freshly cooked artichoke with drawn butter, a lobster tail and baked Alaska for dessert. Pretty good for a four year old! The purser had been with American President Lines for ten years and was a charming host. Two other couples at the table were steamship company executives and wives. Mary and I felt a little out of our class at first, but we were quickly made to feel at ease and we became fast friends with our dinner companions during our passage to Honolulu. Because we were seated with the purser, we received a special invitation to the captain's reception the next evening and the purser went out of his way to insure that we were included in all the special events during the voyage. In answer to our concerns about our status on board, we were definitely not in steerage on this trip.

Arrival in Hawaii by passenger ship is a very special experience. The ship moors at the Aloha Tower, which is a landmark in the Honolulu harbor. A Hawaiian band accompanies hula dancers and as you depart the ship, the dancers present each passenger with a beautiful lei of exotic flowers. Our good friends Ron and Linda Burdge and Tom Hopper, the commanding officer of the Daniel Webster and his wife Meribeth and several other officers from the ship and their wives, met us. We received leis from all who were there to welcome us, and were really overcome with the Aloha spirit of Hawaii.

Aloha Tower

Boomer Off-Crew Training

I reported to the Blue Crew of the USS Daniel Webster as the relief of the Executive Officer, Lieutenant Commander Jim Partlow. The timing couldn't have been better as the crew had just finished a three-week stand-down and leave period and was starting the two-month off-crew training cycle in preparation to flying out to Guam to relieve the Gold Crew in early September. During this period, new members of the crew were assimilated into their watch and duty sections. Shore based trainers and simulators were available to ensure that each new member of the crew became a contributing member of his watch section and battle station. The submarine force had been operating two-crew ballistic missile submarines for ten years, and the training cycles were well established and the experienced hands knew what had to be accomplished during this period. It was all new to me, so I found that I had a lot to learn.

My turnover with Jim Partlow, the outgoing XO went very smoothly and we were able to report my relief to the CO, Tom Hopper a week later. Shortly afterward, the CO called me into his office and told me that my first SSBN patrol would probably be the best one that I would ever have. He went on to explain that the Blue Crew would be conducting a Follow-on Operational Test (FOT) firing of four Polaris missiles during the next patrol. Few SSBN crews have a chance to actually fire the missiles, and this would be a great opportunity for the entire crew. The CO told me that we could not tell the crew what was planned until we actually commenced our patrol scheduled in early October, but there were several aspects of our off-crew training that warranted special attention. We went over the details, and I was very involved in crew training for the next two months.

On the home front, Mary and I were still living in temporary housing while looking for a place to live. We had hoped to move into Navy housing, but we were only eligible for two bedroom quarters and what was available was not suitable. We opted to rent a house in Kailua, which is nice community on the windward side of Oahu, about ten miles from Honolulu over the mountain range splitting the island. The commute to Pearl Harbor was fifteen miles, and then we had to catch a ferryboat or personnel boat to get to Ford Island, which is in the middle of Pearl Harbor where our off-crew training offices were located. I was able to car pool with the Weapon's

Officer of the Blue Crew who also lived in Kailua. Our commuting time was
70 to 90 minutes each way.

Ford Island

I was impressed with the quality and quantity of training provided to
the crews of SSBN submarines. Not only were the attack trainers and
simulators excellent, but the quality of the classroom instruction was superb.
My only other submarine experience was on an attack submarine, the USS
Shark and there was very little classroom training available in her homeport
of Norfolk. There was also very little time devoted to outside training in
attack submarines, as in-port maintenance requirements and the constant
pressure to meet at sea commitments left almost no time for training. During
this particular period of off-crew training, we placed a good deal of emphasis
on missile launch procedures and command and control.

We completed our training period and prepared to fly out to Guam to
meet the ship as it came off patrol in late August. Each member of the crew
was given five family gram forms for his immediate family to keep him
posted on his family events during the two months that we would be on
patrol. A family gram is a message of 25 words that a wife or other member
of the family can send to the crewmember while the ship is underway. It
certainly cannot replace a letter from home or a phone call, but it was all that
was available in 60s and 70s. Today, internet messages are routinely sent to

submarines at sea and the crewmember at sea is able to send emails home as well.

Our nine hour flight to Guam was on a Boeing 707 military charter which was going on to the Philippines and then to South Vietnam. We arrived at Anderson Air Force Base in the late afternoon and were bussed to Polaris Point where the submarine tender USS Proteus was berthed. Temporary berthing on the tender was provided for the entire crew until after the crew exchange which would take place in five days and then we would move aboard the submarine. I looked forward to the next morning's arrival of the USS Daniel Webster, which would be my home for the next two and a half years.

USS Daniel Webster (SSBN 626)—A funny looking submarine

USS Daniel Webster (SSBN 626)

It was an early morning in September 1971 and the officers and leading petty officers of the Blue crew were crowded on board a tugboat in Apra Harbor, Guam on our way to meet the USS Daniel Webster, which was returning from a two-month strategic deterrent patrol. Daniel Webster was a unique submarine as it did not have the traditional horizontal control surfaces on its sail (sail planes), rather it had a strange looking structure on its bow with the sail planes (now bow planes) attached. Even though I had seen several pictures of the ship, I was still taken aback by this strange looking submarine heading our way. The bow planes were an experiment to see if the ship had better depth keeping characteristics when operating at periscope depth in heavy seas. The skipper of the tug was very cautious coming alongside the Webster for our personnel transfer as he did not want to hit the protruding bow planes, which would definitely do some damage to his tugboat.

The Gold crew of the Daniel Webster was undergoing the final stages of an Operational Reactor Safeguards Examination (ORSE), which is an underway evaluation of the ability of the nuclear engineering department conducted annually. The Blue crew was aboard to conduct its own inspection of the ship prior to crew turnover. We observed a Battle Stations Missile exercise and had an opportunity to evaluate the readiness of the Weapons and Navigation systems. After we moored alongside the USS Proteus, we continued our inspection of the ship and would commence turnover with the Gold crew the next morning.

The next two days of turnover with the Gold crew went very smoothly. Although the ship was new to me, most of the senior members of the Blue crew had served on the ship for the last three or four patrols and knew the ship quite well. It was just a matter of finding out what had changed in the operating status of the equipment over the last three months. We also went over the planned work for the forthcoming three-week upkeep period. At 0600 on the following day, both crews mustered topside on the missile deck for the formal exchange of command and then the Gold crew grabbed their sea bags and boarded the bus for Anderson Air Force Base and their flight back to Hawaii. We moved aboard the ship and went to work.

Three weeks later, we had completed an extensive upkeep and refit period. The Proteus had completed the change out of a major piece of equipment, the trim pump that was due for a periodic overhaul. We had loaded all the stores and food for the forthcoming two-month patrol and had taken on board three exercise torpedoes for use during our sea trial period. Sea trials involved a test depth dive, angles and dangles to check the ship for stowage and to get the crew used to large angles. We tested all the navigation and weapons systems and went to battle stations to fire our exercise torpedoes at a target ship, in this case, a tugboat. I had an opportunity to fire one of these torpedoes and I got a constructive hit and felt good about it. Exercise torpedoes do not have an explosive warhead and are set to run under the target. At the end of run, the torpedoes float to the surface and are retrieved, refurbished and put back into the inventory as warshots.

Two days later, we were underway for patrol. After we cleared the harbor, the ever-present Soviet AGI (intelligence collection trawler) intercepted our course and gave us its usual close look, including crossing through our wake for several miles collecting water samples. We were in international waters and the AGI had every right to conduct its surveillance, but that didn't stop us from gritting our teeth as she paralleled our course about 50 yards off our starboard beam. Later we submerged, went deep and cleared the area on a new course. The next evolution was a flyover by a U.S. Navy P-3 aircraft, which dropped a series of sonabuoys in our wake to ensure that we were not being trailed by a Soviet submarine. We would repeat this "delousing" effort two or three times during the patrol.

The captain told the crew that this would be a shorter patrol than usual and that we were scheduled for a four missile Follow-on Operational Test (FOT). He also announced that we would be crossing the equator in order to reach our firing position for the FOT and that the shellbacks would conduct an initiation ceremony for the pollywogs. I had already checked the service records of the crew and was dismayed to find only eight shellbacks aboard. The captain had never crossed the equator, so I was the senior shellback. I wasn't at all sure that we could control a pollywog revolt. We had our work cut out for us.

Crossing the Line Enroute to the Launch Area

Midway through our strategic deterrent patrol, in the fall of 1971, we received a message from COMSUBPAC directing USS Daniel Webster to terminate patrol and return to Guam to prepare for the planned Follow-on Operational Test (FOT) of four missiles. We had been at sea for five weeks and the crew was looking forward to a few days liberty in Guam. But unfortunately, that was not the case, as the procedures for the conduct of an FOT required all hands to remain on board for the short time that we were in port. One of the objectives of the test was to insure that there was no disruption in the operational environment on the ship. In other words, we were to maintain "at-sea" watch rotation, the reactor plant was kept on the line and the navigation systems were maintained operational. A roll of the dice chose four of the sixteen ballistic missiles randomly. Technicians from the submarine tender, USS Proteus were allowed on board to remove the nuclear warheads on these four missiles (three per missile) and replace them with instrumented exercise warheads. Sixteen hours after returning to Guam we were underway again enroute to the designated missile launch area that was northeast of the Solomon Islands and south of the equator. It would take about five days to reach the launch area.

Shellback Certificate

I was the senior shellback aboard and along with the other eight shellbacks planned the initiation ceremony for the 135 pollywogs in the crew. I had a discussion with the Captain about the timing of the ceremony. He said that the squadron commander, who would be aboard the Launch Area Support Ship (LASS) during our missile launch, would be transferring to the Daniel Webster after the missile launch and had recommended that we defer the initiation ceremony until after the missile launch. This made sense in that we would be able to keep the crew focused on the mission at hand, but I was concerned about a pollywog revolt that traditionally occurred the night before the crossing of the line. I had no control over the timing of the "revolt" and if it occurred as expected, then I recommended that we hold the ceremony the next day rather than wait several days until after the missile launch. We agreed to remain flexible.

I could tell that there was something afoot after dinner on the night before we reached the equator. Mess decks intelligence (MDI) told me that a pollywog revolt was underway. I elected to stay behind a locked door in my stateroom and prepare a diversion regarding my intentions. There was an overhead storage area above my stateroom that was accessible through a removable panel in the overhead. There was also a shower and head (toilet) between my stateroom and the Captain's stateroom. The shower stall had a door that lead to a storage area outboard the shower. I opened the panel in the overhead and left it ajar and removed the handle from the door in the shower stall, so that once I had exited the shower to the outboard storage area I could close the door behind me and no one could open it.

I received a call from the Chief of the Boat (also a shellback) telling me that he was about to be taken hostage and I was probably next. I went into my hiding place outboard the shower to await further developments. A few minutes later, I heard banging on my stateroom door, then voices.

"The door is locked."

"Do we have a key?"

"No."

"Let's go through the Captain's stateroom."

I heard a knock on the Captain's door. "Enter" said the Captain.

CO: "Engineer, what can I do for you?"

Engineer: "Good evening Captain. I am sorry to disturb you. Have you seen the Executive Officer?"

CO: "The XO is in his stateroom."

Engineer: "Could we have permission to go through the head and see if he is in his room?"

CO: "Permission granted," then "Good evening Weps, Nav, Chief Hughes and Chief Hodges." "Good evening Captain," they responded.

I now knew who the ringleaders of the pollywogs were. Revenge will be sweet!

There followed much activity in my stateroom, including a thorough search of the overhead storage area. They asked the CO again if he knew where I was, and he told them that the last that he had seen of me, I was in my stateroom. Finally, they spotted the door in the shower stall and its missing handle. Much banging on the door followed, but they couldn't open it.

"XO, we know that you are in there."

"What do you want? I am trying to sleep." I responded.

"We want you."

"Well, you can't have me."

"Could we negotiate terms for your surrender?"

"I don't negotiate with riff-raff. I will not surrender, but I will discuss terms of a truce with the Captain." I responded.

The Captain and I then agreed to a truce. I went with him and the five pollywog revolt leaders to the Lower Level Missile Compartment where I found my eight trusty shellbacks tied up and under guard. We agreed that the revolt was officially over and the shellbacks were set free. The next morning at 0400, I sounded the General Alarm and the ship went to battle stations. The shellbacks were prepared in the crew's mess to commence the initiation ceremony and the Captain was first in line followed by the pollywog revolt leaders who then assisted us in initiating the rest of the crew. Breakfast was served at 0700. The ship entered the launch area the next day.

I have relieved the Diving Officer of the Watch so that he could make a "Head Call". To my left is Petty Officer Wiley on watch on the stern-planes. We may seem rather relaxed as we are. Ballistic missile submarines proceed at slow speed (3 or 4 knots) and rapid depth changes are unlikely.

Battle Stations Manned for a Missile launch

On November 7, 1971, USS Daniel Webster entered the designated missile launch area northeast of the Solomon Islands in the South Pacific. Our target was the ballistic missile test range near Midway Island, 2,500 miles to the north. We established our ballistic missile submarine patrol routine: 4 knots at 150 feet. Our navigation fixes were obtained from the navigation satellite system and bottom contour navigation. The Navy had completed an extensive mapping of the oceans using precision fathometers. In areas where there was a clearly defined gradient or slope to the ocean floor, a submarine could use its own bottom contour charts and a precision fathometer to generate enough sounding data to obtain an accurate position.

The Launch Area Support Ship (LASS) arrived on station the next day, and we commenced our wait for orders from the National Command Authority to launch our four missiles. The LASS maintained station about three miles from our position and we communicated by "Gertrude" which is an underwater communications system. The LASS was necessary to ensure that the launch area remained clear of surface ships and to initiate a missile destruct signal in the event one of our missiles malfunctioned and veered off course.

After the third day of waiting, we were all convinced that we would receive "lunch orders" on the next day. So we decided to watch a movie after dinner. During the movie, the captain's phone rang and there was a simultaneous announcement on the 1MC system "Alert One. Alert One"." This announcement meant that the ship was receiving "Flash" message traffic in radio. The captain proceeded to the control room to direct the actions of the ship, and I went to radio to evaluate the incoming message traffic. We had indeed received a launch order from CINCPAC (Commander in Chief, Pacific Command) to launch our four exercise missiles. I took the message to the captain for his review. He ordered the ship to condition 1SQ for missile launch operations. The general alarm sounded as I proceeded to the two-man control safe where another officer and I opened our two combination locks and removed the captain's firing key from the safe along with the sealed authenticator codes. We returned to the control room and again reviewed the launch order message with the captain. After we all agreed that this was a valid message, we opened the sealed authenticator codes. The codes matched the codes in the message, which is the last step in authorizing the launch of missiles. We gave the captain his firing panel key, and he gave the weapon's officer the keys to missile tubes 2, 7, 10 and 11, which were the designated test missiles.

During the period that we were verifying and authenticating the launch order message, the ship had proceeded to 120 feet, the normal launch depth, reduced speed to less than half a knot as required for missile launch, and engaged the hovering system which is designed to maintain ship's depth during missile launching operations. In addition, the guidance systems in missiles 2, 7, 10 and 11 were energized and received the necessary target information. In fewer than 15 minutes after receiving the initial radio message traffic, the crew was at battle stations, the missile and navigation systems were operational and ready to launch missiles.

We advised the LASS that we were about to launch missiles and requested an "all clear" in the launch area. The LASS gave us an "all clear" and the captain ordered the launch of missiles 2, 7, 10 and 11. The status indicator for the missile tube door on tube 2 went from shut to intermediate and then we heard a muffled clunk as the door fully opened and the status indicator went to open. A series of monitoring lights for the missile went from red to green as the missile countdown continued, and after ten seconds, the tube fired, launching the missile up to the surface. After the missile clears the surface of the ocean the main engine ignites and the missile rapidly gains altitude and heads down range. Sonar reported hearing the main rocket engine ignition. The missile weighed 35,700 pounds or 18 tons. The ejection of this weight from the ship creates quite a jolt and the ship sinks about three feet as a result. The hovering system corrects this and accommodates the change in weight of the ship as the now empty missile tube fills with seawater.

Just as soon as missile tube 2 fired, the missile tube door started to shut, the door for missile tube 7 started to open, and we went through the launch sequence again. Thirty seconds later missile 7 was on its way downrange. In two minutes, all four missiles were on their way and we secured from battle stations. It took 17 minutes from receipt of the authorizing message to the completion of the launch. A launch of all 16 missiles carried by a Polaris submarine can be completed in less than 25 minutes.

Polaris A-3

We were too excited by these events to go back to the wardroom and finish the movie, but we did spend the next several hours recounting the events. We looked forward to receiving the report from the missile range on the accuracy of the missiles.

Presentation to Admiral John S. McCain

On our return trip to Guam, a few days after our Polaris Missile Follow-on Test (FOT), we received a message from the missile test range with the details of the accuracy of the missiles. Each of the four A-3 missiles carried three warheads or re-entry bodies. If each of the twelve re-entry bodies had been targeted at the hot dog stand in the open court in the center of the Pentagon, then the missile range data showed that all of them would have hit somewhere within the perimeter of the Pentagon building. This degree of accuracy was well within the specifications for the Polaris missile.

When a Polaris missile is launched, it is expelled from the missile tube by rapidly expanding exhaust gasses from a rocket engine built into the missile tube. The main engine of the Polaris missile doesn't fire until the missile is well clear of the surface of the ocean. The missile tube rocket engine has a stainless steel protective cover that breaks open when the rocket is ignited. This cover appears like a partially opened toilet seat and was so nicknamed by the missile technicians.

Our captain, Commander Tom Hopper had each of the four missile tube "toilet seats" mounted on a plaque and decided to keep one for himself and present the other three to Commander Submarine Force Pacific (COMSUBPAC), Commander in Chief Pacific Fleet (CINCPACFLT) and Commander of the Pacific Command (CINCPAC). After our turnover to the Gold Crew in Guam, and we returned to Hawaii, I called COMSUBPAC's office to arrange for these presentations. The captain wanted all those who were involved in the successful operation to be part of the presentation ceremony, which included the weapons officer, his assistant, the Chief of the Boat and the weapons department chief petty officers and me.

Our call on COMSUBPAC, Rear Admiral Paul Lacy went very well. He was not only a submarine officer who served in World War II, but also commanded a nuclear submarine, the USS Ethan Allen (SSBN 608) which fired the only test shot of an actual nuclear ballistic missile in May 1962. He was very interested in the results of our test and complimentary about the results. As we were leaving his office, he asked me to wait for a minute. He asked if our next call was on Admiral Clarey, CINCPACFLT. I told him yes it was in about 45 minutes. Admiral Lacy then told me that none of the officers, except the Captain, was in the proper uniform and that I needed to get the problem corrected before our call on Admiral Clary. He went to explain that Admiral Clarey had been the Vice Chief of Naval Operations and had changed the uniform policy to prohibit officers from wearing round neck "T" shirts with open collared shirts. He didn't think that it was appropriate for an officer to "have his underwear" showing. He did not change the rule for Chief Petty Officers. I thanked Admiral Lacy for the warning and caught up with the rest of the group. We did not have enough time to buy v-neck "T" shirts so we did the next best thing and borrowed a pair of scissors from Admiral Lacy's yeoman to cut out the offending piece of underwear showing above our shirt collar.

Our next call on Admiral "Chic" Clarey went very smoothly. He was also a WWII submariner with a distinguished record including four war patrols in command of the USS Pintado. He was very appreciative of the success of our missile launch and of the presentation of the plaque. We must have all passed inspection as no mention was made about our recently modified uniforms.

Our final call that morning was on Admiral John S. McCain, Jr. CINCPAC. He had been CINCPAC since 1968 and would serve in this position for one more year until his retirement in 1972. His son, Lieutenant Commander John S. McCain III, who is one year older than me, had been a POW since 1967. Admiral McCain had command of all military forces in the Pacific, including those in Vietnam. Admiral McCain was a man of small stature but with a commanding presence that filled the room. He was very much aware of our successful missile test firing and was extremely complimentary as he greeted each of us personally. We were all quite taken with him. But, we couldn't help but notice his round neck "T" shirt showing above his collar!

After the Captain made his presentation of the "toilet seat" plaque, Admiral McCain turned to us again and said, "I am sure that you have all been noticing my round neck "T" shirt. I just wanted you to know that I am well aware of the Navy uniform regulations as recently amended by my good friend "Chic" Clarey. But, my staff has had trouble controlling the air-conditioning in this room and it is too cold for me, so I have taken to wearing thermal underwear in order to stay warm. The only problem is that they don't make thermal underwear with V-neck collars." None of us felt that it was necessary to tell Admiral McCain how we solved our uniform "problem."

Admiral McCain Presentation

Christmas in Hawaii with Mr. Science

The Blue Crew of the USS Daniel Webster returned to Hawaii from Guam in early December 1971 and commenced a three-week stand-down period that would last through the Christmas holiday period. Mary had planned a special homecoming meal of roast turkey with all the fixings as we had not had Thanksgiving together and she knew that turkey was one of my favorite meals. Unfortunately, the day after I came home, I came down with a fever and was sick for the next several days, which really put a damper on our homecoming plans. But I wasn't the only one sick from the crew and when I discussed this with the captain, he said that there were two time submariners became sick with flu-like symptoms. Just after we came home from an extended patrol (greater than month) or just after the ship submerges for an extended patrol. He explained this phenomenon by pointing out that when a ship submerges all the viruses that everyone will be exposed to are present and after a few weeks, everyone has become sick or they had already developed an immunity; and there is virtually no sickness for the remainder of the patrol. The opposite is the case on completion of patrol, one is exposed to a new set of viruses and everyone gets sick again. This explanation made sense to me and I would see this cycle of sickness with flu-like symptoms repeat with every patrol.

Shortly after I was back on my feet, my parents arrived from the mainland and they would be with us as we celebrated our first Christmas in Hawaii. The Hawaiian phrase for Merry Christmas is Mele Kalikimaka and you hear it everywhere on the islands. You have three choices for Christmas trees: an artificial one, a real one cut down in September and shipped to Hawaii or a live Norfolk pine, which is spindly and looks similar to a Christmas tree but is really a tropical plant and not a fir or spruce tree. Artificial trees in 1971 were not as realistic as the ones you can get today and really looked cheesy, so we settled for a spruce tree from the mainland. It cost a fortune and it lasted about two weeks before all the needles had fallen off.

We were used to visits from my parents every time we moved to a new Navy town, as Dad was something of a minor television celebrity and would be able to get a booking on a local TV show. He had a long career in public relations with the Union Carbide Corporation and had developed several very informative and educational presentations built around many of the products of Union Carbide. He had appearances on major network shows such as the Today Show, the Tonight Show and several daytime talk shows. He was also very popular on children shows such as Captain Kangaroo and on this visit to Hawaii, he appeared on a local children's show: Checkers and Pogo. This show was a favorite of our 4-year-old son William and we all gathered around the TV to watch my father as "Mr. Science" demonstrate the magic of super-cold (liquid nitrogen).

Interesting — Informative — Fun

That is Pete McKinney, Union Carbide's

"Mr. Science"

Guest on over 200 television shows—Today Show, Captain Kangaroo, Bill Veeck, Mike Douglas, Jim Conway, etc.

Speaker to scores of schools, service clubs, churches, etc.

Pete, now a consultant to Carbide, has time to give great demonstrations and talks to groups of 20 to 200 people.

His topic is the "Cold World of Cryogenics." He shows with liquid nitrogen, 320° F. below zero, what it's like in outer space. And how this amazing cold is used in food cooling and processing. And how it will be used in transmitting electric power.

He tailors his talks to any group — Boy Scouts, Ladies, Businessmen or Science Classes.

Get Pete for a speaking date for your group.

PETER T. McKINNEY
37 SOUTH WAIOLA AVENUE
LA GRANGE, ILLINOIS 60525
Telephone — FLeetwood 2-5199

There were several kittens on the show from the local animal shelter. When my father walked in the front door of our home later that afternoon, he had one of the kittens in a small box for our son William who was thrilled to have a new pet. The only problem was that we were renting the house and the landlord was very specific about "no pets." We kept the kitten, that we named Popoki (Hawaiian for cat), until after my parents left for the mainland and then we gave it away to another family from the ship.

The remainder of the off-crew period was taken up with crew training except for a weekend that Mary and I spent in Maui in late January. In addition to being a romantic weekend getaway, we found travel to the other Hawaiian Islands to be very interesting and we were looking forward to more trips during our tour in Hawaii. We left Hawaii in late February for Guam. As I was embracing Mary before getting on the plane, she told me that she had a surprise, but would wait to tell me after I had arrived in Guam.

Have a Daniel Webster Cigar

We commenced a three-week refit period in Guam in early March 1972. This would be my second patrol on USS Daniel Webster and I found that the planned maintenance schedule on ballistic missile submarines was an important element in keeping these ships operationally ready even though they spent over 60 percent of their time at sea. Each piece of machinery on the submarine was carefully monitored for performance and noise characteristics. Noise monitoring is used to evaluate the overall performance of the machine and the potential for noise transmission through the hull of the submarine that would make the submarine vulnerable to detection. During each refit period, machinery would be routinely replaced and overhauled on the repair ship (tender) and then reinstalled on another submarine in a later refit. There were six Polaris submarines operating out of Guam with four at sea and two in a refit status at any one time. The machinery on these submarines was interchangeable which enhanced the planned maintenance routine conducted by the tender.

In mid-March, I received the news from Mary that I had been expecting; we were going to have another child with a due date in late October. We both agreed that our romantic weekend on Maui had truly been a special weekend.

With Mary expecting, our eligibility for housing changed and we were now eligible for three bedroom quarters. Mary reapplied for housing and we were placed on a waiting list for a three-bedroom townhouse on the water overlooking Pearl Harbor. Living on Pearl Harbor meant that I could walk to the landing, catch a boat to Ford Island, and eliminate the long commute from Kailua on the other side of the island. If the timing worked out, we would be able to move during my off-crew period in June, July or August. Also, since we were moving from civilian housing into government quarters, the Navy would pay for the move.

I decided to celebrate this good news with a Daniel Webster cigar. Although I had given up smoking cigarettes, the year before, I still occasionally had a cigar, and the ship was supplied Daniel Webster cigars by the Bayuk Tobacco Company of Philadelphia. During each off-crew period before flying out to Guam, I would write a letter to the President of the Bayuk Tobacco Company and request a supply of Daniel Webster cigars to replenish the wardroom humidor. The humidor had been a gift to the ship from Bayuk, Inc. upon commissioning with the promise to keep it always full of Daniel Webster cigars. When we flew out to Guam, we would have a case of 500 Daniel Webster cigars, which was more than enough for the crew during the patrol as only a few enjoyed smoking cigars.

The refit and subsequent patrol passed routinely and I was glad to return to Hawaii to the warm embrace of family in June. Mary was in her second trimester of pregnancy and was doing very well. We had no idea of the sex of the child that she was carrying but we were hoping for a girl. William, who was five, was curious about what was going on, but seemed to take the news of a new baby brother or sister in stride.

The Navy came through with an offer of quarters: a three-bedroom townhouse overlooking Pearl Harbor on Aloha Avenue. What could be more Hawaiian than living on Aloha Avenue? We had a door-to-door move in late June and settled into our new quarters. William made fast friends with the boy next door and learned the fine art of fishing and crabbing in the waters of Pearl Harbor. We had a large Banyan tree in the side yard and banana trees in the yard near the water. It was really a picturesque setting and we would enjoy this set of quarters for the rest of our stay in Hawaii.

As I write this story, I realize what a special woman that I had the good fortune to marry in 1965. The mother of our son, William, and at the time of this story, expecting our second child. Taking in stride the many moves that we had already made in the first seven years of our marriage, the birth of our first child while I was at sea in the North Atlantic and now facing the same prospect with our second child, only this time I would be in the North Pacific. Always supportive of my career and the many separations that we faced during the early years of our marriage.

What can I say, other than Mary, I love you.

The Lone Ranger and Way Past Halfway Night

Ballistic missile submarines generally conduct 60-day patrols. Two months underwater can be a very long time when enclosed inside a 35-foot diameter steel cylinder 450 feet long with another 145 men. The daily routine of standing watch eight hours a day, sleeping another eight hours and conducting various training evolutions for the remaining eight hours occupies most of one's time. There are daily emergency drills (such as fire and flooding) for training purposes. Weapons System Readiness Tests (WSRTs) three or four times a week at random times. Some WSRTs are initiated by the ship and others by a message from COMSUBPAC or CINCPACFLT. During a WSRT, the general alarm is sounded and the ship mans battle stations and a practice missile countdown is conducted. The drill lasts about thirty minutes. Data is collected on each of these WSRT's and is provided at the end of the patrol to COMSUBPAC for further evaluation of the ship's readiness.

The training of the nuclear propulsion plant watchstanders is very intensive. Review training sessions are a daily occurrence and in addition, three days each week a series of emergency drills and evolutions are conducted for each watchsection. These drills involve all the nuclear-trained personnel. Critiques are held at the completion of each drill set.

The ship's engineering officer came to me early in the patrol to see if there could be some way to give his watchstanders a break and reduce the number of times that they had to respond to ship-wide battle station drills. He made a good point that the WSRT's were essentially drills to evaluate the weapons system readiness and that the engineering department had very little impact on these evaluations. I agreed with him and proposed to the commanding officer that for ship initiated WSRT's, over which we had some control, only the weapons and navigation department personnel would be required to man battle stations. The engineering department watchstanders could sleep-in. The captain agreed with my proposal, but we weren't sure how to make it clear that only some of the crew needed to respond to the general alarm, which is sounded for all ship emergencies, as well as battle stations.

I had several tapes of classical music that I enjoyed listening to and that night I listened to the William Tell Overture by Rossini, better known as the "Lone Ranger theme song." It is a rousing piece of music and played over the ship's general announcing system would certainly get your attention. We had the solution to our problem. If the ship sounds the General Alarm, all hands are expected to respond to the emergency, but if we played the William Tell Overture and then announced Battle Stations Missile, only the Weapons and Navigation personnel would be expected to respond. We put this new procedure in place and the crew got a great deal of enjoyment out of listening to the music that we all grew up with: "The Lone Ranger rides again. Hi Ho Silver!"

Most ballistic missile submarines have some type of celebration at the halfway point in the two-month patrol and the crew of the USS Daniel Webster was no exception. Halfway night was always a special event with a great steak and lobster dinner followed by musical entertainment and skits by members of the crew. I found that halfway night was too early in the patrol for much celebration as we still had a month to go before the end of the patrol. So during my third patrol on Daniel Webster I proposed a "Way Past Halfway Night" to be held six weeks into the patrol, which meant we only, had two weeks to the end. The crew liked the idea and this became the routine for our crew. I also would organize the officers to perform some type of skit or routine for this event.

The picture was taken at one of our "Way Past Halfway Night" performances, but I have forgotten the reason for my "four-star" uniform.

A Bundle of Joy at the end of my Third Patrol

My third strategic deterrent patrol on the USS Daniel Webster was in the fall of 1972. I left Hawaii in late August. Mary and I both knew that I would be at sea when she delivered our second child sometime in late October. We had moved into our new quarters on Aloha Avenue and had made many new Navy friends in the local community and I was sure that she would be well taken care of, but that certainly did not make it any easier to get on the airplane and fly off to Guam. I immersed myself in preparations for the next patrol and spent a great deal of time getting caught up on some neglected service records and administrative work. Although I was the Executive Officer of the submarine and second in command, I had very few people working directly for me—just two, a senior yeoman and his assistant. I was fortunate to have a great leading yeoman, Petty Officer First Class Rex Harrison and we had added a Yeoman "Striker", Seaman John Duckworth who had been a member of the deck gang, but had taken typing in High School and was anxious for a chance to move up the ladder. As it turned out, two patrols later, I recommended (then) Petty Officer Duckworth for Flag Writer's School as a reenlistment incentive. He learned shorthand at the school and was transferred to an Admiral's staff in the Atlantic, and never looked back. He retired from the Navy twenty years later as a Master Chief Yeoman and had been a key member on the staffs of several Admirals during his Navy career.

I received a message just after our "Way Past Halfway Night" celebrations that I was the father of a new baby girl, Elizabeth Austin McKinney, born in Tripler Army Hospital on October 26, 1972. I was relieved to hear that Mother and daughter were doing fine. I passed out Daniel Webster cigars to the crew and couldn't wait until the patrol was over and we were headed back to Hawaii.

The Blue Crew of the Daniel Webster got back to Hawaii in late November and Mary, our son William and the newest member of our family were there to meet me at the airport with an Aloha lei.

Ship's Office Staff

Meeting Elizabeth for the first time

Command Training and a MEDEVAC

With long duration patrols the norm for nuclear submarines, the Navy had to address the potential of medical emergencies while on patrol. Initially, in the early 60s, doctors were assigned to all Ballistic Missile submarines. But it quickly became apparent that there was very little for these specialists to do as the crew were for the most part in their twenties and were quite healthy. As a result, by the end of the 1960s the doctors were assigned to higher priority missions. The Vietnam War was in full force during this period and there was a much greater need for doctors in support of this war effort than on submarines.

Independent duty corpsmen were assigned to submarines when the doctors left. These specially trained individuals could perform diagnostic procedures, advanced first aid, basic life support, nursing procedures and minor surgery. They could treat illnesses associated with the enclosed submarine environment, diving and high-pressure conditions. They also served as the Radiation Health Officer and were trained in the medical aspects relative to personnel exposed to ionizing radiation. The Corpsman or "Doc" was an important advisor to the commanding officer regarding the diagnosis and treatment of injured crewmembers.

On my fourth patrol on USS Daniel Webster, I had completed my command qualifications and expected command of a submarine within the next six months. This patrol was also the last patrol for the skipper, Commander Tom Hopper. He felt that it would be good training for me if I were to "take command" of the ship during this patrol. All reports that would normally go to the commanding officer were to go to me instead. I would direct all actions of the ship and be responsible for all aspects of the patrol. The one area where Tom would retain control was the release of nuclear weapons, which was essentially a two-man control situation, and he would have to agree in any decision in this area in any event. This period in the Navy (1972-1973) was dominated by a new approach to personnel issues spearheaded by a new Chief of Naval Operations, Admiral Elmo Zumwalt. He encouraged commanding officers to meet with the members of their crew and work at solving race, discrimination and similar human relations issues. Tom devoted his efforts throughout the patrol to these issues and left the command of the ship to me. It was a real vote of confidence and a great opportunity for me to gain insight and experience in command.

Halfway through the patrol, Chief Missile Technician Doug Mullins had a bad fall and injured his leg. Chief Hospital Corpsman "Doc" Bailey came to me after he had treated Chief Mullins and told me that he had a badly sprained ankle, but felt that the chief might have fractured his ankle as well, but couldn't tell, as we did not have an X-ray machine. He could set the leg in a soft cast, but Chief Mullins would have to stay off the leg for at least a month. To be safe, "Doc" Bailey recommended a medical evacuation. I agreed with this recommendation and advised the Captain of my decision. He concurred.

Ballistic Missile submarines maintain radio silence throughout the patrol, but were allowed to transmit in the event of a medical emergency. This was before the days of satellite radio transmission, but we had a specialized burst transmission system that would send a short encrypted message in a two second burst that would be received by special receiving stations located around the world. We prepared our message for COMSUBPAC and sent it. Within a few hours they acknowledged receipt and directed us to proceed to a location about two hundred miles from Japan where we would be met by a helicopter. Since this situation was not a life threatening one, we maintained our alert status, which meant that we were limited to a speed of four knots, and it took us a few days to reach the rendezvous point. We came to periscope depth and spotted the helicopter waiting for us. After surfacing, manning the bridge and evaluating the sea conditions (light wind and three foot swells), I determined that the personnel transfer would be from the missile deck and ordered the hatch from Auxiliary Machinery Room 1 opened. The ship's helicopter transfer team came on deck and assisted Chief Mullins topside. The helicopter (a CH-46 Sea King) was directed to come in, which it did smartly and commenced a rock solid hover, lowered a litter and Chief Mullins was strapped in and lifted off. The team on deck lay below and we secured the bridge and submerged. Total time on the surface was about 40 minutes.

Helicopter Transfer

Chief Mullins was in Hawaii two days later, well ahead of his shipmates. He met us at the airport when we arrived a month later fully recovered from his sprained ankle.

The Royal Navy in Guam

The Blue crew of the USS Daniel Webster flew to Guam in early September 1973 to relieve the Gold crew. This was to be my fifth and last patrol. We had received orders for my relief, LCDR Sam Badgett, to report in December and I was expecting orders to go on to command of a submarine for my next assignment. My skipper, Tom Hopper, would have his change of command in Guam, and his relief, Commander Leo Wright had reported aboard and flew to Guam with us. Usually the change of command ceremony occurred during the off-crew period in Hawaii and was well attended by the submarine community, family and friends, but the timing did not work out and I would have to plan for the change of command ceremony in Guam. Although this was an unusual occurrence in Guam, it was actually easier to set up the ceremony, as there would not be many guests attending. The biggest problem would be the weather as September in Guam is the beginning of the rainy season and tropical downpours were everyday occurrences. As it turned out, we did have some unusual guests for the ceremony as the Royal Navy's first nuclear submarine, HMS Dreadnought, was in port and Daniel Webster was designated as the host ship for this port visit.

HMS Dreadnought

The day of the change of command was cloudy, hot and humid. The ceremony was set for 1300, at 1000 the heavens opened up, and we had about

196 | Flotsam & Jetsam

two inches of rain in about half an hour. The sun was out by noon and the ceremony went off without a hitch. The officers from HMS Dreadnought and the USS Woodrow Wilson, and the officers and their wives from the USS Proteus and Submarine Squadron Fifteen along with Tom Hopper's wife and three children (who had flown out from Hawaii) were the audience for this ceremony. We all attended a very nice reception at the Naval Base Officer's Club.

The next day we commenced our refit in preparation for the next patrol. I met with the new skipper, Leo Wright, and we planned the refit period, the sea trials and crew training for the next three weeks. One of the complications would be our responsibility as host ship for the port visit of HMS Dreadnought. Leo made it clear at this point that he did not drink alcohol, that he expected that there would be many parties with the "Brits", and that he would be uncomfortable in this environment. He would attend the cocktail party that night on HMS Dreadnought and the Commodore's reception for the officers of Dreadnought, but I was to plan the rest of the events on my own and not to include him, as an active participant and he would worry about the refit.

That night, we attended the cocktail party on HMS Dreadnought. They had invited the officers of Daniel Webster, the squadron officers and wives and many officers and wives from the repair ship, USS Proteus. Also attending was Commander Naval Forces Marianas, a 2-star admiral and his wife and members of his staff. In all, I would say about fifty of us were crowded into the control room and wardroom of Dreadnought, a space not much larger than the living room and dining area of a small house. To complicate matters, there was nuclear repair work going on aboard Dreadnought throughout the evening with workers in yellow anti-contamination suits coming and going through the control room as we were enjoying cocktails and hors d'oeuvres. I had never seen anything like this in our submarine navy, but the Brits seemed to take it all in stride. It was quite an evening. Leo Wright left early, but I stayed on until the wee small hours of the morning to ensure all of the Daniel Webster officers made it back to the ship.

The next night was the squadron commander's reception at his quarters in honor of the officers of HMS Dreadnought. It was pretty much the same cast of characters as the night before on Dreadnought, but we did have a little more room. I enjoyed getting to know the Captain of Dreadnought, Commander Patrick "Paddy" O'Riordan and his number one (Executive Officer), Lieutenant Commander David Barraclough. A British submarine wardroom is dominated by the personality of the skipper and Paddy O'Riordan was no exception. Toward the end of the evening, after the ladies had left, Paddy O'Riordan organized us into teams and we competed in some very physical activity, from arm wrestling to building human pyramids that the other team would try to knock down. None of us was feeling any pain at the time, but the next morning we had some very sore muscles.

The Dreadnought Letter

A copy of a letter written by a Chief Petty Officer aboard HMS Dreadnought was given to me by Dreadnought's Executive Officer. It was written just prior to their arrival in Guam and we both found it very amusing. I met Chief Goodbody later that day and he attested to the facts of the letter.

HMS Dreadnought
At Sea

The Commanding Officer
HMS Dreadnought
11 September 1973

Sir:

I regret to report the events leading up to and the subsequent loss of General Service Medal (Malay Peninsula).

I was given the medal whilst serving in HMS Repulse in 1967, and a home was found for it inside a shrunken head converted into a cigarette box which I obtained by swapping two tots and a submarine cap tally with a drunken marine sergeant in a Borneo Long house, we both being the guests of the Seventh Ghurka Rifles. After my return to the UK, the shrunken head with the medal inside was transferred to an unlocked glass case in my house in Helensburgh. Here it reposed in peace for 12 months and would no doubt continue to do so had there not been a christening party celebrating the birth of our third child. At some time during the party one of our more witty underwater guests removed the shrunken head from the glass case (complete with medal), wrapped it in a napkin, and set about it with a bottle of milk. On being asked by my wife what he thought he was doing, he replied, "I'm feeding the effing baby". In all fairness to him the baby, then only three days old, was a bit wizened, but my wife who was sober and not feeling very well at the time was not amused. On returning home from work the next day, it had come to pass that a decision at the wife/eldest daughter/gang of nosey vindictive women level had been taken to get rid of my shrunken head by way of the Helensburgh Rural District Council Garbage Disposal Vehicle. However, this was not to be. I removed the medal from its place of rest and laid it on the shelf, still inside the cupboard. To cover my losses I exchanged the head with a neighbor a CERA(P) for two tots, two pints and a Rover 75 workshop manual (1953) and considered I had made a profit. Had the Tiffy arranged a transplant, he would have profited too.

My eldest daughter, then nine years old, and a fully fledged member of the Brownies, had become very keen on the nursing profession and with the quick sightedness of all little girls had noticed on a recent visit to the local hospital that the nurses wore watches on their clothes and that some of them even wore a medal on their left tit, or as she put it "On their Jacksies Dad". To cut a long story short her next birthday present was a nurse's uniform, complete with carving knife, saw and entire medical torture set – only one thing was missing, a medal like real nurses have, and where better to get one than the glass case. All went well for many weeks of dedicated nursing, carried out on patient dolls and on the odd occasion our long-suffering, much bandaged and splinted/tied up boxer dog, until at last the sad day came when all nursing failed and one of the dolls (Walking Talking Chatty Kathy from three Christmases past) departed this life. At the time of this unhappy event, I was on patrol in HMS Repulse, and although I was informed of the medical failure and subsequent bereavement by family-gram, I had other things on my mind and did not mourn too long for Chatty Kathy. Immediately on my return to harbor I moved into a house I had purchased in Worcester, my wife having packed, etc. in my absence, and it was not until the second week of my leave that I noticed that the glass case did not contain my medal. On asking my wife where the medal was (Divisions were looming) she said she thought I had taken it to sea with me, and began casting "Don't say I didn't warn you glances" at the brat. After threats, bribery, and a final speech informing them that should I not be able to find the medal I would be disrated, flogged and court-martialed prior to being sent back to Borneo to earn another one, and that would take some time as I would have to wait for another war to start, and I wouldn't get paid while I was waiting—the horrible truth finally emerged.

In the several weeks of agony suffered by poor Kathy prior to her untimely demise, she had not so much as uttered a complaining word, but suffered in silence to the bitter end (not surprising as I had removed the talking bit on Boxing day after the three thousandth "Da Da Squeak Squeak") and she was deemed by family, the neighbors and no doubt approved by the dog to have been an extremely brave doll, and worthy of recognition. What better way to recognize heroism of a dying doll than by lending her Daddy's medal that he got from his submarine in Singapore "when the nasty men were going to come and shoot us". This was all well and good but as things are never done by half in my house, the doll was to be given a good Catholic funeral, and that Sir, is what happened to the medal. It too was given a good Catholic funeral, and it now lies in a grave, amongst the heather on a quiet hillside in Scotland. There one day it may be found, perhaps, the circumstances of its finding will remain forever a mystery. But that sir will be the finder's problem, not ours.

I have the honor to be, Sir,
Your obedient servant,

J.P. Goodbody
Radio Supervisor

Queen Elizabeth visits HMS Dreadnought

The next two stories, the first about Her Majesty, Queen Elizabeth and Prince Phillip and the second about a young telejournalist who we nicknamed "Miss Weather Guam", describe a common problem for women visiting submarines.

One evening during the visit of HMS Dreadnought to Guam, I was a guest in the wardroom of Dreadnought for an after dinner glass of port. The commanding officer, Commander Paddy O'Riordan asked me to sign their guest book and I was honored to do so. After signing the book, I was leafing through the pages when I came upon an impressive signature: a script "E Rex" which took up the entire page. I asked if that was the signature of the Queen and Commander O'Riordan replied that it was and there was an interesting story that went with it.

In April of that year (1973), HMS Dreadnought observed its tenth year of commissioned service in the Royal Navy and Commander O'Riordan invited the Queen to visit the ship and cut the birthday cake in honor of the occasion. She accepted the invitation and about two weeks before the event was scheduled, one of Her Majesty's ladies-in-waiting arrived to visit with the Captain and scope out the event in advance to prepare the Queen for her visit to the ship. Commander O'Riordan said that he met the lady topside and they discussed the arrival honors and ceremonies that would take place as Queen Elizabeth boarded the ship. He then led her down a ladder into the control room. Once there, the lady-in-waiting remarked that the ladder was "rather awkward" and possibly a staircase with a railing would be more appropriate. The Captain responded that climbing down a vertical 15-foot ladder could be potentially embarrassing for Her Majesty and that most ladies solved this problem by wearing slacks. "Oh no!" responded the lady, "that would never do, Her Majesty never wears slacks. Are you sure that you couldn't arrange for stairs?" she asked again. "No madam," the Captain responded "stairs are out of the question."

The Captain then offered a compromise. He told the lady-in-waiting that he would station his very best Seaman at the foot of the ladder in the control room and that he would be standing at rigid attention with his eyes staring straight ahead, and that he would ensure a proper area of decorum. No one would be within ten feet of the bottom of the ladder in a position to look upward as the Queen descended. The lady-in-waiting agreed that this would have to do and that she would brief the Queen on the event.

The big day arrived and Commander O'Riordan met Queen Elizabeth, accompanied by Prince Phillip, on the pier. Prince Phillip was an experienced Royal Navy veteran having been involved in some extraordinarily dangerous missions in World War II and as a commander, after the war, had command of a destroyer. He also had a ready wit and a well-known bawdy sense of humor. After arrival honors, the Captain led the Royal Party to the top of the ladder leading down into the control room. Queen Elizabeth said, "You may proceed down the ladder Captain, I have been briefed about what to expect." The Captain proceeded down the ladder and his best Seaman was at the bottom of the ladder standing at rigid attention, eyes staring straight ahead and there was no one else in the control room. The Queen came down the ladder followed by Prince Phillip. After a short discussion in the control room, the Captain announced that his officers were assembled in the wardroom for the official cake cutting ceremony. Queen Elizabeth told the Captain to lead the way and he did, but as he was leaving the control room, he noticed that Prince Phillip was having a few words with the Seaman stationed at the bottom of the ladder.

The rest of the ceremony proceeded as planned and about thirty minutes later, the Captain escorted the Royal Party topside and they departed the ship with appropriate side-boys, boatswain pipes and honors. The Captain returned to the ship and went down the ladder into the control room, where his trusty Seaman was still stationed standing at rigid attention. The Captain asked him what Prince Phillip had said to him earlier. The Seaman replied that Prince Phillip had leaned over and whispered, "They're black."

Miss Weather Guam

The visit of HMS Dreadnought was ending. Acting as liaison with the Dreadnought's Captain, Commander Paddy O'Riordan, during their stay, was demanding on the "social" side, but I still had to carry out my duties as Executive Officer of the USS Daniel Webster as we were very busy with a refit preparing for our next patrol. My duties as Executive Officer performed during the day and my liaison duties in the evening. I was burning the candle at both ends and was beginning to feel some heat in the middle. But there was a light at the end of the tunnel as we planned a joint crew beach party to be held on the day before they sailed.

Dreadnought's First Lieutenant (Executive Officer) David Barriclough and I worked together in the evening planning the activities for our beach party. I suggested softball, volleyball and horseshoes. Swimming on the beach was not recommended due to the poisonous fish and shellfish in the waters around Guam and the ocean temperature of 84 degrees did not make for a very refreshing swim. David wasn't sure about the softball game, as most of his crew had never played. He then suggested cricket, but we concluded that few of his crew played the game and none of my crew had even seen the game. He then suggested "Marrow Paddling" which would be a great icebreaker for both crews. I had no idea what this game involved, but David said that they would bring all the necessary equipment if I would provide a ten-foot pole placed in the ground. He also said that each team would be made up of ten players.

As we concluded our planning, Paddy O'Riordan asked us to join him and a few officers from the submarine squadron staff for dinner at the Officer's Club. Several of the squadron wives joined us and the Admiral's Flag Lieutenant (an aviator) and his girlfriend joined us as well. She was known to us all as "Miss Weather Guam", a most attractive young blond who appeared on the local Guam television station each evening with the local weather report. I am sure that she was chosen to make this report as it never seemed to change, "High temperature today will be 94 degrees with a low tonight of 84 degrees. It will sunny, hot and humid with occasional showers and thunderstorms with heavy local downpours. The chance of rain is 80%."

After dinner, the Captain invited us all back to HMS Dreadnought for after dinner drinks. We had a very nice evening, and just as I thought it was going to break up and I would be able to go back to my ship for some much-needed sleep, the Captain suggested that we all sober up by going over to "Daniel" (his nickname for USS Daniel Webster) for an early morning breakfast. All agreed that this was a great idea, so I had little choice but to go along with the crowd. I called the duty officer and told him to "Rig ship for lady visitors" and get the stewards up in the wardroom pantry and standby to make breakfast. He diplomatically pointed out the hour (2330) and I thanked him for the time check and told him that we would be arriving at 2345.

About ten or twelve tipsy officers and their ladies arrived just before midnight and we were met topside by the duty officer. He told me all was set up in the wardroom and that our Captain had sent his regrets and would not be joining us for breakfast. Three squadron wives went to work in the wardroom pantry with two stewards preparing eggs and bacon. I sat at the wardroom table with several officers from Dreadnought, Daniel Webster, the submarine squadron, the Flag Lieutenant and Miss Weather Guam. We were involved in fairly loud and boisterous conversation, but I kept hearing other voices (almost whispers) and some quiet laughter but I couldn't place where it was coming from. I finally realized the voices were coming from underneath the wardroom table. The table was set with a heavy linen tablecloth. I discretely pulled the tablecloth aside in front of my chair and saw a familiar face of one of the seamen from my crew sticking his head up through a hatch below the wardroom table. It then dawned on me that one of the crew's berthing areas was just below the wardroom and that there was an emergency escape hatch into the wardroom in case of fire.

I quietly excused myself from the wardroom and went below to the crew's berthing area. It was completely dark when I entered the area, but when I turned on the lights several of the crew were getting back in their bunks. I announced that the show was over and we quietly shut and dogged the hatch, and I received assurances from the senior man in the compartment that all would remain under control. I returned to the wardroom, had breakfast and escorted our guests off the ship, and as far as I could tell none were the wiser about the shenanigans going on under the wardroom table. The next morning at quarters, the members of the crew were trading stories about the shapely legs of Miss Weather Guam.

Marrow Paddling in Guam

The day before HMS Dreadnought was to depart Guam, the combined crews of Dreadnought and Daniel Webster had a beach party in the afternoon. Our first crew contest was to be a British game called "marrow paddling." The Brits were not giving us any clues as to what the game involved, but they provided a keg of beer and pint glasses all around as we set up the game. We placed a long pole in the ground with a rope attached to the top of the pole about ten feet above the ground. A pillowcase filled with sand and rags was attached to the other end of the rope hanging about three feet above the ground. The pillowcase represented the "marrow" which turns out to be a British word for pumpkin. The game was much like ten pins, except the pins would be members of the two teams.

We flipped a coin for who went first and I won the toss and elected to let the Brits take the field first. They arranged their team in a triangle formation, filled up their pint glasses with beer and held them on top of their heads. Each of our players then had two throws of the marrow from the opposite side of the pole and if the marrow hit one of their players and he spilled his beer, then he was eliminated from the field of play. In between the two throws by a team member, the players were allowed to drink as much of their beer as they wished and thus reduce the chance that they would spill their beer on the subsequent throw of the marrow. But we would then "top off" the beer of the remaining players on the field before the next player's two throws of the marrow. This continued until all the players in the field were eliminated, and the team's score was the number of throws of the marrow taken. The other team then took the field. The team with the lowest score was declared the winner. We needed something like thirty throws of the marrow to eliminate all of the Dreadnought team.

As our team took the field, I selected the smallest members of the team and placed them as far away from the pole as was allowed, thus reducing the chance that they would be hit by the marrow. Our engineering officer was the shortest member of the crew and known for being able "to hold his beer" and he was placed on the outside point of our team. My strategy worked and even though the Brits did their best to "Top off" the engineer's beer on every occasion, he was able to duck below their marrow throws and held out until they exceeded our score from the first round. As a result, the crew of the Daniel Webster was declared the winner of the first Pacific Anglo-American Marrow Paddling contest. I should also note that the members of both teams had done their best to polish off the keg of beer, but the Brits had more kegs in reserve.

Our beach party was enjoyed by all. The crews of both ships had made many friends and had traded many sea stories about their submarine exploits. I would meet several submarine officers from the Royal Navy in the future and all had heard about Dreadnought's trip to the Pacific.

XO's on the beach

The next day Dreadnought left Guam and I went back to work. Our departure date was ten days away in early October and I had a lot of work to do. I still had not heard about my next assignment and I was getting anxious to hear about what submarine I would be assigned for my command tour. We got underway for patrol and still no word. A nice bit of news was received shortly after we left port; the Commander selection list came out and I had been early selected to the rank of Commander. About a month later we received a message with my orders to report to the Bureau of Naval

Personnel in Washington, DC as the Assistant Nuclear Power Personnel Manager for Enlisted Personnel; a desk job! What a letdown. Selected for early promotion to Commander and then assigned to a desk job in Washington. It would be another month before we returned to port and I could call Washington to find out what happened to my orders to command. Leo Wright, my new skipper told me that he was sure that I had received orders to one of the top jobs in Washington for post XO submariners. I didn't know, but I had my heart set on command of a submarine, not command of a desk.

Chapter VII - Hawaii to DC to PCO Training to Charleston, SC

From Hawaii to Washington DC

Detached in late 1973 from the USS Daniel Webster, my orders were to report to the Bureau of Naval Personnel (BUPERS) to relieve as the Assistant Nuclear Power Personnel Officer for Enlisted Personnel. I had never heard of this position and it sure sounded like a dead-end bureaucratic desk job to me. Rather than command of a nuclear submarine, I would command a desk in some dusty remote office in BUPERS. I flew back to Hawaii and celebrated Christmas with Mary and our children (William 6 and Elizabeth 15 months). I learned more about my new assignment from my previous skipper, Tom Hopper, who was assigned to the COMSUBPAC staff. He told me this was a very carefully screened assignment that required Admiral Rickover's personal approval and that he was sure that I would find it a challenging job. This was encouraging, but I was still skeptical.

We left Hawaii just before the New Year loaded down with leis and best wishes from our shipmates and friends. Enroute to Washington, we visited my brother and his family in Los Angeles and my parents in La Grange, Illinois. After two and a half years in Hawaii, we found the Midwest in January to be mighty cold. Mary stayed with my parents while I went on to Washington, DC to look for a house. We had never owned a house and were looking forward to buying our first. The housing market in the DC area was as overpriced in 1974 as it is today. The realtor I was working with had little to offer that we could afford. After a discouraging week of looking at the houses available, I got a call from Captain Joe Metcalf who was a friend from our days together at the Naval Post Graduate School in 1963. He and his wife Ruth owned a two-bedroom Cape Cod style house in North Arlington that they had rented out for the last ten years. The current tenant had not cared for the house, was not keeping up with the rent payments and was about to be evicted. The house needed a lot of work, but if I was willing to take it on, Joe was willing to work out a loan arrangement that we could afford. I arranged to see the house the next day and it was not in very good shape as Joe had already told me; in fact, it was worse than I had anticipated. The house was full of cats (at least 30) that came and went through a broken window. The house was one big litter box. All the hardwood floors would need resurfacing, all the woodwork needed painting and the walls would need a new coat of paint or wallpaper. Structurally, the house was sound, but we would have to invest a lot of sweat equity in cleaning and painting. I knew that I would have a difficult time convincing Mary that this was our "dream" house.

Mary arrived with the children the next week and we stayed in temporary lodging. After a few days seeing what housing was available, Mary agreed with me that the offer from Joe and Ruth Metcalf was really very generous and we both agreed that it would be a great project for us both to work together to restore an older home. This was before the popular TV show "This Old House" so we had little idea what was in store for us. After sanding all the hardwood floors and varnishing them, we moved in about three weeks later. We would spend the next two and a half years restoring and refinishing every surface in the house. We were to discover in this assignment in Washington that military families sacrifice a lot to make ends meet on a very limited budget. We fell in love with our "new" house and left it with regret in 1976.

I reported to my new assignment after we moved into the house and I was to find out quickly that this was not going to be the routine desk job that I had anticipated.

Command of a Desk (Prelude to a Sea Command)

As it turned out, the next two and a half years was a great opportunity for me. I learned my way around the bureaucracy of the Pentagon and Congress and was able to develop a legislative proposal, which was approved by Congress and enacted into law that established a special incentive pay for nuclear-trained officers. This nuclear officer incentive pay act of 1976 has been modified several times since then, but it is still the basis for special pay for nuclear submarine officers today, 34 years later.

In the spring of 1976, the submarine assignment officer (detailer) started to discuss my next assignment, which would be command. He pointed out that he still had a few problems getting my assignment approved by Admiral Rickover. When I asked him what the problem was he told me that I had never completed my nuclear engineer qualification. I was surprised to find out that this was a problem. I remember when the requirement to complete this qualification was laid down I was the director of officer training at Nuclear Power School, and my commanding officer, Frank Kelso specifically asked Admiral Rickover's staff if I would have to complete this qualification. The response was no, and that I should devote my full attention to officer training.

The detailer said that was all well and good, but Admiral Rickover had a list of names of all those officers who did not complete nuclear engineer qualification and it had become increasingly difficult to obtain Admiral Rickover's concurrence for command assignment as this list got smaller. The list now contained just one name -- mine -- and the detailer was carefully reviewing which submarines had the strongest Executive Officer and Engineer Officer in order to convince Admiral Rickover that I would have a strong back-up team while in command. I felt a little uncomfortable with the idea that I was not considered strong enough to go to command, but when I thought about it -- that I would be assured of the best Executive Officer and Engineer Officer available, I decided I was getting a good deal. A few weeks later, the detailer told me that I had been approved for orders to command the USS Seahorse (SSN 669), homeported in Charleston, South Carolina. Before I got to Seahorse, I would go through the Nuclear Submarine Prospective Commanding Officer (PCO) Course at Naval Reactors (Rickover's office) and then the Submarine Atlantic PCO course in Norfolk. This would be a total of about 5 months of training, but after two and half years of shore duty in Washington, DC I felt that I needed every bit of this time to "get up to speed" before taking command.

I reported to Naval Reactors in July for Nuclear PCO Training. Captain Dick Smith was our mentor and he met with me on the first day and reiterated the concern that I had not qualified as a nuclear engineer and that I had been a "tough" sell to Admiral Rickover who would be carefully watching my progress. There were ten of us going through the course together, all the others had qualified as a nuclear engineer and most had served as a submarine engineering officer. Captain Smith had assigned me to study with Dick Lee who had served as engineer and on the Nuclear Propulsion Examining Board. Dick was going to command of USS SUNFISH a sister ship of Seahorse and in the same submarine squadron in Charleston. The course was entirely self-study. We poured over reactor plant technical manuals, nuclear engineering textbooks and the schematics and diagrams of the nuclear propulsion plant for our assigned submarine. We were expected to put in ten-hour days (0800-1800) five days of the week and from 0800 to 1300 on Saturday. At the end of each two weeks, we were tested. The first exam was on mechanical systems. Dick Lee was a great help in helping me focus my study, reading on what were the important issues, and I did very well on this exam. Captain Smith met with me afterwards, very pleased with my progress, and told me to keep up the good work. I felt that the pressure was off, but I still had a long way to go before I could rest easy.

Admiral Rickover's Graduation Speech

Our three-month training session in submarine nuclear power plants was ending in September 1976. I was one of ten Prospective Commanding Officers (PCOs) who had survived ten two-hour written exams and several individual oral exams and we had only the final eight-hour exam to complete. We had grown into a cohesive group with a sense of humor and hope that the end was in sight. As the senior officer in the group, Captain Smith called me into his office.

"Tomorrow afternoon Admiral Rickover will give his graduation remarks to your group." and he continued, "There a few ground rules I want to go over with you."

"This is the first time since you have been here that any of you have seen the Admiral. He had a heart attack a year ago, that has slowed him down, and at 76, is really showing his age. That doesn't mean that he has lost any of his keen intelligence and insight into the Nuclear Power Program. His comments to you will focus on maintaining the standards of the training you have had and the need to be vigilant in the security and safety of operation of the Navy's nuclear propulsion plants."

He continued, "Now the ground rules. You will be in a small classroom next the Admiral's office. Sit in the first two rows in the middle. Wear your coat and tie. Don't chew gum, don't cross your legs and don't look out the widow while the Admiral is talking to you. Look at the Admiral and listen to what he has to say. Don't take notes. He will ask you at the end of his talk if you have any questions. I recommend that you remain silent as questions often set the Admiral "off" and there is no predicting what the outcome will be. He is not expecting you to ask any questions. Do you have any questions of me?"

"Should we rise when the Admiral enters the room?" I asked.

"Good question." he replied, "We will all be standing before he enters the room. As soon as he is seated, he will tell you to sit, if not, you take the lead and sit down the rest will follow. At the end of the session, when he gets up to leave, you and the rest of class rise as well. No need to call 'Attention on Deck' as that will only set him off as well."

The next day about 1330, the word came from the Admiral's office that he would meet with the PCOs. We assembled in the designated room and stood by our desks. The Admiral entered and sat down and we sat down. He clearly had aged in the last few years. After he looked at each of us, he launched into his remarks…with no notes. He said that he really did not look forward to giving these remarks, primarily because he did not know us on a personal level as he had known the commanding officers of the earlier submarines. He said that it appeared that we would all complete our studies satisfactorily and he would have to pass us on to command. He continued **"What really bothers me is that I know thirty percent of you will fail as commanding officers and if I knew which of you will fail, then I would not let those individuals go on to command. Unfortunately, I have no way of predicting who will fail, so I have no choice but to let you all go on to command."** He went on for another thirty minutes giving his philosophy of safe operation of nuclear power plants and what he expected of us. When he was finished, he asked if we had any questions and we remained silent. He got up to leave the room and we all stood as Captain Smith escorted him back to his office. Captain Smith came back into the room and asked us what we thought of the Admiral's remarks. We were still in a state of semi-shock from his prediction that thirty percent of us would fail in command. Captain Smith smiled and said actually we were better than the last class for which the Admiral had predicted forty percent would fail in command.

The odd thing about this prediction is that four years later, after the ten of us had completed a command, three had had significant incidents during their command tour. A grounding and a near loss of the ship while submerged in well-charted waters because of a navigational error. A loss of two men over the side while conducting a non-essential personnel transfer by helicopter in heavy seas. And a collision with a tug and tow in restricted waters during daylight with good visibility that resulted in the loss of the sonar dome. In each incident, the commanding officer was held fully accountable. Although Admiral Rickover's graduation speech was certainly not the most uplifting, he delivered a message and a warning about the perils of command. We were not to see the Admiral again before we left Naval Reactors, but his message about failure in command was still with us as we started the last phase of our training, which would be intensive review of submarine tactics, a lot of time in the attack trainer practicing periscope techniques and sonar approaches. Then we went to sea to find out what we learned.

Admiral Rickover exiting the deck hatch of the USS Nautilus

Soviet Yankees and Crazy Ivans

October 1976, aboard USS Finback (SSN 670). Submerged about 300 miles off the East coast of the U.S. we had just detected a passive sonar contact bearing 065 degrees. At this point, the range was unknown. I directed the Officer of the Deck to station the fire control tracking party and change course to 065. To Sonar, I gave the following order: "Sonar – Conn, designate new contact Sierra 27, track and report."

After ten minutes, S-27 was now on a bearing of 067, drawing right. We changed course to North (000) in order to generate an increased bearing rate and to get an estimate on the contact's range. Ten minutes later, Sonar reported, "Conn – Sonar we have definite discrete frequency signatures on S-27 that indicate it is a probable Yankee class submarine. Broadband noise is increasing. S-27 is now on a bearing of 071, continuing to draw right."

Soviet Yankee Class missile submarine

We now had enough data in our fire control computer and our manual plots to get a good estimate of the contact's range at between ten and twelve thousand yards. We would refine this range as we continued to close the contact.

Our mission was a typical Cold War mission for attack submarines: to detect, localize and track Soviet missile submarines. This Yankee Class submarine was tracked by a P-3 Orion ASW aircraft flying out of Bermuda, and after we had established a firm trail of the Yankee, we would come to periscope depth, communicate with the P-3, and take over the trail. The objective of the mission was to maintain continuous contact and surveillance of the missile submarine, and if necessary prevent a Soviet missile strike against the U.S.

Two hours later, we had determined the Yankee's course and speed (200/6 knots) and we had maneuvered deep in his starboard quarter at a range of 5,000 to 7,000 yards where we had solid passive sonar contact. In this position, almost astern of the Yankee, we were in the baffled area of his sonar system and he was unable to detect us. We had no way of determining his operating depth, but intelligence reports indicated that Soviet Yankee submarines generally operated at depths of 50, 100 and 150 meters, so we chose a depth of 550 feet to be well below these depths. Once we were firmly in trail, we went briefly to periscope depth, raised a radio antenna to contact the P-3 aircraft and relieved him of the trail. He wished us "Good luck and good hunting." and headed back to the "barn" in Bermuda.

We continued trailing the Yankee. About two hours later, Sonar reported, "Conn – Sonar, the Yankee appears to be increasing speed and changing course." We came right about 45 degrees to clear his track. "Conn – Sonar, the Yankee continues to increase speed, heavy cavitation with significant up-Doppler on all frequencies." then "Conn – Sonar, Crazy Ivan! The Yankee is at flank speed and appears to have reversed course." We continued to pull off his track.

Soviet submarines were significantly nosier than U.S. submarines and their Sonar systems not nearly as sensitive as ours were. As a result, we had a significant advantage in detecting and trailing Soviet submarines. They had a good idea that we were trailing them, but their repeated attempts to counter-detect our submarines generally failed. The aptly named "Crazy Ivan" maneuver was a course reversal and a flank speed run back down their track and in attempt to cause the trailing submarine to panic and clear the area. At flank speed, the Yankee's sonar was completely blanked out and was unable to gain any sonar contact. We learned not to panic, but to gradually maneuver off his track.

After the Yankee passed down our port side, sounding like a freight train, he slowed down and resumed the previous course and speed. We maneuvered back to our usual trail position and continued to track and monitor his activities. At this point, Captain J. D. Williams, our PCO instructor stepped in, asked the captain of the USS Finback to have his officers relieve us at our watch stations, and proceed to the next event of the operation order. The Finback would assume the role of the Yankee submarine and our counterpart PCOs on board USS Pargo would conduct the next trailing exercise. There were four PCOs in USS Finback and each of us would have the opportunity to assume the role of Commanding Officer in a variety of realistic training exercises.

Torpedo Firing in the Tongue of the Ocean

After open-ocean submarine trailing evolutions in the fall of 1976, USS Finback, our PCO training ship arrived at the Atlantic Undersea Test and Evaluation Center (AUTEC) range near Andros Island in the Bahamas. To the east of Andros Island is a 500 square mile underwater range located in the Tongue of the Ocean (TOTO). TOTO is a 7,000-foot deep underwater canyon extending about 30 miles into the Bahamas Islands with Andros Island to the west and Nassau Island to the northeast. The land based control center of AUTEC is located on Andros Island. This unique underwater range has been in operation since the 1960s. The range can track over 60 submarines, surface ships and aircraft simultaneously as they interact in various combat exercises.

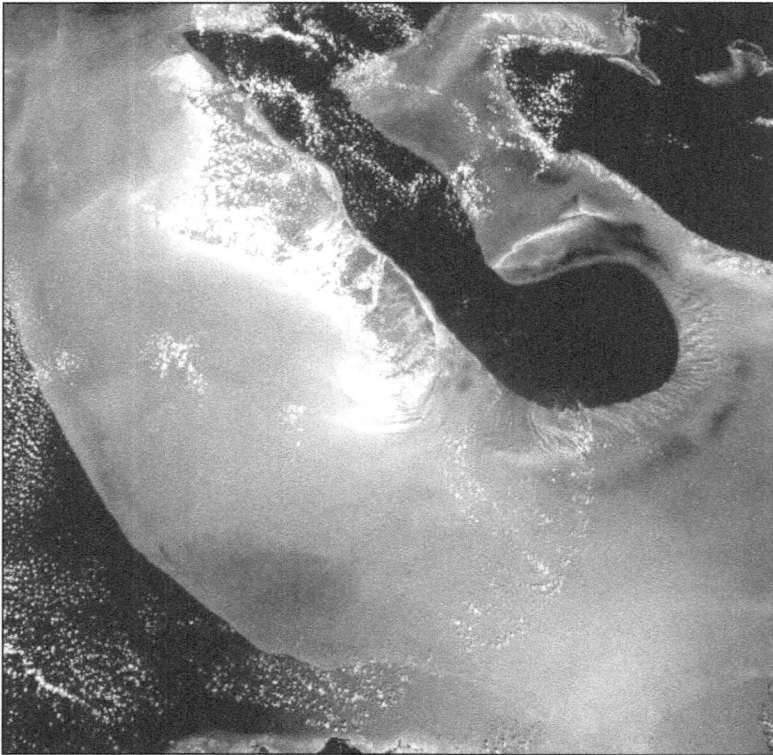

Tongue of the Ocean

As PCOs, we would be evaluated in firing exercise torpedoes at other submarines and surface ships in advanced combat conditions. We would employ the Mark-48 torpedo, which is the standard torpedo still in use today. The Navy cycles through its entire inventory of Mark-48 torpedoes regularly, replacing the explosive warhead of the torpedo with an inert exercise warhead. After the torpedo completes its run, the exercise head fills with air and the torpedo rises to the surface, is picked up by a torpedo retrieval vessel, returned to a torpedo servicing facility and then placed back in the "warshot" inventory. By using all the torpedoes in this way, each torpedo in the inventory is regularly tested, evaluated and proven effective.

The Mark-48 torpedo weighs 3650 pounds, is 19 feet long, and has an effective range of 20 miles and travels at speeds up to 55 knots. It is designed to attack both surface ships and submarines. It is wire-guided, which means that there is a wire attached to the torpedo that pays out during its run and remains attached to the submarine so that guidance commands can be fed to the torpedo throughout its run. The warhead is 650 pounds of high explosive and a single torpedo will sink any submarine and surface ship, cruiser size or smaller. In short, it is an extremely effective offensive weapon.

The Captain of a submarine is in total charge of the attack center team during torpedo battle stations. From the initial detection of a possible enemy target, throughout the approach and attack phases of a torpedo attack, the Captain makes all the decisions using the recommendations of the fire control party. It is a coordinated team effort, and a well-trained team is essential for success. Each of my fellow PCO's had served on several submarines and we had all been key members of the attack center team. Now we were to be evaluated as the leader of this team and judged on our ability to make critical decisions under the stress of simulated, but very realistic, combat conditions. The surface ships, submarines and anti-submarine aircraft participating in this exercise were all hostile and their task was to seek out and "sink" us before we could "sink" our target.

USS Finback carried 20 exercise torpedoes, which meant that each of us would have the opportunity to be the "Captain" for five torpedo launches. As it turned out, for each of us, two torpedoes were launched at submarine targets and three at surface ships. The surface ships were definitely the more challenging targets as we were shallow (at periscope depth) and exposure of the periscope made us vulnerable to radar and visual detection from opposing ships and helicopters. Periscope observations had to be short (5 seconds or less) and accurate. During a periscope observation, it was essential to measure the bearing of the target and get a solid reading of the target's course and range. Getting a good range is very difficult at long distance (greater than 5 or 6 miles). But as the target got closer, we were much more vulnerable to counter detection, so it was essential that we launch the torpedo early and use wire guidance to make mid-course corrections as the target closed. Excessive exposure of the periscope was almost certain to invite counter detection by a helicopter and once they held contact, you had no choice but to go "deep and fast" to avoid an attack and this would abort the torpedo attack on the surface ship.

Each of us had successful attacks and some spectacular failures during our week at AUTEC. In the end, we all graduated from our PCO training course and were on our way to command.

Mark-48 Torpedo testing

A Move to Charleston and a Trip to Italy

In mid-November 1976, we completed the COMSUBLANT PCO course and had one more course on command leadership, but first I had two weeks of leave during which time Mary and I would move from Arlington, Virginia to Charleston, South Carolina, the homeport of USS Seahorse. We had purchased a new house in Charleston, near Charlestowne Landing, west of the Ashley River. As everyone in Charleston will tell you, the city of Charleston is on a peninsula between two rivers, the Cooper and the Ashley. We were on a tight schedule as I had orders to report to the USS Seahorse (SSN 669) and relieve as Commanding Officer in mid-December—Seahorse was currently deployed to the Mediterranean.

We sold our Arlington house to Captain Wayne Hughes and his wife Joan who had provided me many home cooked meals when I was a lonesome bachelor at Navy Postgraduate School in Monterrey, California. Mary and I had become good friends with Wayne and Joan during our time in Arlington. We were sorry to leave our first house, but were pleased that Wayne and Joan would be the new owners. Thanksgiving was upon us, so we had a nice Thanksgiving dinner and started packing out the house on Friday. By early the next week, the moving van was loaded up and on its way to Charleston and we were not far behind in two cars, with two children, a Siamese cat named Charlie and loads of house plants.

Our household goods had not arrived, so we checked into a Ramada Inn. I had to leave on Sunday to drive to Norfolk for the Command Leadership course and Mary took on the task of moving into our new house. A week later, I was back in Charleston, but Mary had done most of the hard work of moving in and I spent the next few days hanging pictures. Two days later, after an emotional farewell with Mary and the kids, I flew from Charleston to New York and then on to Rome and finally to Naples, Italy where I reported to Commander Submarine Group Eight for further orders to USS Seahorse. The Seahorse was at sea and I would spend the next week in Naples waiting her return. During this period, I stayed with Commander Tom Harper and his wife Sandy who were close friends from our time together at Monterey. Sandy, like Joan Hughes, had taken good care of me during my bachelor days in Monterey. Now that I think about it, I was not that lonesome as a bachelor in Monterey because there were so many wives of my classmates who took me in and gave me a good home cooked meal. What a life!

Waiting for the Seahorse, and with Christmas just around the corner, I was looking for an appropriate gift for Mary. A gold Seahorse charm caught my eye in a local jewelry store. I wasn't sure of the Italian word for "Seahorse", but I knew that the word for "horse" was "cavallo." So I approached the lady behind the counter, and in my best Italian asked to see the "Cavallo di Mare" or loosely translated "Horse of the Sea."

She smiled and said "Si, Signore." The Seahorse charm was just what I wanted.

I told the lady, "Sono il Capitanno sommergibile Cavallo di mare." Loosely translated, I am the captain of the submarine Seahorse.

She responded "Cavallo di Mare -- no." and pointing at the Seahorse charm, she said "Questo, Cavalluccio marino, non Cavallo di mare. Il Cavallo grande e cavalluccio piccolo."

After some thought, I finally understood that a seahorse was a small creature and cavalluccio must mean small horse. I responded, "Grazie Signora," and pointing at the charm repeated "Questo cavalluccio marino," and continued "Sommergibile non piccolo, ma grande." We had a good laugh together and I had survived my first Italian language lesson.

Chapter VIII - USS Seahorse (SSN 669)

Change of Command

USS Seahorse (SSN 669)

After my one-week stay in Naples, Italy, I received word that Seahorse would make a brief stop in Augusta Bay, Sicily for some electronics repair work, and flew to the Sigonella Naval Air Station, near Augusta Bay and I reported aboard Seahorse the next day. We spent a day in port, left the next day after successful repairs, and spent the next three weeks at sea. We were the "duty" submarine at sea in the Mediterranean over Christmas (1976) and the New Year's (1977). Although our mission was to track Soviet submarines, we were not able to find any during this period. However, it was an excellent opportunity for me to learn the ship and get to know the crew. The commanding officer, who I was to relieve, was Commander Nate Heuberger, who was well respected and liked by his crew, which he had trained to a high degree of readiness for this Mediterranean deployment. The Executive Officer was Lieutenant Commander Bill Habermeyer who was probably the best-organized officer I have ever had the pleasure of serving with. As a result, my turnover and relief of the commanding officer was greatly facilitated by Bill's efforts. Bill and I had gone through Nuclear Power School together in 1964.

One of the requirements for relief of the commanding officer of a nuclear submarine is a turnover period of one month, which seemed a very long time considering the readiness of the crew and the superb administration of the command, but we had to follow the rules. Nate Heuberger and I agreed that the Change of Command ceremony would take place on January 22, 1977 in LaMaddalena, Sardinia, Italy where Seahorse would be undergoing a refit period alongside the submarine tender, the USS Howard W. Gilmore (AS-16). Normally a change of command is scheduled in the ship's homeport so that family, friends and other commands may attend the ceremony. When Nate had taken command of Seahorse in December of 1973, the ship had been surge deployed to the Mediterranean due to the Yom Kippur War and the subsequent Oil Crisis and he relieved as Commanding Officer on December 11, 1973 in Naples, Italy. So once again, only a few people would be present at a Seahorse change of command.

Piping Aboard

The change of command ceremony has been the same ritual for most of the history of our Navy. Our national colors are paraded and the national anthem is performed, followed by an invocation by a local chaplain. The outgoing CO makes his remarks to the crew and reads his orders, the incoming CO reads his orders and formally relieves the outgoing CO with a salute and the words, "I relieve you sir." The relieved CO returns the salute and says, "I stand relieved." The new CO reports his relief to the Senior Officer present, in this case, Commander Submarine Refit and Training Group, LaMaddalena, the Commodore, who then makes his remarks in praise of the performance of the just relieved CO. The Chaplain provides a benediction, and the ceremony concludes with the departure of the official party.

Following the ceremony, there was a reception for the guests and the crew, which was hosted (paid for) by the two commanding officers. As you can imagine, Nate and I did not have to lay out a lot of money for our "cake and cookies" reception.

Change of Command

Command at Sea

"Only a seaman realizes to what great extent an entire ship reflects the personality and ability of one individual, her Commanding Officer. To a landsman, this is not understandable – and sometimes it is even difficult for us to comprehend – but it is so!

A ship at sea is a different world in herself, and in consideration of the protracted and distant operations of the fleet units, the Navy must place great power, responsibility and trust in the hands of those leaders chosen for command.

In each ship, there is one man who, in the hour of emergency or peril at sea, can turn to no other man. One alone is ultimately responsible for the safe navigation, engineering performance, accurate gunfire and morale of the ship. He is the Commanding Officer. He is the ship!

This is the most difficult and demanding assignment in the Navy. There is not an instant during his tour as Commanding Officer that he can escape the grasp of command responsibility. His privileges, in view of his obligations, are almost ludicrously small; nevertheless, this is the spur, which has given the Navy its great leaders.

It is a duty which richly deserves the highest, time-honored title of the seafaring world – Captain."

Joseph Conrad
Command at Sea: the prestige,
privilege and burden of command

This quotation of the noted author and seaman Joseph Conrad was presented to me by COMSUBLANT upon completion of Prospective Commanding Officer training just before reporting to command of USS Seahorse. Framed, I now display it proudly next to a picture of USS Seahorse. Every past and present commanding officer of a ship in our Navy and of many of our allied Navies has been presented with the same quotation. In three words: Prestige,

Privilege and Burden, it sums up the unique experience of Command at Sea. An experience often called "the loneliness of command."

I was very fortunate to take command of USS Seahorse early in her Mediterranean deployment in January 1977. The ship had been well trained and "worked-up" for this deployment by my predecessor, Nate Heuberger and the Executive Officer, Bill Habermeyer. The Engineer Officer, the Navigator and the Weapons Officer were extremely well qualified and all would go on to very successful careers in the Navy when they left Seahorse. Though well supported, I really did sense the loneliness of command. There was no one to turn to for advice and counsel; the decisions on how the ship carried out its mission were mine.

Our mission for the next several months was to counter the growing Soviet submarine threat in the Mediterranean. Starting in the early 70s the Soviet submarine force started to deploy into the Mediterranean and for these attack submarines, it was their first significant deployment outside of home waters. On the other hand, for the last twenty years, U.S. submarines had routinely been conducting operations in the Barents Sea north of Murmansk, gaining a great deal of intelligence and operational experience against Soviet submarines. The commanding officers of the Soviet submarines in the Mediterranean were now gaining a great deal of operational experience primarily focused against our carrier task groups. In addition to our carrier task groups and logistics support ships, the U.S. maintained five attack submarines in the Mediterranean and generally one or two ballistic missile submarines as well. We had a submarine repair ship permanently stationed in LaMaddalena, Sardinia, Sixth Fleet headquarters in Gaeta, Italy, a large naval support base in Naples Italy, and a large Naval Air Station in Sigonella, Sicily. U.S. Navy ships routinely made port calls throughout the Mediterranean. In short, the U.S. had maintained control of the sea throughout the Mediterranean since the end of World War II; however the Soviet Navy, particularly the submarine force, was challenging this control and the underwater Cold War had a new battlefield, the Mediterranean.

Seahorse would be actively involved in operations against Soviet submarines in the Mediterranean for the rest of our Med deployment. It was a great way to start my tour in command. It wasn't too long afterwards that we would find our first Soviet submarine.

Victor Trail in the Med

In early February 1977, we were operating south of Sicily when we received a radio message from Commander Submarine Group Eight (CSG-8), the Admiral in Naples commanding submarines in the Mediterranean. Directed to proceed to the western Mediterranean near Gibraltar we were to intercept and covertly trail a Soviet submarine enroute from the northern fleet.

Undersea areas throughout the Mediterranean were allocated to specific submarines and this waterspace management was coordinated by CSG-8. This involved multinational cooperation as the U.S., Great Britain, France, Italy, Turkey, Greece and Israel all had submarines operating in the Med. Moving USS Seahorse from south of Sicily to the Gibraltar area involved routing us through several areas already allocated to other submarines. In some cases, other submarine areas were reduced in size to allow us to get by and in other cases; we were assigned to a deep zone (e.g. greater than 500 feet) to get through a specific area and the other submarine would be assigned to a shallow zone (e.g. less than 300 feet) in the same area. Obviously, Soviet submarines were not part of this waterspace management system.

The Soviet submarine being tracked in the Atlantic was a Victor class which was a second generation Soviet nuclear attack submarine, an improvement over their early submarines, but still quite noisy. It had been first detected just West of North Cape, which is the northern most point of Norway, by our underwater sound surveillance system (SOSUS) which is a vast array of hydrophones located throughout the Norwegian Sea and the Atlantic for the express purpose of tracking Soviet submarines. After detection by SOSUS, P-3 ASW aircraft flying out of Iceland were vectored out to establish contact on the submarine and track and identify the class of submarine with airdropped sonobuoys. Tracking of the Victor continued with SOSUS and P-3 aircraft flying out of the Azores and Spain.

Victor Class

Gaining passive sonar contact on a submarine passing through the straits of Gibraltar is a difficult task as there is a high concentration of shipping contacts in this vicinity. In fact, tracking submarines in the Med is challenging because of the number of interfering sonar contacts throughout. One advantage we had was that we knew the class of the submarine we were hunting (Victor Class) and had specific information on various sonar frequencies associated with this class. This allowed us to separate the wheat from the chaff.

Within about six hours of the projected time of arrival, sonar reported hearing compressed cavitation, generally associated with a Soviet submarine and we started picking up some of the typical Victor class frequencies. In about half an hour, we had an accurate bearing to the Victor and began maneuvering to close the contact and establish the range. After a few course changes across the contact's line of bearing we had enough information to establish the range as 8,000 yards or four miles and sonar also had a turn count on his propellers which gave us his speed as twelve knots. The only unknown regarding the contact was his operating depth and to reduce the risk of collision it was important for us to establish our depth different from his. Over the years of surveillance of Soviet submarines, we were confident that his depth during this transit was 100 or 150 meters and I directed the Officer of the Deck to establish our depth at 575 feet, well below his maximum expected depth. This depth separation issue would continue to be an unknown factor for the rest of the trail of the Victor.

Once we had established a solid trail deep in the Victor's port quarter at about 6,000 yards, we came to periscope depth to report by radio to CSG-8 that we were in contact and the course and speed of the Victor. Shortly after we returned to 575 feet, the Victor slowed and maneuvered to check for contacts and then went shallow. Our intelligence data indicated that this was a normal communications period for Soviet submarines in the Med. Our next communications from CSG-8 indicated that the other submarines operating close to our projected track had been alerted and had cleared the area so that we would not have to worry about submerged interference.

We stayed with the Victor for about ten days as he transited to the Eastern Med and then maintained loose contact with the carrier battle group for a few days. He then broke off and headed toward the Soviet surface support group for replenishment and we went on to Naples for a scheduled port visit.

Port Visit to Athens, Greece

In addition to our port call in Naples, Italy, USS Seahorse visited three other ports in 1977 during our 5-month deployment to the Mediterranean. We spent about three weeks in LaMaddalena, Sardinia where we were alongside the submarine tender USS Howard W. Gilmore for a scheduled upkeep period. We also visited La Spezia in northern Italy for a one-week port visit and Athens Greece for a 5-day visit.

Mary and our son Bill, age 10, flew out to Italy for a one week visit while were in La Spezia. It was Bill's spring break from school. We traveled by car from La Spezia to Florence, Pisa, Rome, Naples, Pompeii and the Amalfi coast. We crammed a great deal of sight-seeing into a five-day period and I dropped them off at the Rome airport for their return flight and drove back to La Spezia. We were underway the next morning. Little did we know that we would return to Italy as a family and spend two years in LaMaddalena and two years in Naples during the 1980s.

After extensive negotiations with the new government of Greece, a submarine visit to Athens was arranged and Seahorse was to be the first nuclear submarine to visit Athens in 7 years. We were not authorized to go into the port of Athens (Pireaus) and were assigned an anchorage about one mile south of Pireaus. After we anchored, the American Naval Attaché and his assistant came out to the ship and briefed us on the situation in Athens and Greece in general. He wanted us to be aware of heightened security throughout the country due to terrorist threats against the government and that our visit was getting a lot of negative play in the leftist press. The Naval Attaché accompanied me on a courtesy call to the Port captain of Pireaus who was very cordial, but he also warned me of the unrest, particularly in Athens. The liberty boat assigned to USS Seahorse was operated by the Greek Navy and operated from the Greek Navy base in Pireaus and the Captain recommended that our liberty party stay in the immediate vicinity of Pireaus and the nearby military establishments and not go into Athens. I asked him for a recommendation for a sightseeing trip away from Athens and he recommended the Poseidon temple about 45 miles south of Athens at Cape Sounion.

Poseidon's Temple

I returned to our shore patrol headquarters at the Pireaus Naval Base and using a ship-to-shore radio contacted Bill Habermeyer, my executive officer who was still on the ship. Given the potential unrest in Athens, and the fact that we were anchored in an open bay, I felt that one of us should be on board at all times. Bill agreed and volunteered to take the first day's duty. I told him about my planned trip to the Poseidon temple and I would call him in the afternoon when I returned. The Naval Attaché provided me with a car for the trip and his phone number if I needed any assistance. One of the junior officers from the Seahorse, Lieutenant Junior Grade Gordon Cremer, and I set out on our trip to Cape Sounion. We had lunch in a local restaurant in Pireaus. About 3PM, with Gordon driving, we had a car accident. We were in a small town, with narrow streets and no sidewalks and buildings built right next to the road. Gordon entered into a blind intersection slowly and a car coming from the right doing about thirty miles an hour smacked us. Fortunately, no one was hurt, but both cars had considerable damage. No one spoke English and we were surrounded by a growing mob of unhappy Greeks. An older gentleman approached me, who had a good command of English and offered his assistance. As the saying goes, "any port in a storm," and I promptly accepted his offer. The Police had arrived by then and the situation started to quiet down. With the help of my newfound friend, I was able to reach the Naval Attaché at home, he said to sit tight, and his assistant, LCDR Nick Glifadis would be with us in about 45 minutes. Nick, who was born in Athens, and was now an American Citizen, showed up on schedule and negotiated with the police and with the other party in the accident. He arranged to take care of the car we had been driving and told the Police that he would take responsibility for the safe return of Gordon and me to our ship. That seemed to satisfy the police and we left for Pireaus. In the meantime, the wind had really picked up and was blowing 30-35 knots in the bay. When I reached Bill Habermeyer by radio on board the ship he told me that all liberty boat runs had been cancelled and that heavy waves were washing over the deck of the ship. All the hatches were shut and the weather prediction was that this blow would last through the next day. Gordon and I had another day on beach! Nick invited us to his house for a great meal prepared by his Greek wife and insisted that we stay at his house that night.

We made it back to the Seahorse the next night and Bill Habermeyer and his duty section went on liberty the next day. As we were preparing to leave the day after, Nick came aboard and asked to meet with Gordon and me. He told Gordon that he had been charged with reckless driving and he had a court order for Gordon to appear in court in about three weeks. If Gordon did not appear, then a warrant for his arrest would be issued. Nick was sure that the lawyers at the American embassy would eventually resolve this case, but in the meantime, he encouraged Gordon to not visit Greece, as he would be taken into custody. About two years later, we received official notification that all charges had been dropped.

As a footnote to our visit to Athens, the unrest became violent in the 1980s and the American Naval Attaché, Captain George Tsantes was assassinated in 1983 and his successor, Captain William Nordeen was killed by a car bomb in 1988.

Keeping Banker's Hours on a Submarine

In April 1977, the Mediterranean deployment of USS Seahorse was ending. We were back in LaMaddalena, Sardinia, Italy for our last upkeep alongside the submarine tender, USS Howard W. Gilmore and we were enjoying a very nice spell of spring weather. One of the special features about LaMaddalena was the submarine officer sanctuary established by the first Commodore, Al Burkhalter. He had arranged for the Navy to lease a villa in the resort community of Porto Rafael, which is just across the water from the island of LaMadallena. The villa belonged to the Rook family who lived in England, and we called it "The Rook House." It had a great view of the islands of the LaMaddalena archipelago and had overnight accommodations for about ten. It provided an ideal sanctuary, away from the cramped living conditions on board a submarine.

View from the Rook House

On a very pleasant afternoon, the officers from Seahorse were enjoying a barbeque on the patio of the Rook House and I decided that it was an ideal time to find out their feelings about in-port working hours in Charleston, SC, our homeport. On my last tour in Washington, DC, I had been very involved in writing a legislative proposal for Congress to approve a special bonus for nuclear submarine officers to help solve a retention problem. Many submarine officers were leaving the Navy and our surveys indicated that one of their principal issues was the long working hours while in homeport which cut into their time to spend with their families. I opened the conversation by noting that we had all left the ship about 1500 (3 PM) and were enjoying a pleasant evening; wouldn't it be nice to be able to do the same thing once we got back to Charleston? This was followed by a long silence from the wardroom. Finally, one of the officers said that getting off the ship before 1800 was just not possible. I said that we had the same responsibilities and work load whether we were in Charleston or in the Mediterranean, yet we left the ship at 1500 today; what was the problem in Charleston? This observation got the conversation going and I heard a lot about the officer workload problems over the next few hours.

The difference between LaMaddalena and Charleston boiled down to significantly less external tasking while deployed, whereas in homeport, the officers had to deal with tasking from the local submarine squadron, COMSUBLANT and Naval Reactors, coordination with the shipyard, the Naval Supply System and many more agencies. By the time they had dealt with all the external tasking, they still had to complete their internal ship administrative assignments, which they would start at 1700 and then hope to finish by 1900 so that they could leave the ship and get home to a late dinner with their families. On top of these daily work load problems, the officers were required to stand in-port duty officer watches which amounted to one day out of every four or five during which they would spend the night aboard the ship. In fact, most of the officers used this extra time to catch up on the work that they had put off.

I asked them for their solutions to this problem, and to a man, they asked for more telephone lines to the ship. This was 1977, before cell phones, the internet and computers. We had four telephone lines: two in the wardroom, one for the CO/XO and one in the control room for use by the crew. During the day, these phones were in constant use and someone was always waiting to make the next call. I asked them if we needed more telephones when we were in LaMaddalena, they said no, as the phones were never busy.

I thought about our discussions overnight and the next day met with the wardroom and told them that my solution to the workload problem wasn't to get more phone lines but to reduce the external tasking to the ship. The way to do this was to cut off the phones after a certain time and to stop outside agencies from coming on board the ship after the same time. I went on to ask them if they had ever tried to go to the local bank after 1500 (remember this was 1977). Banks pulled down the shade on their windows and doors at 1500 and closed for business. That did not mean that they had all gone home. In fact, they had a great deal of internal business, balancing the books, counting their cash and locking everything up so that they could go home a 1630. I told them that we would be just like the First National Bank of Charleston and pull down that shade at 1500 by cutting off all phone calls (in and out) and restricting access to the ship so that we could all go home at 1630. The officers liked the idea, but felt that 1500 was too early and we compromised on 1600. When we got back to Charleston, I briefed the Commodore on my plans, and he agreed to support me and we put "banker's hours" into effect on USS Seahorse. It worked and I started to see the officers leaving the ship at a reasonable time. This solution worked then, but will not work today with our ever-expanding inter-connectedness with cell phones, smartphones and the internet. Even the banks have given up closing early. I am not sure that this is progress.

Homecoming to Charleston, South Carolina

USS Seahorse left the Mediterranean for our transit back to homeport in April 1977 and we returned to Charleston, South Carolina in early May on a glorious day. This was my first experience navigating Charleston harbor and the Cooper river up to the Naval Station (about 9 miles), so I requested a bar pilot whom we picked up before passing Fort Sumter at the entrance to Charleston harbor. The pilot had twenty years experience in Charleston and a wealth of information, which he passed on to me. Charleston has significant tides and the currents that can be very tricky to navigate, but I felt confident that I would be able to forego the services of a pilot in the future. The best time to make a landing at the Naval Station is at high slack water when the current of the Cooper river, is minimized. This requirement dictates one's arrival time at the Naval Station, which in this case was early afternoon.

The best part of this homecoming day for me was leaving the ship and coming home to our new house, which Mary transformed, from a sterile new construction house to a beautiful and warm family home. I was really taken with all she had accomplished. The transition from living in the cramped confines of a submarine for the last five months to finally being at home with my family was an experience that I will always cherish.

Wives and families were all there to meet us and it was a very emotional time for all as we reunited with loved ones. My 10-year old son Bill is in the foreground, he is now a Commander in the Navy.

Lieutenant (Junior Grade) Dave Alford completed his qualification in submarines and the Commodore and Dave's wife Mary pinned on his new dolphins.

We were met by the Commodore of Submarine Squadron FOUR, Captain Claude C. Cross and the Commander of Submarine Group SIX, Rear Admiral Stan Anderson.

Midshipmen Training

After the USS Seahorse returned from its Mediterranean deployment in May 1977, we were in port for about a month and then commenced three weeks of Midshipmen training operations. During the summer after their sophomore year in college, NROTC and Naval Academy midshipmen receive indoctrination training in Naval Aviation, the Marine Corps and submarines. We took twenty-five midshipmen to sea for two and a half days and then another twenty-five for the second half of the week. In order to provide berthing for the midshipmen, we had to leave to leave twenty five of the crew in port which meant that most of the crew stood port and starboard watches (six hours on and six hours off) at sea. This added workload on the crew and the officers concerned me, but we were able to rotate other crewmembers ashore during subsequent weeks.

On the first day at sea, we submerged and conducted submerged operations, battle stations with simulated torpedo firings, casualty drills and general submarine indoctrination. On the second day at sea, we conducted an emergency surfacing evolution and then spent the remainder of the day on the surface. I had remembered my midshipman submarine indoctrination twenty years earlier in 1957 on the USS Entemedor, a diesel submarine and the special time we had on the bridge with the skipper, Commander Joe Skoog, shooting sharks with an M-1. That special one-on-one time with the skipper made a real impression on me, and I wanted to duplicate that for the midshipmen on Seahorse but I knew that we would not be able to shoot sharks. The Gulf Stream of the Atlantic Ocean off the coast of Charleston is a deep blue and generally quite calm in the summer. Standing on top of the sail, twenty feet above the surface of the ocean with the submarine doing 15 knots is quite an exhilarating experience. The wind is in your face, there are generally dolphins leaping in and out of the bow wave, which piles up on the deck just forward of the sail and the ship leaves a wide white wake astern for about half a mile. There is no noise from the submarine, just wind and the waves breaking over the bow. This is a unique experience to submarines; unlike any that, I have had on surface warships, and I wanted to share this experience with the midshipmen.

USS Seahorse on the surface

We conducted man-overboard drills, using a dummy in a life jacket nicknamed "Oscar." When a ship has an actual man-overboard, it flies a special signal flag which stands for the letter "O" which is "Oscar" in the military phonetic alphabet, hence the name Oscar for our man overboard dummy. We had two midshipmen on the bridge with me, one to conn the ship and the other to observe and then to conn the ship on the next run. I explained to them that there were three standard maneuvers to return to the spot where a man fell over the side. A "Williamson turn", in which the ship turns right or left 60 degrees and then reverses the rudder to the opposite direction and turns 240 degrees until it is on the reciprocal from the original course to return to pick up the man in the water. The second is a circle turn in which the ship makes a full circle to return to the man in the water. The third is a Y-backing maneuver in which the ship turns 60 degrees and then backs down with opposite rudder and then maneuvers to pick up the man in the water. I left it up to the individual midshipman to decide which maneuver to use. A 6,000-ton submarine has a lot of momentum and it takes a long time to stop it dead in the water. This was a difficult aspect of ship control for the midshipmen to master. Directing the ship from the top of the sail via a microphone to the helmsman who was stationed below in the control room was also a challenge for many of the midshipmen.

Each evolution required twenty to thirty minutes and with twenty-five midshipmen, we spent most of the day conducting ship-handling training. I shared my time on the bridge with the executive officer, Bill Habeymeyer. We both felt that it was time well spent, as we were able to have quality time with each of these young officer trainees. Many of the midshipmen remarked at the end of the week, that this experience was the highlight of their summer training.

Passing on a Seagoing Heritage

During the summer of 1977, USS Seahorse conducted local operations in waters off Charleston, Florida and the Bahamas. We conducted three weeks of Midshipmen training and were one of the school ships for Prospective Commanding Officer training, so I saw two ends of the spectrum; young officer candidates and experienced submarine commanders about to go to their first command. In addition to taking these individuals to sea, I was able to take two very special people, my ten-year-old son Bill and my 72-year-old father, Peter T. McKinney.

My son in the galley

My father at the periscope

Bill went to sea for a week during the midshipmen-training phase. The Chief of the Boat, Master Chief John Shettles also had his son aboard for this week. The two boys were assigned to mess cooking duties in the galley and were responsible for setting up the mess decks for each meal, washing the dishes and general cleaning under the supervision of the leading cook. The crew was well aware of who these youngsters were and I was assured that they "cut them no slack." Bill spent a great deal of his spare time on the bridge watching man overboard drills and by the end of the week his "page boy" haircut was in complete disarray with his hair permanently windblown and plastered to the side of his head with salt spray. Some of this experience must have made an impression, as he went on to graduate from the Naval Academy and is now in command of a Trident submarine, USS Wyoming (SSBN 742).

In September, Seahorse was assigned to make a port visit to Fort Lauderdale, Florida and then conduct operations on the underwater tracking range (AUTEC) in the Bahamas. I invited my father to ride the ship from Charleston to Fort Lauderdale, which is about a 24-hour trip.

My father grew up as a boy in Sault Ste. Marie, Michigan and spent his teenage years (early 1920s) as a deck hand on freighters carrying iron ore from Duluth to Gary, Indiana and Cleveland, Ohio. After he graduated from the University of Michigan in 1927, he shipped out as an Able-bodied Seaman on ocean-going freighters and made several trips to Europe and through the Panama Canal to Australia. By 1930, he had satisfied his wanderlust and settled down in New York to work in a bank on Wall Street. As I grew up, I would hear his stories of adventure on the high seas, which included a visit to Pitcairn's Island where the mutineers from HMS Bounty finally settled in 1789. The descendents of the mutineers and their Polynesian wives are still living on this remote Pacific island. My father's stories had a great deal to do with my seeking out a seagoing career.

When we left the Navy base in Charleston, my father was on the bridge with me and he was as thrilled as I was for us to be together on a glorious late summer day on our way to sea. After we cleared the harbor, we went to the wardroom for lunch with the rest of the officers and later on in the afternoon, we submerged with my father controlling the fairwater planes during the dive. He had never been aboard a submarine at sea and this was a great moment for him and for me. I then directed the officer of the deck to conduct some large angle depth changes (30 degrees up and down) and some high speed turns to demonstrate the underwater maneuverability of a nuclear submarine. After dinner, we played some cards and watched a movie and then Dad went to bed as we had an early breakfast the next day so that we could surface the ship and arrive at Fort Lauderdale on time.

Taking both my young son Bill and his grandfather to sea that summer on the submarine that I commanded was a once in a lifetime experience for me. The seagoing heritage that my father passed on to me, I was able to pass on to my son that summer. It just doesn't get any better than that.

Life Raft Race

After our visit to Fort Lauderdale, USS Seahorse was assigned to support the operational evaluation of another submarine about to deploy to the Mediterranean. The other submarine conducted tracking operations of Seahorse on the Atlantic Undersea Testing and Evaluation Center (AUTEC) range off Andros Island in the Bahamas. We spent three days on this exercise and the other submarine then departed for other operations. We had about six hours before we were to start our transit back to Charleston, SC. The Chief of the Boat asked me if I would authorize a swim call for the crew. I thought this was a great idea, and after we surfaced, we found that the weather was ideal, 85 degrees with a slight overcast and virtually no wind.

As we were rigging, a cargo net over the side of the ship so that the swimmers could get back aboard, I asked the First Lieutenant if he had recently tested our life rafts. He told me that they were due for an inflation test in three months, and I told him that I was concerned about whether they would pass this test and that I would like to test them today. He gave me a funny look and then it dawned on him that I wanted to use the life rafts today as part of swim call and the life rafts were promptly delivered topside.

A submarine carries two inflatable four-man life rafts, which is clearly not enough for a crew of 135 men. A submarine has two escape hatches and if the submarine is sunk in relatively shallow water (less than 400 feet) then it would be possible for the crew to make an emergency escape to the surface. The two life rafts are stored at the escape hatches. An ascent to the surface from 100 or 200 feet is dangerous but possible. A few might survive an ascent from 400 feet. Survival from deeper than 400 feet is unlikely. Nuclear submarines operate in deep ocean water (greater than 1,000 fathoms or 6,000 feet) almost all the time. If the submarine suffers a casualty causing it to sink, then all hands would be lost. Carrying a life raft is about as useful as carrying parachutes on a modern jet passenger plane, but nevertheless we still carry two life rafts which as far as I know have never been used in an emergency.

As we inflated the life rafts, the crew gathered around wondering what was up. I explained that I had heard the nuclear engineers bragging about their ability to paddle a life raft and that they had challenged all comers to a race. Well, it didn't take long for the operations/weapons (ops/weps) personnel to accept the challenge, and the race was on. I then explained the rules. The race was one lap around the ship and would be a relay race. Each team would have two sets of crews of five men each—four men to paddle the raft and one to steer. The race would start port side amidships, proceed down the port side of the ship, around the stern and back up the starboard side. When the life raft reached amidships, the next crew would enter the water and exchange places with the crew in the raft and continue the race around the bow, returning to the finish line on the port side amidships.

Life rafts at the starting line

The race started with both rafts even at the start. The engineers had quickly figured out how keep the life raft going straight, and by the time they got to the stern of the ship, they had a commanding ten yard lead. As the life rafts came up the starboard side of the ship, the engineer relief team was ready to go into the water. I told them to wait until I told them to go in.

When the engineers' raft reached us, I told the ops/weps team to go in the water, and they didn't hesitate.

The engineers cried foul "Captain you made a mistake, that's our raft." I replied, "I know that, this is to even up the race."

Well, it did more than even up the race. The ops/weps personnel were doing their best to sabotage the engineers' raft and by the time the engineers got in the water, the ops/weps raft had arrived and the engineers went after it. Both rafts were deflated and semi-submerged and neither one made it around the bow, much less to the finish line. The race was officially declared a tie and a great success by all hands.

The Continental Shelf

USS Seahorse was heading back to Charleston, SC from our visit to Fort Lauderdale, Florida and the Bahamas. This would be my last period at sea in command of Seahorse for the next year and a half. We would be entering Charleston Naval Shipyard in November 1977 for an extended nuclear power plant refueling and overhaul that was scheduled for eighteen months. The shipyards were having a hard time keeping up with the number of overhauls scheduled for submarines and the conventional wisdom was that our overhaul could easily extend to two years. This was not news that I wanted to hear.

About 2400 we were entering, the Charleston submarine operating areas, which are, located about 60 to 100 miles off the coast of South Carolina. This is because the continental shelf extends out from the coast a considerable distance and the water over the shelf is too shallow to operate nuclear submarines. George Voelker, the engineer officer had requested that we conduct about 4 hours of full power (flank speed) operations to collect and record required pre-overhaul data on the engineering plant. I wrote my night orders directing the OOD to obtain a navigational fix to confirm our position in our assigned submarine operating area and then to conduct flank speed operations at 600 feet in accordance with the engineer's requirements.

About two hours later, I woke up to the vibration of the ship, which is normal at flank speed. I rolled over to glance at the remote log reading above my bunk to confirm the speed and then stared at the compass repeater that indicated we were on a course of 300 headed directly at the continental shelf. This got my attention and I got out of bed and went into control, which was just forward of my stateroom. I asked the OOD what were his intentions. He responded that he planned to continue to close the coast until we were 20 miles from the shelf and then reverse course. His plan was to time his course reversals so that when the full power testing was done, we would be close to the coast and we would surface and proceed on the surface to Charleston. Not a bad plan, but not what I had in mind when I wrote my night orders. I realized that I had not been specific enough in what I wanted.

A submarine is blind when submerged and running at high speed. The sonar system is designed to detect the noise made by other ships and does not detect shallow water. The fathometer is used to detect the depth of water, but the fathometer installed in Seahorse in 1977 was an older model, which was not effective at high speeds. So the OOD's plan was based solely upon the known position of our navigation fix obtained several hours earlier. We were operating in the Gulf Stream where the currents were unpredictable and strong. To add to my uncomfortable feeling was the news that a sister ship of ours, the USS Ray (SSN 653) had just run aground while transiting at flank speed in the Mediterranean. She had apparently hit a submerged seamount that was well known with an accurately plotted position.

I directed the OOD to change course 90 degrees to the right (030) so that we were paralleling the coast of South Carolina and to not close the Continental Shelf, keeping us at least 30 miles off, reversing course as necessary to remain within our designated operating area. It was his lack of experience and my error in not being more specific in my night orders that led to this situation.

About three months later, USS Ray returned to Charleston after a surface transit across the Atlantic and went into drydock near Seahorse in Charleston Naval Shipyard for replacement of her sonar dome and extensive repairs to her bow. She was in drydock for over a year. The junior officer who was the OOD from the Continental Shelf experience and I toured the Ray's drydock and viewed the incredible damage to the sonar dome. It was a lesson learned and reinforced for both of us.

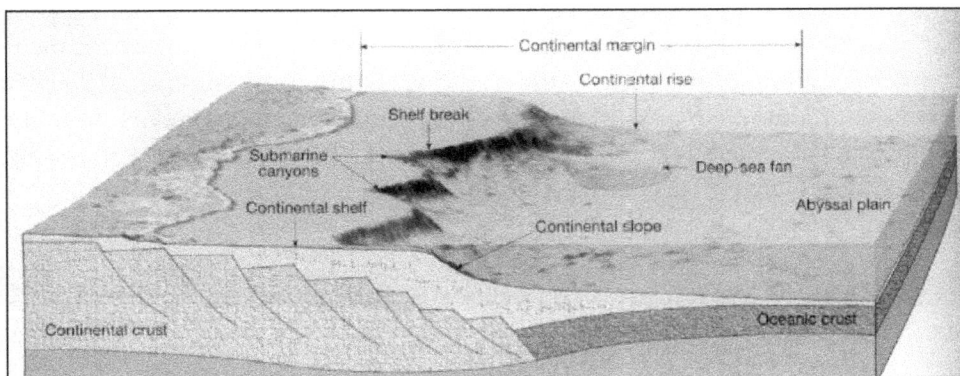

Continental Shelf

Preparations for a Refueling Overhaul

October 1977 was spent alongside the pier preparing to enter Charleston Naval Shipyard for a refueling overhaul. The nuclear reactor core would be replaced by a new advanced core, which would last more than twice as long as the first core. In addition, a new digital computer aided sonar would be installed and a new digital torpedo fire control system would be installed on the ship. Major equipment in the engineering spaces were either replaced or removed and overhauled. In essence, Seahorse would leave the shipyard after eighteen months as a completely updated and modernized submarine fully able to match the capabilities of any of the newest Los Angeles class submarines that were under construction at that time.

The control room, sonar room, sonar equipment space and sonar dome would have the majority of equipment removed and then reconfigured to accommodate the new equipment to be installed. The ship would be in drydock for about a year with large holes cut in the hull in strategic locations to allow for equipment removal and installation. A reactor access house was built over the reactor compartment to accommodate the refueling of the reactor. All access to this house was by a tunnel connected to a building next to the drydock to ensure security in this area and to monitor for potential radioactive contamination. The crew was moved off the submarine to live in shore-based accommodations and we were provided with a special support barge next to the drydock for office space, workshops and a galley for meal preparation. All spare parts were removed from the ship for a special inventory and upgrading with new spare parts integrated into the inventory to support newly installed equipment. In short, the crew was very busy throughout October preparing for our move into the strange industrial environment of a shipyard.

In early November, two tugs took us under tow and moved us from the Naval Station to Drydock #2 in the shipyard. After we were placed over the keel blocks in the dock, the caisson was put in place and the shipyard docking officer lined up the ship in the dock and started the process of pumping out the dock. Once Seahorse was firmly in place and resting on the keel blocks, there was not much to see and I was ready to go over to the support barge to have lunch. The docking officer advised that he would not put over a gangway so that we could leave the ship until the dock was pumped dry and that would take another three hours. There were three officers as well as myself trapped on the ship, so we decided to play a game of Uckers, which is a board game, a sort of simplified form of Parcheesi, which we all enjoyed. Unfortunately, the Uckers board was on the support barge. We spotted LTJG Ben Morgan, our supply officer, on the drydock wall and told him our problem. Ben didn't need any more direction and ten minutes later, he was giving directions to the drydock crane operator, who responded by attaching a small parcel to his giant hook designed to lift loads of fifteen tons. The parcel was swung over to the deck of Seahorse. Inside the parcel, we found our Uckers game, sandwiches and soft drinks.

We retired to the wardroom for lunch and spent the next few hours playing some spirited games of Uckers. An inauspicious start to our overhaul.

USS Seahorse in drydock the day after docking. The shipyard was already placing scaffolding around the ship. In two weeks, the ship would be completely covered and unrecognizable.

My First Christmas in Charleston

USS Seahorse had started its shipyard overhaul in early November 1977, and we wouldn't be going to sea for another year and a half. So what is a submarine crew going to do during this period? As it turns out, there is lot for a submarine crew to do during overhaul. Even though most of the work on the ship is the responsibility of the shipyard, the crew is still responsible for certain reactor plant systems and safety of the nuclear reactor. The ship still is the responsibility of the crew and ship cleanliness in an overhaul is a never-ending problem. Early in the overhaul period, there is a great deal of flame cutting of the hull to provide access to equipment that needs to be removed. Members of the ship's crew are assigned as fire watches for each flame cutting and welding operation to ensure that a fire is not started. These are tedious watches, but essential for ship safety.

The biggest concern of mine was the training of the crew. Over one third of the crew would be rotated off the ship during this period and their replacements would need extensive training and indoctrination so that when we left the shipyard, we could safely operate the ship. In addition, the new advanced digital sonar system and fire control system would require extensive training for the entire attack party (Officers, sonarmen, fire control technicians, quartermasters and electronic technicians) in the operation of these new systems and new procedures for Battle Stations. Finally, during every overhaul, Naval Reactors required that all nuclear power plant watchstanders complete an extensive basic engineering requalification program and we would have an exam conducted by Admiral Rickover's staff before we started up the nuclear reactor and conducted power range testing. In short, we would be very busy for the next year and a half.

Fortunately, I had been the director of the Officer's Department at Nuclear Power School for two years, and was very well grounded in nuclear reactor theory and nuclear power plant engineering. This background allowed me to conduct a series of seminars on the theoretical aspects of nuclear engineering for the officers and senior enlisted personnel in the engineering department. Most of the material was supposed to be review for the officers and new for the enlisted personnel, but I was to find out that the officers had forgotten much of what they were taught at Nuclear Power School, so these seminars were valuable for all. I liked this approach of combining officer and enlisted training and I extended it to the training sessions that we were to have on the new sonar and fire control systems. My goal was to have the best-trained and knowledgeable crew to have completed an overhaul, and a year later, I believe that we had achieved that goal.

Seahorse was deployed in the Mediterranean for Christmas 1976, so this was a special time for all hands to be home for Christmas 1977 with our families. The shipyard had a stand-down for two weeks over Christmas and we had a liberal leave policy for the crew. It was the first Christmas for Mary and me in our new home, and we enjoyed making this a special Christmas for our children, Bill (10) and Beth (5).

Beth decorating the tree

Bill decorating the tree

As you can see from the pictures, decorating the Christmas tree was one of the highlights of our Christmas celebration.

How does Santa Claus get into a Submarine?

We were having dinner on Christmas Eve when our five year old daughter Elizabeth, who we called Boo asked me that question. Before answering, I looked across the table at Mary, she smiled, but I could tell that this question was definitely one that I was expected to answer. Our ten-year-old son Bill had long ago figured out who Santa Claus really was and if I didn't respond quickly to Boo's question, he would be all too happy to tell her the real story of Santa Claus.

I looked at Boo and asked her, "Why do you ask sweetheart?"

She said "Daddy last Christmas you were gone at sea in your new ship, the Seahorse, and we had Christmas with Grandfather and Grandmother and Santa Claus came to their house. Did he come to the Seahorse too?"

"Yes he did." I replied. "After dinner we will read *Twas the Night Before Christmas* and hang our stockings and before you go to sleep, I will tell you how Santa Claus visits a submarine." That seemed to satisfy her for the time being, and it gave me some time to come up with a plausible story that would make sense to a five year old. I also had a word with Bill and told him that he was to keep his thoughts on this subject to himself, or else he would find some coal in his stocking tomorrow morning. He got the message.

We all sat before the fire and I read *Twas the Night Before Christmas* and then we hung our stockings and before I carried Boo up to bed I told her how Santa visits a submarine.

I started "When Santa visits our house tonight he will have a sleigh pulled by eight tiny reindeer. When Santa visits a submarine, he has a special boat pulled by eight seahorses."

"Just like your Seahorse Daddy?" Boo asked.

"Yes, but much smaller." I replied.

"But how does he get into the submarine? You don't have a chimney and a fireplace."

"That's right, but what we do have is a snorkel."

"What's a snorkel Daddy?"

"Remember when we go to the beach and Bill and Daddy put on face masks and put a long tube in our mouth and then swim in the water looking at the fish? Well that tube allows us to breathe and it is called a snorkel tube. A submarine has one just like it, only bigger, so that the men inside the submarine can breathe air from above the water even though the submarine is under water." Boo let out a big yawn and I could tell that I was about to lose my audience.

"On Christmas Eve, the submarine goes very slowly and listens for Santa's sleigh bells."

"Are the bells on the seahorses?" Boo asked sleepily.

"Yes they are. As soon as we hear them, the submarine comes up near the surface and raises the snorkel. Santa comes aboard down the snorkel and quickly goes through the ship placing gifts in all the stockings hung by everyone's bed. We never see Santa, but we do hear his laughter as he runs through the ship. When he's finished, he goes up the snorkel and sonar reports hearing the bells fade away and then a voice saying "Merry Christmas to all, and to all a good night."

Boo drifted off to sleep with visions of seahorses in her sweet little head.

Beth wondering about Santa

Split Rail Fence and a Split Phone Line

An obvious advantage of being assigned to a Navy ship in overhaul in a shipyard is that you are home every night and on the weekends. It is almost like having a civilian job. My next-door neighbor, Phil Sawyer, was in charge of the local J. C. Penney store and we would see each other in the morning as Phil went off to his store in the Northwoods Mall and I went off to my ship in the Charleston Naval Shipyard. We would see each other on the weekends as we worked in our yards. Both houses were brand new, and there was a considerable amount of work to complete the landscaping around the houses. We both felt that a split rail fence around and between our back yards would be an attractive addition and we agreed to share the costs and labor to install the fence.

The split rail fence posts and rails were delivered a few weeks later and on Saturday, Phil and I measured off the property lines and determined where we would place the posts for the fence. The soil was sandy and soft, so that we would have no difficulty digging the postholes. Before starting, we checked to see that electric power was provided to our two houses by overhead power cables. The water supply was from the water main near the street in the front of the house and would not be a problem for our digging in the back yard. So we went to work digging our postholes and setting the fence. By five o'clock that afternoon, the job was done.

It occurred to me that I had not received a phone call from the duty officer on the ship at any time during the day, which was not normal. Cell phones did not exist then (in 1978) and there was only one way for him to call me. I went inside the house to check our phone, and sure enough, there was no dial tone. I asked Phil if his phone was working, and it was. It was obvious that we had cut my phone line when we were digging one of the postholes, but the problem was, which one was the culprit.

Phil and I did a more thorough search of the back property line and found the telephone connector box hidden behind a bush. We then sighted a straight line from the connector box to the phone connection on my house and noted that one of the new fence posts was smack dab on this line. In removing the fence post, and cleaning out the excess dirt in the hole, we came across the remains of about ten inches of telephone cable cut when we installed the post. Expanding the hole, we were able to locate the other two ends of the phone cable buried about 18 inches underground.

At that point, I probably should have called "Ma Bell" (as we referred to the phone company back then). And asked them to come out and repair my phone line, but quite frankly, as the Commanding Officer of a nuclear submarine and the manager of the local J. C. Penney store, Phil and I were too proud (and embarrassed) to admit that we made such a bonehead error. So we went down to the local hardware store and bought a length of phone cable, spliced and restored the existing cable. The post went back into the same hole with the phone cable slightly offset. I tested the phone, called the ship and contacted the duty officer who was wondering where I had been all day. I told him that I had spent the day shopping at J. C. Penney with my wife and then had gone on to a movie.

I have often wondered if, after thirty years, my splice to the telephone cable, for the house at 25 Bainbridge Drive in Charleston, South Carolina, is still holding up. Maybe I should call the current residents.

First Prize at the Submarine Birthday Ball

On April 11, 1900, the United States purchased its first submarine from inventor John Holland. This submarine was ultimately named the USS Holland (SS 1), and the birthday of the submarine force is celebrated on April 11. The typical celebration is a Submarine Birthday Ball, separate Officer and Enlisted Balls during most of my career, but now these birthday celebrations are combined. The Submarine Birthday Ball is a formal affair, the men in formal military attire and the women in long gowns. In addition to a great meal and a military band for dancing, the most recently qualified submariner and the longest qualified submariner cut a submarine birthday cake.

The officer Submarine Birthday Ball in April 1978 was at the Charleston Naval Base Officer's Club. My wife Mary and some of the Seahorse wives were planning our table decorations and she asked me for any ideas I might have. I thought something that included a seahorse would be appropriate. As we discussed this idea further, we hit upon the idea that Charleston was well known for its horse-drawn carriage rides of the historic downtown of Charleston. A Charleston carriage pulled by a team of seahorses would be a unique table decoration.

The judges of the table decorations thought so as well, and we were awarded first prize, which was six bottles of wine. We finished off our prize by offering toasts to all of the other submarines in the squadron and by the end of the evening, a few of the junior officers were feeling no pain. I wouldn't say that we were the rowdiest table at the ball as we had competition. We were lured into a dinner roll fight by the officers of one our sister submarines, the USS L. Mendel Rivers (SSN 686) and by the time the dinner rolls stopped flying, most of the other submarine tables had joined in. The next day, the Commodore had both Ray Jones, the skipper of the Rivers and me to his office for a dressing down. Because of our shenanigans, both wardrooms were assigned tables in the back room at the next birthday ball. Ray and I felt that we had a reputation to uphold after this event and we continued our friendly rivalry for the remainder of our command tours.

I have attended many submarine birthday balls from New London, Connecticut, to LaMaddalena, Italy to Pearl Harbor, Hawaii, but this particular submarine birthday celebration stands out as one of my favorites.

Seahorse officers, wives and girlfriends show our winning table decoration and the three wives responsible for it: Mary, Marty Troutman (Navigator's wife) and Karen Mullins (Weapons Officer's wife). One of the bachelor junior officers, Don McCamey is holding the remains of our first place prize.

Uckers and the Port Visit of HMS Conqueror to Charleston

HMS Conqueror, a Royal Navy nuclear submarine, made a port visit to Charleston in 1978, and USS Seahorse was the host ship for the visit. We were still in the shipyard and I welcomed the opportunity to break out of the shipyard routine for a week and enjoy our counterparts in the Royal Navy. My experience with the HMS Dreadnought in Guam had taught me to expect a full social schedule, as the "Brits" know how to enjoy themselves in port.

As always, the "Brits" enjoy upstaging the Yanks by holding a cocktail party on their submarine, as they know that we are not allowed to have alcohol on our ships. That was OK with me, as I have always enjoyed a good party no matter who the host is. The Commanding Officer of HMS Conqueror was Commander Roger Trussell, and although I had not met him before, we got on very well as we planned his social calendar for the next week in Charleston. After the cocktail party on Conqueror, the Commodore of our Squadron, Claude Cross, had invited all to his quarters for another cocktail party on the next evening. We planned a couple of nights on the town as well as tours of Fort Sumter and the local plantations. Our last evening would be a party at our home for both wardrooms and other invited guests. I happened to mention that the wardroom of Seahorse enjoyed the game of Uckers and asked Commander Trussell if his wardroom was up to a challenge match. He didn't need any encouragement as he immediately responded that the officers in his wardroom were some of the top Uckers players in the Royal Navy and would enjoy showing us upstart "Colonialists" how the game should be played. The next night at the Conqueror cocktail party there was considerable bantering between the two wardrooms regarding our upcoming Uckers competition and this kept up for the remainder of the week.

At this point, I will digress from the story of the Charleston visit of HMS Conqueror and provide a little background and insight into the game of Uckers. It is a board game played with dice, which was developed by the Royal Navy in the early 1900s from the game of "Ludo" which was a children's version of the Indian game of Parcheesi. It is very popular in the Royal Navy, particularly in the submarine force, and many U.S. Submarines have picked up the game from our British counterparts. I had never seen nor played the game before I reported to Seahorse, but in my first year in command I had become a great fan of the game and always found time to play a game with the officers of Seahorse after lunch. Four players, two on each team, play the game and the members of a team cooperate in moving their pieces around the board attempting to block the other team from advancing their pieces. The object of the game is for a team to get all of its pieces home before the other team. It is really a simple game and one learns the rules without any difficulty. Rule number 1 of the game is my favorite; "The Captain is always right."

Although the rules are straight forward, the strategy of how to beat your opponent is complex and subject to endless debates by the players in the game and by those watching the game. In fact, this aspect of the game is the most enjoyable for me as everyone has an opinion on each move as the game progresses and I would encourage these opinions from all watching the game. If we had senior guests in the wardroom, senior captains or admirals, they were encouraged to play the game, and many times a junior ensign would provide his unsolicited opinions and advice to an admiral. Although, the ensign was respectful to the Admiral, and didn't call him a "knucklehead" for a bonehead play, it became clear to the Admiral that he had a lot to learn from the ensign. I have much the same feeling today when I have to ask my children how to solve a problem that I am having with my computer.

Commanding Officer, Commander Dennis Murphy of the USS Tucson (SSN 700) and his executive officer playing a game of Uckers with two submarine commanders from the Chilean submarine force in 1999.

The Anglo-American Submarine Uckers Championship

My wife Mary and I had invited both the wardrooms of HMS Conqueror and USS Seahorse for a pizza party at our home. In addition to the wardrooms, the British Naval Attaché and his wife from Washington and some of his staff attended as well as our commodore and his wife and all the wives and girlfriends from Seahorse. All told, about 40 people were included. I was just finishing making 20 pounds of pizza dough and Mary was cooking the tomato sauce when the front door bell rang and our daughter Boo answered the door. The next thing that we heard was an excited Boo running through the house telling us at the top of her voice "Captain Conqueror is here!" Boo was convinced that Roger Trussell was some sort of comic book hero named Captain Conqueror, and we didn't want to disappoint her so we played along with her fantasy and of course, Roger enjoyed his hero status.

Once all our guests arrived, I explained that we would provide the wine and beer and other beverages for the evening, but it was up to the guests to make pizzas for all to enjoy. In addition, those making the pizzas would be identified by wearing their choice of hats, which I provided from my collection of hard hats from the shipyard, midshipman hats and assorted hats from Halloween parties. The Brits enjoy wearing odd hats and they were first in line to make pizzas.

As you can imagine forty people fill up a house rather quickly, but we had them evenly spread through the family room, the dining room and the living room, with those making pizzas in the kitchen. Compared to the crowded conditions for the cocktail party on HMS Conqueror, we all fit rather comfortably.

After two hours, all the pizzas had been cooked and consumed, Roger and I got together to set up the Uckers match that would decide the Anglo-

American submarine championship. The British team was headed up by "Knuckles" Smith, the First Lieutenant (Executive Officer) on Conqueror. I am not sure why he was called "Knuckles" but Roger indicated that the nickname came about from a small altercation between two sub-lieutenants ten years ago. Our engineer officer, George Voelker, headed up the American team. Roger and I met with the team captains and we agreed upon the rules of the game. The biggest problem we faced was Rule Number One...The Captain is always right. We finally decided that as the "Home Team" Commanding Officer that this privilege was mine and all would accept my rulings in case of controversy.

After the Uckers game got underway, there was a good deal of interest in the competing teams' strategy and tactics and a great deal of advice, both good and bad, given to both teams. After about a half an hour of watching the game, I could tell that this was going to be a long and close game and I went off to join a group around the piano singing English drinking songs. Ten minutes later, I was called back to the Uckers match. George Voelker reported to me that he had just caught "Knuckles" Smith cheating. He had moved one of his playing pieces ten squares and the roll of the dice was eight. "Knuckles" response was that was right, he always cheated with the count if he could get away with it. He maintained that it was part of the game. Well I was shocked! I had never heard of such under-handed and disreputable play, particularly in my home, where this behavior might influence my children. I asked Roger if he supported this type of skullduggery in his wardroom. Roger said that they always cheated playing Uckers, didn't we? I said no, never in Uckers, but we always cheated playing Cribbage. Roger said that they never cheated playing Cribbage, as that was a gentleman's game. Well, we were at an impasse and the only way out of it was to invoke Rule Number One. So I told the players that no cheating was allowed for the rest of the evening. There was some grumbling from the Brits that the Yanks were taking unfair advantage of them, but Roger reminded them of the agreement we had made on Rule Number One.

It was a close finish, but Seahorse emerged victorious and claimed the Charleston Anglo-American Submarine Uckers Championship. We were to maintain this championship title throughout my command of Seahorse and defend the title on a later visit to Portsmouth, England, but that is another story.

Plank Owner or Keel Owner

Shipyard overhauls are not a positive experience for submarine crews. The ship is uninhabitable; the crew lives, eats and has office space on a temporary living barge. In addition to the shipyard work going on, the crew is responsible for several maintenance jobs on the ship, and an extensive retraining and requalification program for the entire crew is mandatory. The nuclear reactor was replaced with a new core and new instrumentation. The operation and testing of the reactor and engineering plant at the completion of the overhaul is the responsibility of the crew, and considerable training is devoted to ensuring that the officer and enlisted nuclear-trained personnel are ready to safely operate the nuclear power plant. We would have a formal examination by Admiral Rickover's engineers before we would be allowed to operate the reactor plant.

In the late spring of 1978, I was inspecting the shipyard work in the drydock, underneath the hull of the ship. I came upon a stack of lead blocks that puzzled me. I asked the ship superintendent what the lead was for and he replied that the lead had been removed from the ballast tanks where it acts as additional ballast for the ship. That made sense to me, as the overall weight of a submarine has to be carefully monitored to ensure that it can maintain neutral buoyancy in all circumstances. During overhaul, much equipment is removed and replaced and these changes in weight will affect the buoyancy of the ship. Adjustments are made by adding or removing some of the lead ballast. The ship superintendent then went on to tell me that all the lead was removed from the ballast tanks during drydocking as the area underneath the lead blocks was subject to corrosion and needs to be inspected and re-preserved. That got me to thinking about "Plank Owners."

There is a tradition in the Navy going back to the wooden sailing ships of the 1700s in the Royal Navy and the American Navy that the members of the commissioning crew of a new ship were designated "Plank Owners" which, loosely translated, meant that they each owned a plank of wood of the ship. Even though today's warships are made of steel, the "Plank Owner" tradition carries on. Seahorse was not a new ship, and would not be re-commissioned at the end of the overhaul, so we could not designate our crew as "Plank Owners." But the lead that I was looking at in the bottom of the drydock, and there were tons of it in sight, gave me an idea. A submarine doesn't have a keel as it is a circular hull, but the lead came out of the bottom of the ballast tanks, and if a submarine did have a keel, that is where it would be, at the bottom of the ship. Why not use some of that lead to create some type of memento to present to the overhaul crewmembers and designate them as "Keel Owners?"

COMSUBLANT had set aside some discretionary shipyard man-hours that I could use for ship improvement and morale items. I needed to develop my ideas as to some type of memento involving the lead ballast. At first I thought of casting a small lead seahorse memento, but that would be complicated and not something that the shipyard could accomplish. I asked the Captain of one of the submarine tenders in Charleston and he seemed to feel that some of his machine shop personnel would have some ideas, and he would get back to me.

A Keel Owner Solution

About two weeks later, the captain of the submarine tender asked me to come down to his ship to see what his machine shop gang had created. They had machined the inverse image of the Seahorse seal into a hardened steel billet and then set up a hollow cylinder above the seal in which they placed a lead disk and then using a sledge hammer, hit the top of the lead disk and the image of the ship's seal was impressed into the lead disk. I was very impressed with the quality of their work and that they had designed this device so that I could make these ship's seals at home. My next step was to ask the shipyard to make 200 lead disks that I would make into replicas of our ship seal. Two weeks later, I had 200 disks in my garage and I started the process of stamping out the ship's seal on these disks.

Although the image of the seal was clear on the lead disk, I decided that I could enhance the image if I painted the image with the colors of the ship's seal. This would take a lot more time, but if I worked at it on the weekends, I could paint ten seals on a Sunday afternoon and in five months, all the seals (200) would be done. So I set to work in the summer of 1978 and was finished by Christmas. I then asked the submarine tender to mount the lead disk on a block of wood and make plaques for the "Keel Owner" and the details about the overhaul. The finished products were very handsome and in late May, after the overhaul was complete, I held quarters for the crew and gave each crewmember a "Keel Owner" memento. I had an extra thirty keel owner blocks and I asked the crew to nominate shipyard workers who made a difference in the quality of our overhaul, and I would personally present keel owner blocks to each. The next week I walked through the shops in the shipyard, made these presentations, and thanked them for a quality overhaul.

Crew Picks a Slogan for USS Seahorse

As we neared the end of our overhaul in Charleston Naval Shipyard in the spring of 1979, several members of the crew approached me with a proposal that we adopt a slogan for the ship. I thought that this was a great idea, and I asked this group to form a committee to come up with a proposal for a slogan. I appointed the Executive Officer, LCDR Bill Habermeyer, to head the committee.

Many good ideas came in from the crew and after a few weeks, the slogan committee had narrowed it down to two slogans: "Thoroughbred of the Fleet" and "A horse you can BET on". I liked both slogans as each emphasized the "horse" in Seahorse and they both spoke of the quality of the ship and crew. I had badges made for each of the slogans and passed them out to the crew and asked them to wear their favorite badge and after a week, we would have a vote as to which slogan was preferred. We held a vote and 75% of the crew liked the "Thoroughbred of the Fleet." I then had 500 bumper stickers made up and sold them to the crew at cost. Our slogan was the envy of all the other submarines in Charleston.

The slogan was so popular that the USS Kentucky (SSBN 737), which is a Trident missile submarine, adopted it years later. Seahorse had been decommissioned in 1995, and USS Kentucky is still in commission and will be for another 15 or 20 years, so our slogan that the crew of USS Seahorse created in 1979 will be honored for several more years. The legacy of the "Horse" lives on in USS Kentucky.

THOROUGHBRED of the FLEET
USS SEAHORSE SSN 669

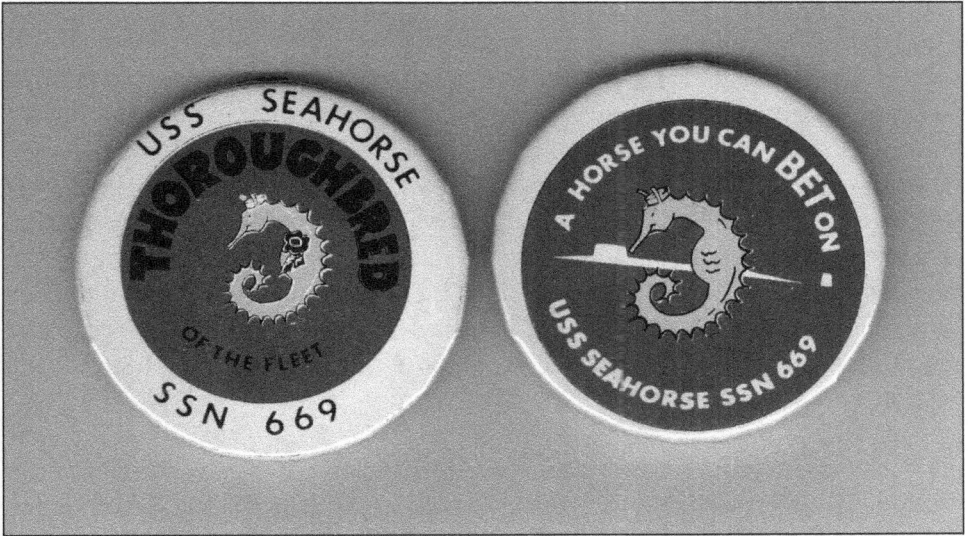

Post Overhaul Sea Trials

USS Seahorse went to sea in early May 1979 for sea trials after completion of our refueling overhaul. It had been 18 months since my crew had operated a submarine but we had been training several months to meet this challenge. The first test was our initial dive. Lieutenant Dave Alford was the diving officer and he was responsible for figuring out the compensation of the ship to achieve neutral buoyancy when were submerged. This was a monumental task, as he had to figure all the weight gains and losses that had occurred during our shipyard period. I told Dave that if he got within 15,000 pounds I would present him with a bottle of the finest single malt scotch. Within 10,000 pounds would be two bottles of scotch.

We submerged very cautiously, and because of the uncertainty of our compensation, the ship was 50,000 pounds lighter than Dave's calculated compensation. Well, we didn't get below 50 feet keel depth, so gradually started to flood water into our variable ballast tanks and the ship responded by slowly going deeper. The whole process took an hour or so, but we finally achieved perfect trim at zero speed and then took accurate readings of our variable ballast tanks. The variable ballast was 12,000 pounds more than Dave had figured and I owed Dave a bottle of scotch when we returned to port. This was quite an achievement on Dave's part. The shipyard calculation was off by about 30,000 pounds.

We were now a submarine again and back in our element under the sea, but we had a lot more to do during these sea trials. The next step was to progressively increase our depth to test depth (greater than 800 feet, the actual test depth is classified). At every 200 feet, we would hold and check all sea water systems for leaks. Once at test depth, all seawater valves were cycled to ensure operation and timed to ensure they met design specs. The torpedo tubes were operated and their launching mechanisms were tested. Torpedoes were loaded into the tubes and removed to ensure the proper clearances of the tubes under full submergence pressure.

During this phase of sea trials we had a surface escort and we were restricted to operate in a relatively shallow area off of Charleston where the depth of the water was about 300 feet deeper than our test depth. This restriction was to ensure that if we had a flooding casualty, the ship would not sink below a depth where the pressure hull would collapse.

Once we had completed all of our required testing at test depth, we released the escort ship. We then conducted a full power run followed by an emergency engine reversal to ensure the operation of our nuclear power plant.

We tested our new sonar system in all phases of operation and all the hydrophones for grounds and continuity. All radio antennas were checked for grounds and at periscope depth all antennas and periscopes were raised, lowered, and timed to make certain that they met specifications. The ship's atmosphere control system was tested and air borne contaminates evaluated.

Our last evolution of the sea trials was to test the emergency ballast tank blow system. This system is vital to the safety of the submarine in a flooding casualty. Operated from the control room, when the system is activated, high-pressure air is admitted into the ballast tanks, forcing out the water in the tanks and the ship gains positive buoyancy quite rapidly. The evolution commences from a depth of 400 feet with the ship doing 20 knots. The emergency blow valves are opened and the ship immediately starts to rise, but this is counteracted by the diving planes that are placed at full dive. After about 10 seconds, the diving planes can no longer hold the ship at 400 feet, and they are shifted to full rise and the ship's up angle is controlled at 30 degrees. Ten seconds later, the ship breaks the surface of the water quite spectacularly, and the evolution is completed.

Emergency Surface

Sea Trials were a complete success and we returned to Charleston with a broom tied to our periscope indicating a "clean sweep" which was a signal of a successful submarine war patrol during World War II.

Beach Towels and Sunscreen in the Engine Room

On a Saturday in early June 1979, we departed Charleston for Groton, Connecticut. USS Seahorse was scheduled for two weeks of refresher training starting on Monday at the U.S. Naval Submarine School. Although we had been to sea for our sea trials and had demonstrated our ability to operate the ship at sea, we had yet to operate our sonar and fire control systems in a combat environment. The sonar watch standers would need a lot of training on the new sonar system and our battle stations team had a lot to learn about our new fire control system. The emphasis during our two weeks of Sub School training would be in these areas.

We surfaced on Sunday morning and it was a beautiful warm sunny day. George Voelker, the engineer officer was the officer of the deck and I directed him to conduct some man-overboard drills for training of our newly reported junior officers. The propulsion plant was put through its paces as the ship was backed down in order to stop and then ordered ahead full speed to make another try at "picking up Oscar" our fictitious man overboard.

After two hours of thrashing around with the man overboard drills, we resumed our transit to Groton for a scheduled arrival time of 1300. Shortly after we resumed our transit, George Voelker got a call from the engineering officer of the watch that there was sand in the engine room collecting around and underneath the "tail shaft." I relieved George as Officer of the Deck so that he could lay aft to investigate. He came forward 10 minutes later and confirmed the report and said "Captain, be sure to bring your beach towel and sun-screen to the engine room because we are creating quite a beach in the shaft alley!"

Each time the shaft made a revolution, it sprayed out some sand from a coupling just aft of the thrust bearing. I ordered the main engines stopped, and George Bardsley, my new executive officer, George Voelker, our Chief Machinist's mate and I had a conference about what to do. We had all read about the incident on USS Tullibee (SSN 597) the previous June when the tail shaft snapped and the propeller with part of the tail shaft attached pulled out of the stern of the submarine. The precursor to this tail shaft failure was sand in the engine room.

The tail shaft about 30-feet long is hollow and connects the propeller to the main turbines and the reduction gear. The outside of the cylindrical shaft absorbs the torque on the shaft and the interior is filled with sand to dampen out vibrations. The USS Tullibee had cracks in the tail shaft due to a corrosion problem and seawater was leaking into the tail shaft and forcing the sand out into the engine room. Our tail shaft had been removed and completely refurbished as part of our overhaul and I doubted that in the two months that we had been out of the drydock that we had corrosion problems that would have caused cracking of the tail shaft. There had to be another explanation. The sand problem did not show up until after the man overboard drills this morning. Did our engine maneuvering during these drills cause the problem? I didn't know, but what I did know was that I had to contact COMSUBLANT and advise the engineers on the staff of our problem and get some advice on how to proceed.

We had just upgraded our communications system during the overhaul so that we could contact COMSUBLANT by secure voice transmission on a communications satellite, which enhanced a rapid turnaround to our request for advice. Cell phones still didn't exist in 1979!

The duty officer at COMSUBLANT patched me through to the engineers in Washington who concurred with me that it was unlikely that we were about to suffer a catastrophic failure of the tail shaft such as occurred on USS Tullibee, but they did advise caution on overstressing the shaft during the remainder of our transit to Groton. We kept our speed down to a stately 7 knots and entered port at 1500. Ironically, our berth assignment was across the pier from USS Tullibee.

Next, the mystery is solved.

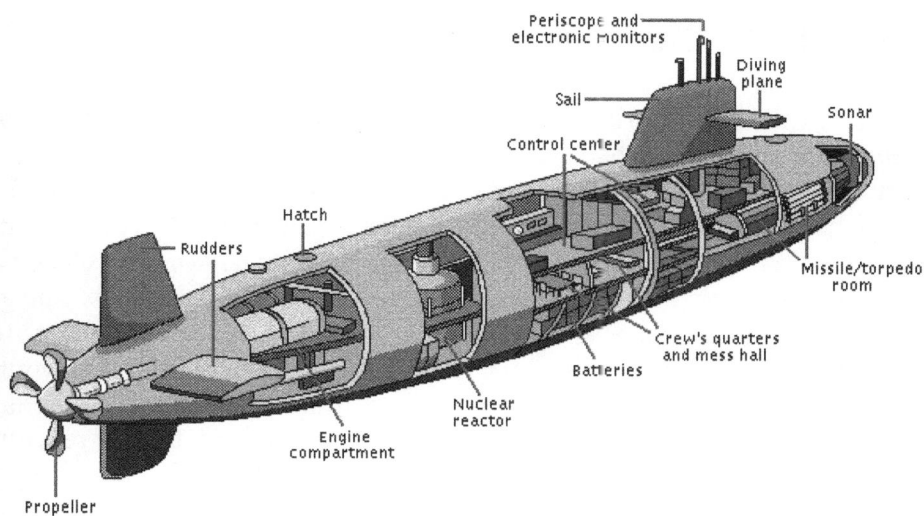

Periscope and electronic monitors

Diving plane

Sail

Sonar

Control center

Hatch

Rudders

Missile/torpedo room

Crew's quarters and mess hall

Batteries

Nuclear reactor

Engine compartment

Propeller

Typical Submarine cutaway diagram

The Tale of the Seahorse Tail Shaft

We arrived at the Submarine Base, Groton, Connecticut on Sunday afternoon in early June 1979 and had quite a welcoming committee to discuss our reported problems with our tail shaft. There is not a lot of room in the after part of the engine room and there wasn't much to see other than a pile of sand under the tail shaft, but all of our official visitors had to have a look. Once the "looking" was over, we got down to laying out a plan of action. We would go into drydock on Tuesday and on Wednesday commence removal of the propeller and evaluation of the tail shaft. Charleston Naval Shipyard would provide their engineers and shipyard workers to do all the work on the tail shaft as it was assumed that our problem was related to the recently completed overhaul in Charleston.

As we worked out the plan of action, I had to remind all that we were in Groton to conduct much needed refresher training and I did not want to lose valuable training time. All agreed and it was decided that once we established nuclear power plant conditions for dry docking, most of the officers, the sonar operators and key battle stations personnel would be available for training. This meant that we would lose a few days of training and we would extend our stay at the submarine base to make up the lost time.

Monday was a full day of getting the ship ready to go into drydock, and early Tuesday morning, at slack water, we transferred from alongside the pier to the floating drydock Shippingport (ARDM 4). By midday on Wednesday, the propeller was removed by crane and we could examine the end of the tail shaft.

The tail shaft is 30 inches in diameter and there is a plug at the end of the hollow shaft to keep the sand in the shaft and the seawater out. The plug was gone and we were looking at a 12-inch hole where the plug was supposed to be. The plug had been threaded into the hole at the end of the shaft and "staking screws" should have been in place to prevent the plug from coming loose. There were no staking screws and no sign that they had ever been installed. It became clear that we had lost the plug during our maneuvering on man overboard drills on Sunday, as that was when we first saw the sand accumulating in the engine room. In hindsight, it was fortunate that we conducted the man overboard drills when we did and then remained on the surface afterward. Had we submerged, the increased sea pressure would have caused minor flooding in the engine room.

This incident should never have happened, as there is a very careful check of all submarine systems and components with inspectors verifying every step in the manufacturing process. Clearly, someone had dropped the ball on the inspection of the tail shaft. I never did hear the outcome of the investigation conducted by Naval Sea Systems Command, but it was clearly a wakeup call for all concerned.

The replacement of the tail shaft is not a simple job and the shipyard spent about two weeks getting it done right. As a result, our two-week training session at the submarine school was extended by a week, but we made good use of the additional time and we left with a much improved battle stations team.

Gone Fishing

After our refresher training at Submarine School in Groton, Connecticut and an unexpected dry-docking to replace our defective tail shaft, our next post overhaul evolution was sound trials in Exuma Sound near Cape Eleuthera in the Bahamas. I had been there before as a trials supervisor for the sound trials of the USS Cincinnati (SSN 693) and had discovered that there was some good fishing for Mahi Mahi available in Exuma Sound, and I thought that we should take advantage of this opportunity if possible.

Sound trials involve running the submarine at various speeds, with various machinery operating, past a series of hydrophones suspended from a noise monitoring ship. The monitoring ship is MONOB I, the acronym standing for MObile NOise Monitoring Barge. The noise levels emitted by the submarine are recorded and analyzed by engineers on MONOB, which is moored to a buoy in the middle of Exuma Sound. Exuma sound is 60 miles wide. There is lots of maneuvering room for a submarine, and Exuma sound is surrounded by islands and reefs which reduces the background noise from the ocean--perfect for sound monitoring. The depth of water is over 6,000 feet. The buoy that MONOB is moored to is in the middle of the sound and the buoy has an anchor chain and cable that extends 6,000 feet to the ocean floor.

I found out on my previous trip that the fishing for Mahi Mahi was particularly good around the buoy as there was a natural habitat for fish developing around the anchor chain. MONOB was normally berthed in Palm Beach and when it was operating on sound trials, the MONOB crew not involved in the trials spent all their time fishing for Mahi Mahi and when MONOB returned to Palm Springs, they sold their catch to the local up-scale Palm Beach restaurants.

MONOB

I called SUBLANT Operations and asked about the schedule of the MONOB. It was currently in Palm Beach and not scheduled to get underway until our sound trials next week. I asked for an early arrival on the sound range one day before the arrival of MONOB to allow for some surface ship handling drills. No problem for SUBLANT as a submarine just out of overhaul needs as much training as possible. I told the Chief of the Boat about my plans and asked him to arrange for our deep-sea fishermen to bring their fishing gear with them for this trip and also that the cooks should bring two Weber grills, just in case, we were successful.

When we arrived in Exuma sound, the water was nearly flat calm and it was a beautiful day. The crew was allowed out on deck and immediately wanted to have a swim call. I told them to wait to see how the fishing went. The first two fish that we landed were four-foot sharks and the interest in swim call promptly evaporated. The officer of the deck asked me what I wanted him to do. I pointed at the buoy and told him to troll past the buoy at about three knots. He gave me a funny look and said that he never expected to go trolling for fish on a nuclear submarine. I told him to relax and enjoy the day and not to come too close to the buoy. A collision with a buoy can ruin your whole day.

We caught a few Mahi Mahi, but not enough to feed the crew, so we broke out the Weber grills and had steaks grilled to order and Mahi Mahi as an appetizer. The crew enjoyed the day on the surface, that night the Chief of the Boat figured out how to rig the movie projector topside, and we enjoyed a movie under the stars. The next day MONOB arrived, we got down to work in earnest, and we ran sound trials around the clock for the next four days.

Mahi Mahi also called Dolphin

Dodging Hurricanes David and Frederick

How close can you get to a Category 5 Hurricane? If you are on a nuclear submarine, the answer is 300 feet. What's that you say? Impossible? Too dangerous! If you were on a surface ship, then anywhere inside of 50 miles from the eye of the hurricane means some rough seas and high winds. But in a submarine, at 300 feet beneath the surface, with the storm raging above you, the submarine may experience a few 10 or 15 degree angles, but other than that, the ride is pretty comfortable. At 500 feet, even the angles disappear.

In late August 1979, USS Seahorse was in the Caribbean for weapons systems accuracy tests. Our first stop was Roosevelt Roads Naval Station, on the eastern end of Puerto Rico. We offloaded our warshot torpedoes and took aboard a full load of instrumented exercise torpedoes. Technicians conducted a series of alignment checks to certify the alignment of our periscopes, sonar and torpedo tubes with our gyrocompass. After the alignment checks in Roosey Roads, we were scheduled to operate on the underwater weapons range off St. Croix, about fifty miles southeast of Puerto Rico.

Hurricane David

I had been watching the development of a major Hurricane (named David) headed our way. "David" was bore sighted on St Croix and Puerto Rico and would arrive in two days. Our weapons system tests were postponed and we got underway to find deeper and safer water north of Puerto Rico. The next day, the wind and seas really started picking up and I made the decision to seek a more comfortable ride at 300 feet. Hurricane David passed south of Puerto Rico that night, with the eye of the storm about 80 miles away. The next day we proceeded through the Mona Passage, then south of Puerto Rico and on towards St. Croix.

The winds were quite calm, but the seas were still running a significant swell of twenty feet. About 15 miles from St. Croix, we surfaced the ship and manned the bridge. As we approached Frederiksted on the western end of the island, there was no sign of life, no traffic seemed to be moving on the roads and we could see considerable storm damage. The pier, where major passenger ships moored, was destroyed. I was reminded of the scene in the movie *On the Beach* as the nuclear submarine approached the city of San Francisco, which was a ghost town after a nuclear war and all of humanity in the northern hemisphere had been killed by radiation. It was a spooky feeling. We called the weapons test range on the radio with no response. Finally, sonar reported contact with the test range on underwater communications. They had seen our approach and told us that they had suffered considerable flooding and wind damage to their buildings. Power was out all over the island. They were using batteries to contact us on their underwater circuit. They did not envision weapons testing for another few weeks. I thanked them for their support and wished them good luck with their recovery efforts.

I then contacted COMSUBLANT in Norfolk on satellite voice radio to request further instructions and clearance for submerged operations. But before I could get on the circuit, it was already in use and I recognized the familiar voice of Commander Ralph Tindall, the commanding officer of USS Dace (SSN 607). Ralph reported that the Dace had suffered a major air conditioning failure and requested a port call to Roosevelt Roads Naval Station. Temperature in the engineering spaces was 135 degrees and his watchstanders were suffering severe heat exhaustion. I then checked in on the radio circuit, explained our situation, and volunteered to follow Dace into Roosevelt Roads and assist. An hour and half later we moored across the pier from USS Dace and Ralph Tindal was the first across the brow. I asked what we could do to help and Ralph said that he could use all the qualified nuclear power plant watch standers I could afford to let him have. Our engineering plants were very similar, there would be no problem in certifying their qualifications, and I sent over 25 nuclear qualified personnel. I kept back a skeleton crew as we had to keep our reactor up and running because the limited shore power in Roosevelt Roads was necessary to shut down and cool down the reactor plant in Dace.

Two days later, the situation was stabilized on the Dace and just in time too, as Hurricane Frederick was on its way following the same path as David, and Seahorse got underway for storm evasion. We left several qualified nuclear watch standers in port to continue assistance to the Dace and we returned two days later. Fortunately, Fredrick was much weaker than David, which had been a Category 5 storm, with winds of 175 mph and the strongest storm to strike the Dominican Republic in recorded history. Over 2,000 people died from this storm in the Dominican Republic.

Reenlistment Ceremony in a Life Raft

USS Seahorse was completing our unscheduled port visit in Roosevelt Roads Naval Station in Puerto Rico in late September 1979 after dodging hurricanes David and Frederick, and scheduled to return to our homeport of Charleston, SC. We were to get underway in the afternoon and George Bardsley, my executive officer, asked me if I would reenlist Petty Officer Steve Centore, a nuclear reactor operator, before we got underway. I said that I would be happy to, but could we wait until after we got underway for Charleston. George said he didn't think so as there was an additional request from Centore. He wanted to be reenlisted in a four-man life raft. That would be a first for me. I had conducted reenlistment ceremonies on the top of the sail, in a torpedo tube, at test depth, but never in a life raft. I said that I would be happy to accommodate Centore's request and asked to have the crew topside at 1300 to witness the reenlistment ceremony.

A good part of the crew was topside to witness the ceremony. I had already made it into the life raft and was waiting for Petty Officer Centore to join me. The crew was enjoying the day but anxious to leave Puerto Rico. When Petty Officer Centore got to the life raft, I administered the reenlistment oath:

"I, Steven Centore, do solemnly swear that I will support and defend the Constitution of the United States of America against all enemies, foreign and domestic; that I will bear true faith and allegiance to the same; and that I will obey the orders of the President of the United States and the orders of the officers appointed over me, according to the regulations and the Uniform Code of Military Justice. So help me God."

After administering the oath, I asked Centore if he was ready to take a swim. He wasn't too sure and told me that he wasn't a strong swimmer. I told him that if he didn't, I was sure that the crew would toss him in anyway, and I recommended that he follow me in and then hold on to the life raft. I went in by falling backwards into the water, and Centore followed me but kept a firm grip on the life raft. Within a few minutes, the rest of the crew topside stripped down to their skivvy shorts and enjoyed a swim as well.

After fifteen minutes of swim call, I told the executive officer to station the maneuvering watch and we were underway for Charleston thirty minutes later.

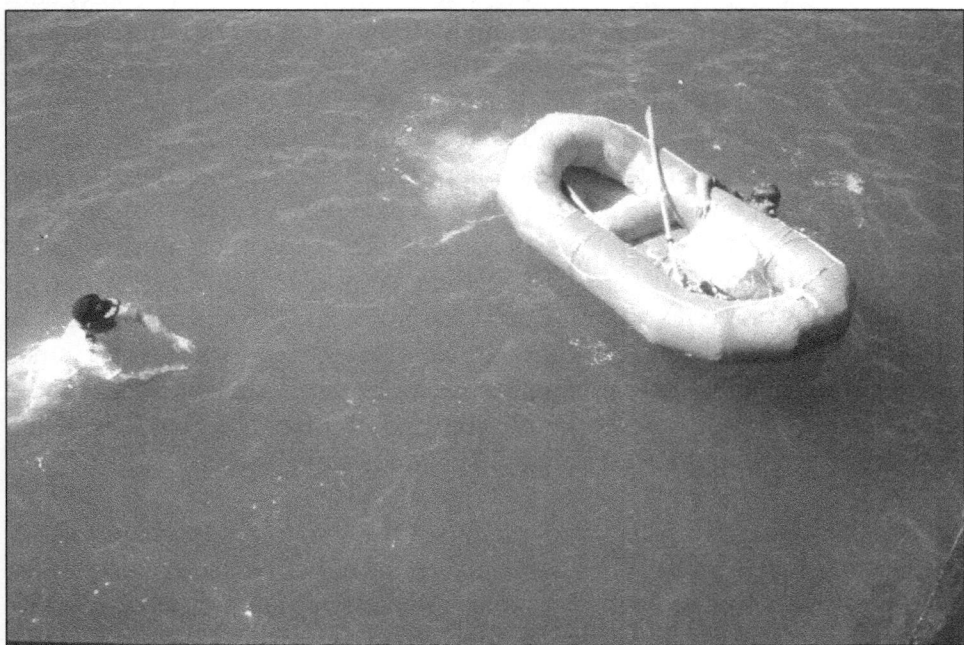

Operational Reactor Safeguard Examination (ORSE)

After our post shipyard trials and evaluations were completed, USS Seahorse returned to our homeport of Charleston, SC in early September 1979 for some well-deserved rest for the crew, as this had been an intensive at sea period that started in April. Long range planning had scheduled us for a six-month deployment to the Mediterranean the next summer, but COMSBLANT changed that schedule and we were now to deploy in April 1980 to conduct special operations observing Soviet Naval training in the Barents Sea, north of Murmansk. Because of the long winters north of the Arctic Circle and winter ice conditions, the Soviet Navy was very limited in training opportunities and April was a prime month to begin their training cycle. It was one of the best opportunities to observe their operations. I was very pleased that Seahorse had been selected to conduct this mission, but we had a lot of work ahead of us to prepare for this operation.

At the top of the list was our Operational Reactor Safeguard Examination (ORSE) conducted annually to evaluate the training, material condition and proficiency of the crew to safely operate a nuclear power plant. We had last had an ORSE in 1977, before the shipyard-refueling overhaul, so we had a lot of training to accomplish in the next six weeks to prepare for this exam. George Voelker, the engineering officer and George Bardsley, the executive officer and I put together our plan of attack. Voelker with an assist from Bardsley would concentrate on casualty drills and operations, Voelker and his key division officers and leading Petty Officers would work on administration, material condition and cleanliness and I would concentrate on training. We had been working on all these areas consistently since completing the shipyard overhaul, but we knew that added emphasis would be necessary if we were to show our best for the Nuclear Propulsion Examining Board (NPEB) who would conduct the ORSE.

Nuclear power plant operations are the key to a successful ORSE, particularly a well-trained crew that can respond effectively to casualty drills. To develop this well trained crew takes time and repeated drills at sea. Our operational schedule had been very intense and as a result, I did not feel that we had devoted enough time to operational casualty drills. I was sure that the crew would be able to pass the ORSE, but we would not achieve the highest standard. On the other hand, we had worked very hard on level of knowledge in preparation for our Naval Reactors crew exam before we could start reactor plant operations during our overhaul, and I felt that I could build on that success in preparation for the ORSE. I had been involved in nuclear engineering training as the Director of the Officer Department for almost three years at Nuclear Power School and I knew that I could conduct a strong training program for the officers and leading petty officers. This training effort would filter down to the rest of the engineering department.

The submarine squadron provided several experienced trainers to assist us in our final at-sea preparations. The squadron's deputy for training, Commander Tom Evans and I both felt that we were ready for the ORSE.

We returned to Charleston, met a Navy tugboat near Fort Sumter, and transferred the NPEB from the tug and returned to sea. The senior member was a post commanding officer of a submarine, assisted by three Lieutenant Commanders who had all served as nuclear submarine engineering officers. The rest of the day was spent reviewing engineering administration, conducting written and oral exams of all the nuclear watch standers, conducting a material and cleanliness inspection of the nuclear engineering plant. The next day was a drill day and each of the three engineering watch sections were evaluated conducting casualty drills including a reactor scram, fire, flooding and radioactive spills. We returned to port the next day and the NPEB completed their review and deliberations and then gave us their evaluations of our examination.

The ship is evaluated in several different areas, including operations, level of knowledge, material condition, and administration. There were no numeric grades, rather descriptive evaluations of Excellent, Above Average, Average, Below Average and Unsatisfactory. Unsatisfactory in any category is an automatic failure and the ship must return to port and shut down the reactor and then go through an extensive retraining program with another ORSE scheduled about a month later.

USS Seahorse received Average evaluations in all categories except Level of Knowledge, where we received an Excellent, with an overall grade of Above Average. The senior member remarked that this was an unusual situation as generally, the grade in Operations drove the overall grade, but in our case, the Level of Knowledge of the crew was exceptionally high and that convinced the board that our overall grade was above average. I was in no position to take issue with this evaluation and was certainly pleased that my efforts in training had paid off. I was very proud of my crew's performance.

Predeployment Preparations

As the saying goes, "Always save the best things for last!" and that was just what happened during my three and a half years in command of USS Seahorse. My last year in command saw us complete a very successful refueling overhaul in the spring of 1979 followed by about four months of post-overhaul shakedown and training operations and then in the late fall of 1979 we started training, preparations and certification for a special operation to be conducted in the spring of 1980. Submariners use the expression "Special Operations" to describe a classified mission that entails covert intelligence collection and surveillance. During the Cold War, these operations were conducted principally against the naval forces of the Soviet Union.

We were scheduled to conduct a surveillance mission in the Barents Sea in April. This is a traditional time for the Soviet navy to conduct training operations after a long winter. The area is north of the Arctic Circle so by April and May there is considerable daylight and by June the sun never sets. Even though this area is just north of the Soviet Union (Russia), all the operations are conducted in international waters and although the Russians don't like our presence, in their "back yard", we are not violating international law and they conduct similar operations in our operating areas off Norfolk. They also routinely have intelligence collection ships off Cape Canaveral to observe our submarine ballistic missile tests.

To prepare for this mission, we took USS Seahorse to Groton, Connecticut in January for two weeks of intensive work-up training at the submarine school. During this period, the officers and members of the fire control and tracking parties went through refresher classroom training and then spent a considerable amount of time in trainers and simulators where we refined our skills making periscope observations and conducting tracking and trailing operations of surfaced and submerged contacts.

The submarine periscope is a critical sensor for a submarine. It not only provides an opportunity to view other ships and aircraft in the immediate vicinity, but it has special electronics sensors that provide for the analysis of all electronic transmissions in the area. This includes early warning of threat radars as well as intercept of all radio transmissions. The periscope also allows the submarine to take high-resolution photographs of ships and television recording of events observed such as missile launches and gunfire exercises. Officers are trained in the use of the periscope as junior officers and by the time, they have reached command they have become quite proficient.

When observing ships in a close-in situation, one has to be very careful for time that the scope is above the surface and how much of the scope is exposed (generally only one or two feet). The standard is to limit observations to six seconds. The reason for this standard is that most surface radars have a sweep rate of 10 revolutions per minute. The periscope is a small target, but it is still detectable on radar, but if it is seen on one sweep of the radar and not on the next, it is likely to be seen a "noise" by the radar operator.

When observing a surface ship, the officer on the periscope (approach officer) calls out "target, bearing mark" and the true bearing to the target is entered into the computer, Then he calls out "range, mark, 1 (or 2.5, etc.) divisions in High Power" and after another few seconds to observe the target he lowers the scope. He then announces "Angle on the bow, starboard 30 (or port 45, etc.)" The periscope assistant then announces the range, which is computed from a formula using the masthead height of the target and the number of divisions seen by the approach officer. This range is entered into the computer and the angle on the bow is entered. The angle on the bow (AOB) is the angle that the bow of the target makes with the line of sight from the periscope. For instance if the target is headed directly at the periscope, the AOB would be zero. If you see the target on the beam, then the angle would be port or starboard 90.

As these observations are made over a period, the computer is able to generate a solution for the target's course and speed. This procedure was standard during World War II and is still in use today. There are no active radar transmissions from the submarine; all information is obtained passively so that the submarine minimizes the chance of counter-detection. Of course, the target is also being tracked passively by sonar and a target course and speed solution is generated and compared to the visual observations.

Training and evaluation of our attack team was conducted in an attack trainer that simulates the actual control room of a submarine. As is obvious from the picture, the attack center is crowded and teamwork is essential to solve the problem. After we mastered observations on one target, multiple targets were inserted into the problem as well as randomly maneuvering targets. The level of threat radars are increased as well as active sonar searches. The increased complexity of the surface picture is designed to prepare us for what we will be up against during our special operation.

Submarine Attack Center

Predeployment Preparations – Part 2

In addition to the intensive attack center periscope observation drills that the USS Seahorse attack team was put through at submarine school, we were also evaluated on our ability to conduct trailing and surveillance of submarines. On the mission that we were preparing for, we would be primarily focused on surveillance of Soviet submarines with particular attention paid to new construction submarines that might be observed conducting sea trials. The objective of these operations was to evaluate and record on passive sonar all the sound signatures of individual submarines. The sonar tapes would then be analyzed after our mission was completed and these sonar signatures would be placed in a data bank so that these submarines could be identified in future encounters.

Trailing of another submarine is a difficult task and requires a great deal of teamwork and training to conduct this type of operation successfully and safely. Training and evaluation in the attack teacher at submarine school is the first step in preparing for this mission. Later we would conduct trailing operations at sea with another U.S. submarine.

Once initial contact is made on another submarine, various early maneuvers are required to establish the range, course and speed of the target submarine. Then Seahorse would maneuver to gain a trailing position astern of the target submarine. Not directly astern, but 20 or 30 degrees on either the starboard or port quarter. Directly astern, there is a stern null in the target's sonar signature, which makes maintaining contact difficult. By staying on the quarter of the target, you are able to maintain good contact and you are in his sonar-baffled area, so that it is unlikely that the target would be able to counter-detect.

There are two other immediate concerns: Trailing range and own ship's depth. Trailing range is a function of the target's noise level and the target's speed. Noisy targets allow for a longer trailing range. Higher target speed also dictates a longer trailing range so that we would have more time and distance to react to any maneuvers by the target. Newer Soviet submarines were a good deal quieter than the early submarines, which meant that in order to maintain contact, we would have to reduce the trailing range. If the ambient noise level, due to other shipping and heavy sea state, was too high and the target was quiet, then trailing range would be reduced to a point that the risk of collision or counter-detection was too great and we would not be able to safely trail the target submarine. These were decisions that I would have to make as Captain. In addition the selection of own ship's depth was an important safety decision, as you did not want to be at the same depth as the target submarine. The problem in this decision was that we rarely knew what the depth of the target submarine was. In general, Soviet submarines were known to operate at even 50 meter depth intervals (50, 100, 150, etc.), so we would chose an operating depth in between these intervals.

On a very cold Saturday morning, we departed Groton to return to Charleston. The temperature was ten degrees below zero, with the wind out of the north and a wind chill of 35 below. The tugboats that assisted us leaving the pier had broken up the ice on the Thames river and once we had left the pier, the only people exposed to these frigid conditions were the Officer of the Deck, a phone talker and me. We were all dressed in exposure suits and crammed into the bridge cockpit on the top of the sail and spent a very cold morning until we reached the diving point.

That afternoon we received a message from the submarine school, which read, in part: "Section tracking party and special party results and wardroom organization show USS Seahorse as the best prepared SSN evaluated for predeployment training in over twelve months. The boat's proficiency is the result of obvious, conscientious effort on the part of the entire wardroom." That message went a long way to warming me up.

An oil painting by artist Jim Christley, a retired submariner, titled "Trailing." Depicted is the artist's conception of the underwater scene of a Sturgeon class submarine (Seahorse was a Sturgeon class boat) in trail of a Soviet Victor III class. The Victor has just maneuvered to "clear" his sonar baffles and the Sturgeon has come to all stop to avoid closing the target submarine and await further developments. A trail can last for an hour, days or weeks and we never see the target submarine. This painting is the best I have seen of what we never see.

The Fox caught in the Hen House

"Conn, Sonar, we have a new contact, probable Soviet Victor class submarine bearing 150 relative on the towed array. Designate this contact Sierra 22."

The towed array was a new sensor installed during our recent overhaul. It is a 250-foot linear array of hydrophones towed about 1500 yards astern of the ship. It was very sensitive and designed to pick up low frequency passive sonar signals at long range. Its major drawback is there is a directional ambiguity that would have to be resolved with each new contact; e.g. 150 relative could also be 210 relative. A relative bearing is not a true bearing but is relative to the heading of the array, which, since it is being towed behind the ship, the array heading is also the heading of the ship. Maneuvering the ship through a 90-degree course change would resolve this ambiguity, but it would take ten minutes to allow the towed array to stabilize on the new course.

"Helm, Right full rudder, come to new course 120." This was a 90-degree course change from our original course of 030. Ten minutes later, the array had stabilized and Sonar reported; "Conn, Sonar we have regained Sierra 22 bearing 030 relative, which correlates to an original true bearing of 180."

Thus began our cat and mouse game of gradually closing an unseen submarine until we could gain a firm contact on our hull sensors. This would take several maneuvers and several hours of tracking while holding onto a tenuous sonar contact. As we closed the range, we lost sonar contact on several occasions due to changes in the ocean environment and changes in the contact's aspect. This is the time for patience. The impatient submarine that attempts to close too rapidly is often counter-detected by the target submarine, which will result in either loss of contact or possibly an aggressive move by the target, and the hunter becomes the hunted.

After two hours, we had maneuvered astern of the target submarine and determined his course and speed and had gained solid broadband contact on our spherical array. The target continued on a steady course of 090, speed of 8 knots, and did not appear to be alerted to our presence, but that was to change within the next few minutes. "Conn, Sonar we have echo ranging from a surface ship sonar to the north. We have identified the active sonar as the new "Horse Jaw" sonar carried on the Udaloy class destroyer, which is a new construction class. Designate this contact Sierra 26"

Udaloy Class Destroyer

I asked sonar for an estimate of range to Sierra 26. They caught a ping steal range of 12,000 yards. A ping steal range is obtained by timing the difference in arrival times of the direct path sonar ping and the bottom bounce sonar ping. The "Horse Jaw" sonar (NATO designation) was a new and more powerful Soviet sonar and we were vulnerable to detection at 12,000 yards. Sonar reported underwater communications between the Victor submarine (Sierra 22) and the Udaloy (Sierra 26). They were comparing ranges and bearings to each other and planning a rendezvous in order to conduct an ASW exercise. I decided that I did not want to be in the middle of an ASW exercise and we started to fall further astern of the Victor and then clear the area. This maneuver apparently alerted the Udaloy as he shifted his sonar beam away from the Victor and on to us. He reported a "stranger" in the area on underwater communications and then increased speed to close us. The fox had been caught in the hen house! We went deep, fast, and cleared the area. Deep in order to get under a thermocline that would deflect his sonar, and fast to cause his sonar to blank out. After a run of about 45 minutes, we slowed and listened. The Udaloy was distant, still pinging on active sonar, but was over 40,000 yards (20 miles) away and no longer a threat and the Victor was long gone. We came up to periscope depth and the horizon was clear of contacts. We recommenced our patrol looking for additional contacts of interest.

This scenario was part of our Tactical Readiness Exam conducted by our Squadron Commander using U.S. Submarines and Destroyers to simulate their Soviet counterparts and was conducted in the waters off of Charleston, SC, our home-port. The Commodore and his inspection team were satisfied with our performance and we were cleared for our upcoming special operation.

Late Breaking News and a Change in Plans

In early March 1980, about two weeks before we were to deploy on our Special Operation (SPECOP) to the North Atlantic, I received a classified message from COMSUBLANT changing our deployment schedule. Rather than the standard two and half month SPECOP deployment, we would be extended another three months to deploy to the Mediterranean after the SPECOP as part of a surge deployment of SSNs to cover the increased Soviet submarine presence in the Mediterranean. The Iranian take-over of the American embassy in November 1979 had a great deal of attention and both U.S. and Soviet forces were increasing their presence and level of readiness.

In a few days, I was to brief the Seahorse wives and families on our upcoming deployment and this news would certainly not be well received. The last year, since leaving the shipyard in May, had been a very busy year and we had limited opportunity to be with our families (about two months spread over the year, a week or a weekend was typical). Now we were going away for over five months and because of the classification, I really couldn't tell them where we would be, or when we would return other than mid-summer, July or August. I also had a personal problem in that I expected to be relieved of command sometime after our SPECOP and we were planning for a change of command in Charleston, but this extension of the deployment would likely change these plans. I discussed these issues with the Commodore and we agreed that I should call the COMSUBLANT operations boss and discuss my concerns.

When I got through to COMSUBLANT Ops, they were still working on our deployment plans, so I had an opportunity to discuss some of the options. After the SPECOP, we would return to Holy Loch, Scotland and off load our classified equipment, patrol report and any additional personnel and take on fresh provisions. They were planning to send us to Faslane, Scotland, which is a Royal Navy submarine base, or to Portsmouth, England, which is an historic Royal Navy, port that goes back to the 1600s. I opted for Portsmouth. We would then depart Portsmouth for the Mediterranean and proceed to LaMaddalena, Sardinia, Italy for a routine upkeep with Mediterranean SSN operations to follow. We discussed change of command plans, and it was possible to delay the change of command until August, but my relief would be available in May and the Bureau of Naval Personnel (BUPERS) was pushing for change of command as early as possible so that I could make the turn over for my next assignment. I had no idea what my next assignment would be nor did the Captain I was talking to; all he knew was that there was a timing problem that had to be worked out. I thanked him for his assistance and then called BUPERS.

I reached the submarine officer assignment desk and was put through to Captain Frank Kelso, who had recently been selected to Rear Admiral. He had been my skipper and mentor at Nuclear Power School, Bainbridge. After I explained the purpose of my call, he told me that they were still working out the timing, but he was pleased to tell me that my next assignment would be Executive Assistant to the Deputy CNO for submarines, relieving Guy Curtis who would be the Commodore of the submarine squadron in Holy Loch. I was floored by this announcement as I knew that this was a highly selective and plum assignment and one for which I had no idea that I was being considered. We discussed change of command timing and decided that LaMaddalena was the obvious choice. Admiral Rickover required a one month overlap for relieving commanding officers, which we would meet if my relief (Commander Joe Sharpe) met the ship in Holy Loch and rode the ship to Portsmouth and then on to LaMaddalena.

I got back to COMSUBLANT Ops and we agreed that the SPECOP portion of the deployment would stay classified, but we could discuss with the families our planned port visit to Portsmouth, England and our Mediterranean deployment with the first port call to be LaMaddalena, where the change of command would take place. As I expected, there were many questions and some unhappy wives at my family night briefing.

Mary and I were also disappointed that the Change of Command would again be overseas in LaMaddalena, but we thought that she could fly over with the children and then we could have a few week's leave to see Italy. When I called Guy Curtis, the individual I was to relieve, he didn't think that this would work as he was scheduled to leave before I could get to Washington and the billet would be gapped. The Admiral was anxious to minimize this gap. Back to the drawing board! We decided that I would leave LaMaddalena as soon as I was relieved and fly back to Charleston to assist in the move to the DC area. During our deployment, Mary would put our Charleston house on the market, drive up to DC, and find a house in northern

Virginia to buy. Not an easy job for Mary, but as the sign in our kitchen says: "Navy Wife, toughest job in the Navy"

Overweight in the Gulf Stream

Seahorse was about to deploy on a SPECOP to be followed by an abbreviated Mediterranean deployment. I decided that we would load out our stores for a three-month cruise, which would fill us up to the limit. In addition to the normal crew, we took aboard ten extra personnel who were various specialists who would support us on our SPECOP; sonar experts; electronics countermeasure analysts, and Russian linguists and an experienced officer-in-charge. We had converted some of the torpedo loading skids to bunks and had thirty sailors hot bunking. The chill box was converted to a freeze box and stuffed to the overhead with frozen food. We had a great quantity of freeze-dried food and canned vegetables that lined the decks of the crews berthing compartments. I was just completing my discussion with the supply officer about the food load out when LT Dave Alford knocked on my door and had a worried expression on his face. Dave was the diving officer responsible for compensation of the ship so that we could submerge safely.

"What's the matter Dave?" I asked. Dave said, "Captain there are 2,000 Oxygen candles on the pier waiting to be loaded that would definitely make us too heavy to submerge safely." I trusted Dave's judgment on this matter as he had been monitoring our load out very carefully, and had been extremely accurate on our post overhaul dive,

Oxygen candles are Sodium Chlorate with small amount of Iron, which are heated in a small furnace and produce oxygen. The ship has an electrolytic oxygen generator that uses electrolysis to separate water into Oxygen and Hydrogen, but I wanted the oxygen candles aboard as a backup. Each candle weighed 25 pounds and 50,000 pounds would sink us as far as Dave was concerned. I asked Dave to let me know if he had enough weight reserve to load a ten-day supply of candles. Dave said, "That would be 5,000 pounds and I think that we can do that.

We were underway three days later, families were on the pier, but a lot families then drove out Fort Moultrie to have a final wave as the ship cleared Charleston Harbor. In another three hours, we were in water deep enough for our initial dive. Dave Alford was supervising the dive and was a little nervous about his compensation computations. To compensate the submarine for added weight we must remove water from variable ballast tanks: the Forward Trim Tank, the After Trim Tank and the Auxiliary Tank (which is located amidships). We dove with about 4,000 pounds total in the variable ballast tanks, which was light on purpose. When we slowed down to get our final trim, we had 500 pounds in FTT, 2,000 pounds in Auxiliary and 3,000 pounds in ATT. The total capacity of these tanks is over 300,000 pounds, so we cut it awfully close. But Dave was smiling as he had a right to do, and we went down to the wardroom for our first dinner of the next sixty days before we returned to port.

I turned in that night at 2300 and left word to be called at 0100 before we came to periscope depth for the navigation satellite pass and the radio broadcast. When the officer of the deck called me, I could tell he was having a depth control problem. The ship was doing 8 knots at 200 feet with a 10 degree up angle and was not going up. When I got to the control room the OOD had increased speed to 10 knots and we were again going up, but slowly. The ship was very heavy, and the Chief of the Watch was pumping the remaining water out of auxiliary and the after trim tank. I called the engineering officer of the watch and asked for injection temperature (temperature of the seawater flowing into the main condenser). His report was 86 degrees! We were in the Gulf Stream and had been for the last 4 hours. I asked for injection temperature when we made our initial dive. It was 56 degrees. Because water at a higher temperature is less dense, the ship was not displacing the same weight of water when we made our initial dive. In fact, we were over 30,000 pounds too heavy for the Gulf Stream. The solution was to increase speed and continue east until we were clear of the Gulf Stream, which we did in about two hours. Back in colder water our weight compensation was no longer a problem.

In the past, we routinely went through the Gulf Stream and never thought much about it, but as result of this incident, I changed my standing orders to have the engineering officer of the watch report every five-degree change in injection temperature and have the diving officer adjust compensation accordingly.

Barents Sea Patrol—Part 1

We rounded North Cape, the northern extremity of Norway, and entered the Barents Sea in late March 1980. Although spring had arrived, we found ourselves in a snowstorm and 40 knots of wind. After riding out the storm for a few days, the weather calmed down and although our visibility was still hampered by the snow, we were riding a lot easier at periscope depth. We started picking up several different radars and after sorting through their frequencies and characteristics, most were Soviet long-range surface to air radars, none of which was threat radars. We also detected a U.S. surface search and air search radar as well as two U.K. (British) surface search radars. I had been expecting all of these radars as we had been advised that the U.K. would have two destroyers in the Barents conducting surveillance and the U.S. would have a specially configured surveillance LST in the Barents as well. These ships were there to conduct overt surveillance of the Soviet Navy's surface operations and were directed not to conduct anti-submarine operations. Our mission was to focus on Soviet submarines. I did not have a vote on these combined allied surveillance operations, but I was worried about our success in carrying out our mission.

This was the first time U.S. and U.K. surface warships would be in the Soviet Navy Operating areas observing their operations and I was sure that their reaction to this overt presence would be to curtail their normal operations. Although the Soviets were well aware of our submarine surveillance, they never sure that we were there or where we were and they continued with their routine training. We were expecting to see new submarine classes during this spring training period, but with the presence of U.K. and U.S. surface ships; these new classes were not observed. Finally, there was always the risk of our counterdetection, not only by the Soviets but also by our own ships. These surveillance missions are very demanding on the commanding officer of the submarine, and I found that the added allied surface warships increased the complexity of our mission and added to my own personal stress.

The Barents Sea is ice free year round along the northern coast of Russia as is the port of Murmansk and the numerous Naval Bases in the area. As a result, the Soviet Navy has year round access to the Atlantic Ocean. But after World War II, the U.S. developed a large underwater hydrophone array in the Norwegian Sea. This Sound Surveillance System or SOSUS is designed to detect submarines departing the Barents Sea and transiting the Norwegian Sea to gain access to the Atlantic. Essentially SOSUS prevented Soviet submarines from having free undetected access to the Atlantic and our East Coast. Once their submarine was detected by SOSUS, a P-3 ASW aircraft was dispatched from Iceland to localize the submarine and then our nuclear attack submarines gained contact and trailed the Soviet submarine. The early Soviet ballistic missile submarines had to operate off our East Coast in order for their missiles to be in range of our key strategic targets. This gave the U.S. a tremendous advantage during the Cold War up to the early eighties.

In the early 1980s, with the development of the DELTA I submarine and the SS-N-6 missile with a range of 1300 kilometers, the Delta patrol areas were moved well out into the Atlantic and by the late 80s they had developed the SS-N-8 missile with a range of 8100 Kilometers and they could be within effective missile range from the Barents.

Delta I Submarine

As Seahorse entered the Barents, I elected to start our patrol near the Marginal Ice Zone (MIZ), which was about 150 miles north of the coast of Russia. There are few ships in this area and I felt this would give us an opportunity to get used to our patrol area. Because we did not receive any under-ice training in our deployment workup, we were not authorized to conduct operations under the ice. Two days later as we were about to head south toward the Kola Peninsula, Sonar reported a distant contact to the south with slight cavitation and a series of frequencies that identified it as a Soviet submarine, probably on the surface.

"Sonar Conn, Designate new contact Master-2, Track and report." After a few own-ship maneuvers, the fire control system had a reasonable solution. "Sonar Conn, Master-2 now on a bearing of 183 is on a course of North, speed 12 knots and the range is 15,000 yards." I directed the Officer of the Deck to come to a course and speed that would take us off his track at a Closest Point of Approach (CPA) of 6,000 yards.

A little over an hour later, Master-2 passed CPA and we visually identified him as a DELTA 1 submarine that also matched the sonar frequencies that we were receiving. He was operating his surface search radar, his active sonar and his under ice sonar, which made it easy for us to track him. He continued to head for the MIZ on a steady course of north (000).

A few hours later, our contact slowed and submerged near the edge of the MIZ. He commenced calling on his underwater communications circuit. After another half an hour, there was a response and our contact had made a rendezvous with a surface ship. They passed a lot of range and bearing information and course and speed data. While we were listening to all of this information, Lieutenant Parnell, the officer in charge of our special detachment which was holed up in radio, came out to report to me that they had just intercepted an area closure message for all ships in the Barents. The closure area was centered on the current position of the Delta 1. LT Parnell said this area closure was for a missile launch for the Delta (Master 2). The time of the closure was from 0800 to 1600 and he felt that the probable time of launch would be between 1000 and 1400. We were about 30 miles from Delta and we could not get any closer because of the ice, but providing the weather held, we would have a good view.

His predictions were accurate, with the launch occurring at 1130 on a clear sunny day. Through the periscope, we tracked the missile as it lifted off vertically and slowly arced off on an easterly course down range. The missile telemetry was recorded and it was all over in about 5 minutes. But we were not done collecting data from Master-2.

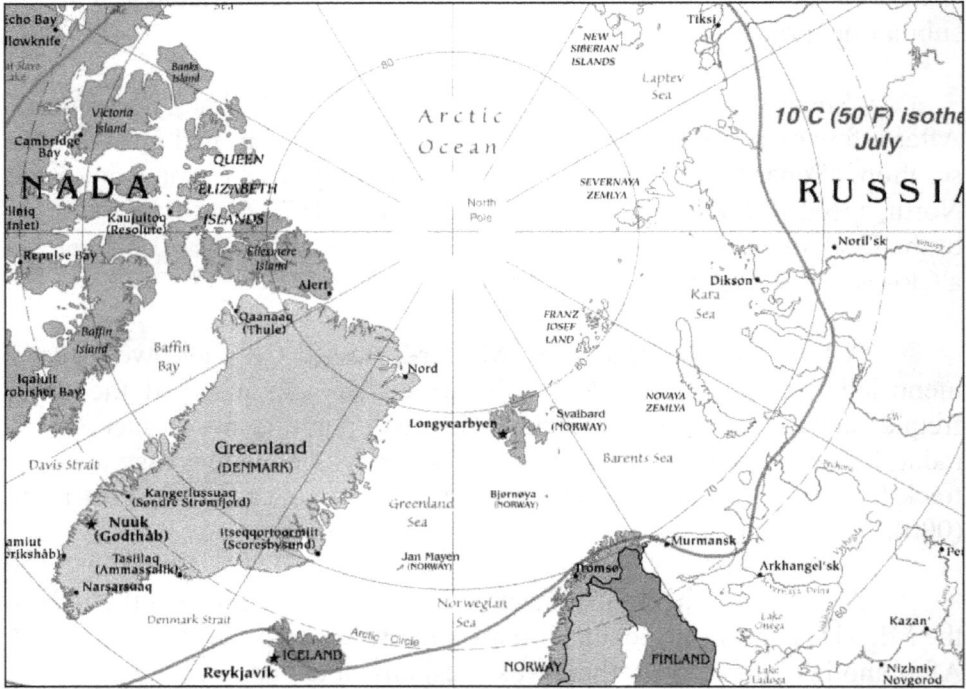

Barents Sea

Barents Sea Patrol—Part 2

Seahorse lingered outside the MIZ for a day as we still had sonar and underwater communications contact on Master 2. The next morning he surfaced and started his surface search radar and completed his communications with what had to be the Launch Area Support Ship (LASS) for yesterday's missile launch. About an hour later, he departed the MIZ and we gained solid broadband contact. He steamed over the horizon about a half hour later, doing a leisurely 8 knots on a course of south, There were several personnel on the bridge enjoying a fine day, and they didn't seem to be in any hurry to get back to the barn. This was an ideal opportunity for us to get a high quality wide band tape recording of Master-2, which was one of our intelligence collection requirements on all submarines that we encountered.

We maneuvered the ship until we were about 1200 yards on his starboard beam. We were at a depth of 200 feet to ensure that the personnel on the bridge could not see us. Sonar started the tape recorder and we slowed to 7.5 knots and let him gradually overtake us as we maintained a constant range to the target. As he passed our port beam, we put some left rudder on and gradually slipped 1200 yards directly astern. Then we opened the range, worked up to 1200 yards on his port beam, and did the whole procedure again, taping his port side. The key to success in this procedure is to go slow, don't cavitate and don't get visually detected. The information is valuable so that intelligence analysts can analyze the patrol data and identify the submarine, as each has a specific sonar signature. Submarines don't have hull numbers painted on the side so that this is best procedure for identification.

As we watched the Delta submarine proceed into port, we went on a search for another high priority target. We didn't have long to wait as we spotted a target barge under tow proceeding out of port and heading north toward an area well known as a surface to surface missile range. We lingered behind the target barge and tug with hope of spotting a potential missile shooter. We were not disappointed as a Kresta I class cruiser came out of port and followed the target barge. The Kresta I carried four SSN 3 (Shaddock) surface-to-surface missiles a long-range cruise missile that requires another ship for terminal guidance as it homes on the target. I elected to stay with the target barge and intercept the terminal guidance radar. Once the target barge was about two hundred miles from the launch area, the tug cast it loose and cleared the area. Radio intercepted a range clearance warning centered on the target barge and we waited for the missile launch. We detected the final guidance radar from an unknown ship in the vicinity and then about five minutes later the cruise missile came in low over the water and impacted the target barge. The tug came back in the area the next day and started to tow the barge back home.

Kresta I

And so it went for the next month. Lots of activity with many Soviet warships carrying out routine exercises. We had to pick which was the highest priority from an intelligence collection point of view. My concerns about the other allied ships in the area diminished as they concentrated mainly on surface ship activities and we focused on submarine operations. We had at least twenty hours of daylight every day, and this made for very long days. Most of time I was in the control room directing our activities and I found that after about five days at this activity level I was exhausted so we would pull off station and take care of a few necessary housekeeping activities and I would recharge my batteries with about eight hours of sleep.

The operations that I have described are typical of the intelligence collection priorities that U.S. submarines have when conducting special operations. They are designed to minimize the risk of collision and of counterdetection, and as a result, there are very few submarine mishaps.

The Holy Loch, Scotland

CO and XO beards are ready for our return to Holy Loch at the end of the patrol

USS Seahorse completed our Barents Sea Patrol in May and headed for the Holy Loch, Scotland for a short refit and resupply by the submarine tender USS Canopus (AS 34). The submarine refit facility in the Holy Loch conducts refits on our Ballistic Missile submarines that operate in the Atlantic and provides support to deploying attack submarines. As we entered the Loch, I assessed the weather—zero wind and almost no current. Two tugs were standing by to assist in our mooring to the tender. The tugs requested permission to come alongside to make up their lines for our landing. I waved them off and advised them to stand by if required, but I intended to make the landing alongside the tender unassisted. The landing was a one-bell landing, meaning that we coasted in alongside the tender and I ordered a backing bell so that we stopped at the designated mooring location. In short, it was a perfect landing, and after over sixty days underway, I was very pleased with the results.

As I left the bridge, one of the tug pilots met me topside and complimented me on the landing. He then asked if this was my first visit to the Holy Loch, and I replied that I had been here in 1967 as a lieutenant. "Well Captain," the tug pilot said, "The rules have changed since then, and submarines are not allowed to make unassisted landings alongside the tender. But I need to tell you that you made one the best landings I have seen in my

20 years as a tug pilot." I thanked him for the "heads up" and went on board the tender to pay my respects to the Commodore.

When I saw the Commodore, I apologized for breaking the rules regarding my unassisted landing, and he told me not to worry about it. He said they normally have someone from his staff ride a new submarine on its first visit, and they dropped the ball. He did compliment me on my landing however. We didn't have any major repairs for the tender to accomplish and we agreed that five days alongside should be adequate for resupply and a good meal and a few beers ashore before we departed for Portsmouth.

Holy Loch Full House

I called home early that afternoon. Mary had just returned from her house-hunting trip to DC and she had lots of news. Our house in Charleston had sold very quickly and we had a firm contract with closing in mid-June. Her trip to DC was productive and she had found a nice three-bedroom house just outside the beltway in Annandale. Pictures were in the mail and would arrive when we got to Portsmouth if not before. She made a bid on the house and would like my OK ASAP. She needed to set up a move to DC. Kids and dog were fine and anxious for me to get home. In the two months I was out of touch, Mary had accomplished a lot. What a woman! What a wife!

Portsmouth, England

Portsmouth, England is southwest of London and just off the English Channel. It is an historic Navy town and a large portion of the Royal Navy is still home ported there. Admiral Nelson's flagship, HMS Victory, from the historic Battle of Trafalgar is maintained in dry-dock in Portsmouth. This is a place I always wanted to visit, so I was very pleased to have the opportunity to see it during my last week in command of Seahorse.

USS Seahorse entering Portsmouth. HMS Dolphin is the building just beyond Seahorse, which houses the Royal Navy Submarine School.

After we moored, several invitations arrived, and suddenly my social calendar was rather full. That morning I was to call on the Port Captain followed by a call on Flag Officer, Portsmouth followed by lunch at his quarters. I was assigned a Lieutenant Liaison Officer to assist me. The Brits always do this sort of thing with class and style. Lunch was followed by a tour of a spectacular rose garden conducted by my hostess. I was then whisked over to HMS Dolphin to call on the Captain commanding submarines Portsmouth. Prior to our arrival in Portsmouth, I had sent him a personal message explaining that Seahorse had become the Anglo-American Uckers champion in a hard fought match with HMS Conqueror, and had challenged any submarine in Portsmouth to see if they could take the title back from us. After we settled down for a cup of coffee, the Captain accepted my Uckers challenge and one of his submarines would meet us on the field of battle on Monday next, which would be our last day in port. He apologized for not scheduling it earlier, but this was a bank holiday weekend and most ships were standing down. He did invite me to a formal dining-in on Friday night after the "Bone of Contention" match, which would take place during the day. He suggested that I arrive a little earlier so that we could work out the toasts. He also asked the Liaison Officer to explain the "Bone of Contention."

On the way back to Seahorse, the Liaison Officer explained the "Bone of Contention." At Portsmouth, In addition to the submarine school, HMS Dolphin, there was also a Mine-countermeasure and anti-submarine school, HMS Vernon. Annually, they meet on the athletic field to battle over the Bone of Contention, which was a large elephant thighbone as I recall with a brass plaque suitably inscribed to the winners and presented at the dining-in that I too was to attend on Friday. A dining-in is a British military tradition that has been adopted by the U.S. military, primarily the Navy and Marine Corps. It is a formal dinner for military officers only. It used to be male only, but now women are included as well. Everyone is dressed in their formal mess dress uniforms. A president of the mess is responsible for maintaining the proper decorum. The meal is typically a large round of beef, which is paraded around the room. I could go on for another couple of pages, but you get the idea. (I hope) At the end of the meal, after the table is cleared, bottles of port are placed on the table, and time for toasts has arrived. The first toast is to the head of state of the (foreign) guest of honor if one is present. And in this instance, that was me. The next toast will be to Her Majesty the Queen, and that led to some concern by the planners for this evening. In the Royal Navy, they never stand for the King or Queen, custom dictates that they will stand for other heads of state. This custom goes back William IV, the Sailor King, who was sent to sea at age 13 and saw active service in America and the West Indies. He was a tall man (over six feet), and he bumped his head on the low overhead of most wardrooms toasting his father He vowed that when he became king no officer would suffer a similar fate. So ever since, the Loyal Toast to monarch is drunk seated. After some discussion, we agreed that after the toast to the President of the United States, and we were all standing, the president of the mess would say "Seats, gentleman." I would wait to all were seated, and then I would rise and propose a toast Her Majesty.

All this planning came out perfectly and the toasts came off without a hitch, But the toasts go on until the port runs out, so we were all feeling no pain by the end of the evening which is just as well because Brits enjoy physical activity at this point such as arm and leg wrestling, building pyramids and seeing who can knock them down.

The next day the Port Admiral invited the Seahorse officers to a private tour of HMS Victory and that was a special treat. The ship is over 240 years old and has been beautifully restored and maintained. It was dismasted and badly mauled at the Battle of Trafalgar but you would never know that today. The place where Nelson died was deep in a hold where the operating room was. He died several hours after being shot by a sharpshooter on the French flagship—knowing they had defeated the enemy

HMS Victory

Where Lord Nelson died

The Royal Navy accepted our offer of an opportunity to regain the Uckers title during our stay in Portsmouth. I chose the Engineer, George Voelker and the Navigator, Greg Serwich as our team. I also suggested that they might choose a character and an appropriate costume to put the Brits off their game. George chose a Samurai warrior, fighting costume and Greg Chose the Swedish Chef from the Muppet Show. The rest of the wardroom attended in appropriate costumes and we brought the ship's bell, portable foghorn, life rings, ships brow banner and assorted noisemakers. The Brits showed up in everyday civilian clothes and were clearly overwhelmed by our enthusiasm. I met with their captain and we agreed on the rules. As the current titleholder, we would be the home team and rule one; the captain is always right would be under my control.

With much fanfare and cheering, the game got underway and it was the shortest game of Uckers I ever saw. Games usually last 45 minutes to an hour and this game was over in 20 minutes. The throwing of sixes with the dice is very important as it gives you extra throws and allows your pieces to move around the board rather quickly. The game was very one-sided as the British team simply couldn't throw a six and we had more than our fair share. The result was our team cleared their pieces off the board before the Brits had gotten all their pieces on the board. The result—A Skunk!

We retained the title as Anglo-American Uckers champions, but we gave them a consolation game and politely lost.

That night I hosted a small dinner party for the senior Royal Navy submarine officers and their wives on board Seahorse. We departed the next morning for LaMaddalena, Sardinia, Italy, via the Straits of Gibraltar.

LaMaddalena, Sardinia, Italy -- USS Seahorse Change of Command

USS Orion (AS 18) moored at Santo Stefano Island. The city and the Island of LaMaddalena is in the background and the Island of Corsica in the distance.

We left Portsmouth on 28 May1980. My relief, Commander Joe Sharpe, was on board and we would use the transit to conduct our turnover and give Commander Sharpe an opportunity to observe the ship underway, conducting battle stations, emergency drills and routine evolutions. He had served as Executive Officer of USS Sunfish (SSN 649) which is a sister ship of Seahorse, so he was already well acquainted with the class of ship. The weather was ideal for our transit through the Straits of Gibraltar and we arrived at LaMaddalena on 6 June. We moored port side to the USS Orion (AS 18) where the submarine in the picture is moored. Joe and I met with "Mac" Hughes, the Commodore of the Submarine Refit and Training Group on arrival and discussed the Change of Command. I asked Mac if there was another submarine due in port before our change of command scheduled for 12 June. Mac said that the USS Greenling (SSN 614) was due in three days. I asked if he could moor the Greenling outboard of the Seahorse. I explained that my first change of command in 1977 had the crew assembled on the pier and the Seahorse hidden out view on the other side of the tender. I would like my crew on the deck of the Seahorse and we could seat our limited number of guests (10 to 15) on the Greenling in a single row of seats along the centerline on the ship. Mac thought that was a novel idea and he saw no reason not to do it, as long as the weather cooperated. If it was raining or we had high winds then he would have the guests watch the ceremony from the main deck of Orion.

The officers gave me great dinner and send off the night before the change of command and a very thoughtful gift. They presented me a bound copy of all the War Patrol reports of the USS Seahorse (SS 304), under the command of Commander Slade Cutter. He was one of the top submarine skippers in World War II (21 ships sunk in four patrols).

12 June was a beautiful day with only a slight breeze. The crew was mustered topside and my Executive Officer, George Bardsley in charge and Master of Ceremonies. The awards and recognition from our recently completed Special Operation would be awarded at a separate ceremony in about two months, but I felt it was important to present an award at these ceremonies, so I singled out Petty Officer Second Class Lance, an Electronics Technician. He performed admirably both as repair technician and watch stander in our recently completed ops. I awarded him a Navy Achievement Medal.

Last time piping aboard as SEAHORSE arriving

Awarding a Navy Achievement Medal to Petty Officer Lance

We received several congratulatory messages; this one from our squadron commander in Charleston:

> "I wish to take this opportunity to acknowledge the tremendous achievements of USS Seahorse during the past three and one-half years while under the command of Commander McKinney. The ship has been challenged by two Mediterranean deployments, a Special Operation, a refueling overhaul, an assortment of Eastlant operations and all the milestones attendant on readying an attack submarine for her mission of anti-submarine warfare. The Seahorse has met each challenge head on and has proven to be a consistently superior performer. Under Commander McKinney's leadership, not only has the ship excelled but the officers and crew have had fun along the way."

I really appreciated the commodore's observation that the officers and crew had fun under my command. Maybe that is not the right approach to command for everyone. But I served under several commanding officers and the most successful clearly enjoyed their command and made it a point to build a strong rapport with their crew. As I look back at my command, many of the highlights are what I have written about. From life raft races to ship slogans to fishing for Mahi Mahi to movies topside to reenlistments in a life raft, I tried to engender a spirit of fun and mutual respect within the crew and I think that it paid off in our sense of camaraderie and our success as a crew.

As I told the crew in my remarks, I was very proud of their performance and that I was turning over to my relief the best crew in the Atlantic Fleet that has earned the title of **"The Thoroughbred of the Fleet."**

Addressing the crew for the last time

I finished my remarks to the crew with a poem by John Masefield who was the Poet Laureate of England and a favorite poem of my Father who taught it to me:

Sea-Fever

I must go down to the seas again, to the lonely sea and the sky,
And all I ask is a tall ship and a star to steer her by,
And the wheel's kick and the wind's song and the white sail's shaking,
And a grey mist on the sea's face, and a grey dawn breaking.

I must go down to the seas again, for the call of the running tide
Is a wild call and a clear call that may not be denied;
And all I ask is a windy day with the white clouds flying,
And the flung spray and the blown spume, and the sea-gulls crying.

I must go down to the seas again, to the vagrant gypsy life,
To the gull's way and the whale's way where the wind's like a whetted
knife;

And all I ask is a merry yarn from a laughing fellow-rover
And quiet sleep and a sweet dream when the long trick's over.

Epilogue

One of the hardest moments for me in my Navy career was turning over command of USS Seahorse. As commanding officer, I was the mentor and leader of a crew of 140 men. They looked to me for all the decisions that would affect their lives on the ship. It is an awesome responsibility and when you accept it, you devote your full energies toward the ship and crew. When the new CO says, "I relieve you, sir." And you say, "I stand relieved." Everything shifts to his shoulders and you become an outsider looking in on a command that no longer belongs to you. This really comes home when you leave the ship and they announce "Commander, U. S. Navy, departing.' And when the new CO leaves the ship and they announce "Seahorse departing." It was at this point that I began to wonder, "Is there life after Command?"

I didn't have to wait long for an answer to that question. I said my farewells to the Seahorse and was on a plane flying from Olbia, Sardinia to Rome then to New York and I arrived in Charleston the next day with jet lag but glad to be home with family. We packed out the house and were on our way to Washington, DC and our new home in Annandale, Virginia. A week later, I received word that I had been promoted to Captain and reported to the Pentagon to become the Executive Assistant to the Deputy Chief of Naval Operations for Submarine Warfare (OP-02). I spent two years in the Pentagon and then was assigned overseas as the Commodore of the submarine squadron in LaMaddalena (sound familiar?) and after another two years we went back to Washington where I was the Nuclear Power Personnel Manager and submarine captain assignment officer (another familiar job!). I was then selected for Flag (Rear Admiral) and sent back to Italy (Naples) (we love Italy!). After two years in Naples, Back to Washington to take over as Commander, Navy Recruiting Command, then Pearl Harbor, Hawaii to take over the Submarine Force in the Pacific and finally back to Washington DC to become the Deputy Chief of Naval Personnel—the last post in my Navy career

Mary and I found that there was definitely "life after command" with lots of travel, and *believe it or not*, a few "new" sea stories as well.

www.ingramcontent.com/pod-product-compliance
Lightning Source LLC
Chambersburg PA
CBHW021043090426
42738CB00006B/160